Unexpected Journey

UNEXPECTED JOURNEY

A Marine Corps Reserve Company in the Korean War

Randy K. Mills and Roxanne Mills

Naval Institute Press
Annapolis, Maryland

Naval Institute Press
291 Wood Road
Annapolis, MD 21402

Library of Congress Cataloging-in-Publication Data

Mills, Randy Keith, 1951–
    Unexpected journey : a Marine Corps Reserve Company in the Korean
War/ Randy K. Mills and Roxanne Mills.
        p. cm.
    Includes bibliographical references and index.
    ISBN 1-55750-546-2 (alk. paper)
    1. Korean War, 1950–1953—Personal narratives, American. 2. United
States. Marine Corps Reserve. 3. Mills, Randy Keith, 1951– I. Mills, Rox-
anne, 1954– II. Title.

DS921.6 .M55 2000
951.904'245—dc21
                                                    00-030487

Printed in the United States of America on acid-free paper ∞

07 06 05 04 03 02 01 00   9 8 7 6 5 4 3 2

First printing

Dedicated to all the men of C Company, 16th Infantry Battalion, United States Marine Corps Reserve, Evansville, Indiana, especially those who gave their lives in Korea: John M. Elliott, Robert "Bud" Fitch, William E. Grove, Jack Perigo, Byron E. Watson, and Eugene Whittaker.

Contents

Acknowledgments

A project of this sort could not have been completed without the help of a great number of people. We wish to acknowledge the following for their assistance in making this story come to life.

First and foremost, the members of C Company, 16th Infantry Battalion, United States Marine Corps Reserve, Evansville, Indiana, and their wives. Thank you for allowing us to attend your regular meetings, visit your homes, and for sharing with us your stories and your hospitality. You will always be special to us.

All of those who shared personal correspondence, photographs, and other materials. (A detailed account of correspondence and other materials can be found in the bibliography.)

Bill Marshall, for introducing us to the larger group and, most of all, for reading each chapter as we wrote it, giving suggestions, and encouraging us to keep at it.

The late Richard Eberle—without his dream, C Company might never have reunited.

James Skinner, for helping us to make some important contacts and for sharing his story of the spring offensive battle in which Bud Fitch died.

The Marine Corps Heritage Foundation at Quantico, Virginia, and its Executive Director, Susan C. Hodges. The foundation provided a grant to aid in the initial research for this work. Also, Mr.

Charles R. Smith at the Marine Corps Historical Center at Washington, D.C., who offered valuable advice regarding this work.

Kristen Coble, for manuscript typing; Rob Spillane, for manuscript typing and editorial suggestions; and Nora Nixon for transcription of interviews.

John Selch, at the Indiana State Library, Indianapolis, who was essential in helping us find local newspaper accounts of the war. Lyn Martin and Carol Bartlett, who made it possible for us to conduct several important interviews at Willard Library, Evansville, Indiana. Robert Sears, at Oakland City University, Oakland City, Indiana, who maintained his usual patience in allowing us to keep materials long past due. Many thanks to you, Bob. Other libraries used in this research include the Central Public Library, Evansville, Indiana; Princeton Public Library, Princeton, Indiana; Oakland City/Columbia Township Public Library, Oakland City, Indiana; and Jasper Public Library, Jasper, Indiana.

The Naval Institute Press and Paul Wilderson, Rebecca Hinds, Randy Baldini, Susan Artigiani, Elizabeth Johnson, and Kristin Wye. Also Karin Kaufman for her solid copy editing. You have been a pleasure to work with.

Col. Joseph Alexander, USMC (ret.), who offered much helpful advice for organizing this work.

Thanks and love go to our kids—Ryan and Andy Mills and Erin and Allison Oxendine—for being so good-natured about this whole wild book-writing experience.

Finally, the Fitch family, who, by selling their house to us, started us down the trail of this story. We think of you and Bud often.

Introduction

This book began with a mystery. We had purchased a home for our family in the fall of 1989 in the small, quiet college town of Oakland City, nestled in the southwest corner of Indiana. Among the items left behind by the previous owners were a few faded black-and-white snapshots, which we found in a dusty corner of the attic. One photo seemed especially fascinating. It showed eight young men in Marine Corps dungarees standing, arms around one another's shoulders, in front of a train station. Obviously they were waiting to be shipped out, perhaps to war. Intrigued, we framed the picture and set it out in our living room so that those boyish and somewhat haunting faces, as youthful looking as those of our own teenage sons, stared back at us each day, moving us to wonder who they were, what happened to them, and how the snapshot came to be left in the attic. Eventually we felt compelled to seek the answers to these questions, and in doing so we discovered the often unfathomable complexities of war.

All wars are brutal. On close inspection, however, we found that the Korean War seemed to stand out more in this regard than other American conflicts. Several reasons bear out this contention. First, the beginning of the conflict came at a time when our country stood profoundly unprepared both militarily and psychologically for war. It is often forgotten that although the attack on Pearl

Harbor came as a stunning jolt, our nation had actually been, for some time, preparing both in spirit and in material for that struggle. Conversely, in the years before the Korean War, the nation found itself in the grips of the largest military downsizing in our history. Too many years of guns made us hungry only for butter. Of the 8 million men in the army when Japan surrendered in September 1945, only 4.3 million were in uniform by the end of the year. Still Americans demanded more reductions. In Washington, D.C., for example, General Eisenhower found himself, in the early months of 1946, beleaguered by mobs of women belonging to "Bring Back Daddy" clubs, complaining that too many men were still in uniform when they should be at home. Congress was bombarded with letters from constituents voicing the same opinion. Such complaints must have been effective, for by the middle of 1946 there were only 1.5 million men in the army and only seven hundred thousand in the navy.[1] Apparently Americans expected no international trouble. *U.S. News and World Report* observed in its first issue of 1950 that the possibility of war breaking out "now seems remote."[2] In the late spring of 1950 Americans believed they were taking a well-deserved rest from both economic hard times and war.

On top of the psychological jolt that came with the Communist invasion of South Korea, the Korean struggle also stands as an especially brutal and bitter conflict because of its relative intensity. Lasting but three years, its casualty numbers all but equal that of our decade-long struggle in Vietnam. Altogether our frustrating endeavor in Korea would claim 54,246 Americans dead, 103,240 wounded, and 5,128 missing. Further, the physical arena of the war, a land of extreme weather and mountainous terrain, was one of the bleakest and harshest in which American troops have ever fought. Summers on the Korean peninsula are most often unbearably hot and humid, with heavy monsoon rains, and winters can turn bitterly, sometimes fatally, cold. A Korean saying describes the landscape as "after the mountains, mountains, mountains." At the time of the war, hardly a paved road existed in the entire country. An absence of understanding regarding why soldiers had to fight over there further added to the negative feelings Americans would eventually come to have about the war. One Hoosier GI offered this harsh, but no doubt popular, assessment of Korea early in the conflict in a letter to the folks back home: "This is the dirtiest place I ever saw. The people look awful, go nude on the street and the place smells terrible." Another soldier, in an interview in a national news magazine in August 1950, demanded to know why in the world he was "fighting to save this hell hole."[3] Perhaps Secretary of State Dean Acheson, in one particularly baffling moment, best captured the frustration of the war in Korea when he said, "If the best minds in the world had set out to find us the worst possible location in the world to fight . . . the unanimous choice would have been Korea."[4]

The final circumstance that seems to make the Korean War especially harsh is its neglected status. To have suffered for one's country and then in turn be honored for that service is one thing; to have served and have one's efforts fall into the category of the "forgotten war" is something entirely different. A few solid efforts have been made to correct this injustice. Clay Blair's *The Forgotten War*, Joseph Goulden's *Korea: The Untold Story of the War*, Donald Knox's *The Korean War, An Oral History*, Martin Russ's *Last Parallel*, Bevin Alexander's *Korea: The First War We Lost*, and more recently John Toland's *In Mortal Combat: Korea 1950–1953* are some of the books that have been written in an attempt to make the general public more familiar with the war in Korea and the sacrifices made there. Yet despite these works and others, one area of the Korean conflict has gone all but unnoticed.

The involvement of Marine Corps reservists in the Korean War stands as unique in the annals of American warfare. Originally praised as "the Minute Men of 1950," the reservists and their special contributions and unique circumstances were quickly forgotten even as the war continued.[5] Those reservists who had also served in World War II received a double blow. Veterans trapped by reserve status into fighting in Korea became known in some circles as "two time losers."[6] Many were struggling at that time to start their own livelihoods. About such reservists, *U.S. News and World Report* noted, "They're already behind competitors in business. They'll never catch up with some who stayed home. . . . Brushing the old uniforms, again, [they] are beginning to wonder what they did to deserve it."[7]

To add to this difficult situation, reservists also discovered that regular marines often looked down on those who served in the nonregular component of the Corps. Reservists found themselves having to contend with being called "weekend warriors" or hearing a regular crack, "What are you, a wise guy or a Reservist?"[8] But the most profound circumstance the reservist faced concerned his lack of training. In no other armed struggle have American reservists been called upon so quickly and been so unprepared to carry out the tasks required by combat. The official Marine Corps Reserve history somewhat understates that assigning reservists so soon to combat situations in Korea "was not what the Marine Corps desired . . . nor planned." However, as the official version concedes, "the harsh necessities of the situation offered no other choice."[9]

Officially, the reservists first sent to fight had supposedly received extensive training. "Combat-ready" included those "of the organized reserves for two years and who had attended one [two-week] summer camp, and seventy-two drills or two summer camps and thirty-six drills and veterans with more than ninety days service in the Corps."[10] In truth, many who joined the reserve had hardly darkened the doors of the local armories where once-a-week training took place. Fewer still attended the volunteer two-week summer camps. Those who did attend training sessions likely found the instruction wanting. Local drill and summer camp training tended to be uneven, and in many cases, especially for the multitude of teenagers who had joined the reserves for every reason under the sun but to fight, did little if anything to prepare them for combat.

Once the war started, those who lacked combat-ready training were supposed to receive adequate instruction before being sent to war. Further, according to official policy, any reservist "who believed he needed more training was to be removed without prejudice from consideration for immediate assignment to combat duty."[11] In reality, this policy, because of circumstances beyond the control of the Corps, would rarely be practiced. Members of C Company, 16th Infantry Battalion, of Evansville, Indiana, for example, were promised six months' combat instruction before going into battle.[12] The first man killed from that unit, however, perished only thirty-four days after leaving Evansville by train for Camp Pendleton. He had received all of two weeks of combat preparation. One marine, 2d Lt. Joseph R. Owen, who stood in charge of training a company of reservists at Camp Pendleton in the early crisis days of the war, offered this bleak assessment regarding Marine Corps reservists' lack of preparedness:

"Rarely have Americans been sent into battle as ill prepared as these men. These young Reservists . . . [were] called abruptly from their homes . . . having . . . had neither active service nor combat training."[13]

Despite the shocking abruptness of the call-up and the lack of actual preparation, marine reservists, in the finest spirit of the Corps, quickly proved their worth when thrown into actual combat. Writing some years after the event, Gen. Lemuel C. Shepherd Jr. noted that "if it had not been for the mobilization of the Reserve to bring the remaining units of the [1st] Division to full strength, I would not have been able to recommend to General MacArthur that he request the assignment of the 1st Division to the Far East Command for his desired employment at Inchon which turned the tide of defeat to one of victory, to the lasting glory and prestige of the U.S. Marine Corps."[14]

By the first campaign to liberate Seoul, about 30 percent of the marine division would include reservists. Three short months later, during the incredibly difficult Chosin campaign, the 1st Division was an even mix of regulars and reservists.[15] This brutal portion of the war included what many military historians believe to have been the fiercest small-arms struggle of any American military engagement.[16] In a ground war in which most of the fighting occurs at the company level and below, Marine Corps Reserves made the critical difference in the desperate fight to escape the Chinese trap sprung at the reservoir. The overall behavior of reservists in these most difficult of circumstances stands as extraordinary. Maj. Gen. Edward A. Craig wrote several years after the bitter Chosin battle, "I came in contact with thousands of Reservists. . . . They had a can do spirit, no griping, not afraid to go forward under fire and take the consequences. . . . They endured hardships probably never encountered by Marines in the past and always acquitted themselves in the highest traditions of the Corps."[17] A few months after the Chosin struggle, these same reservists would again face the Chinese juggernaut and this time help stop the Chinese offensive along the thirty-eighth parallel in some of the heaviest fighting of the war.

C Company, 16th Infantry Battalion, of Evansville, Indiana, makes for an especially important case study of what Marine Corps Reserve units and their families endured during the Korean War. Located near the demographic center of the nation at that time, the majority of C Company's

240 members came from Evansville, a city of about one hundred thousand people. Some, however, called nearby smaller Hoosier communities, such as Oakland City, Tennyson, Boonville, Tell City, Newburgh, Spurgeon, Poseyville, and Fort Branch, home. The balance of C Company reservists, like their counterparts across the nation, were teenagers who had joined the reserves not only for the extra money but also for the travel and adventure reservist duty offered, as well as the glory that came with wearing a marine uniform. Inspired by the patriotic afterglow that followed World War II and by movies, such as 1948's *Sands of Iwo Jima,* these teenagers desired to play marines in the worst way. Many of them were underage but convinced a parent or guardian to sign for them.

For their part, parents likely believed their sons safe from actual harm since reservists of that time did not even face the rigors of Marine Corps boot camp. Evansville enlistees, like their counterparts across the nation, were also promised they could "turn their suits in anytime they wanted."[18] What was rarely stressed, however, was that this promise was null and void in the event a national emergency was declared. Most, of course, could not have possibly imagined that any such emergency would occur. Joining seemed to offer foolproof fun for the teenagers and a little extra money for the older, more practical reservists. Thus, like others throughout the nation who joined the Marine Corps Reserve in the late 1940s, the young men who enlisted in C Company hailed from places both large and small and joined for reasons both practical and frivolous. And like the young boys whose faces were forever frozen in the snapshot found in our upstairs attic, not one of them could possibly have imagined what lay in store for them on the bitterly cold shores of the Chosin Reservoir and, later, on other barren mountains of Korea.

Told in the larger context of international and national events and gleaned from dozens of extensive personal interviews, letters, diary accounts, high school yearbooks, newspapers and magazines, personal poems, and novels, this work relates the struggles, heartbreaks, and triumphs of an ordinary group of American men and their families in extraordinary times. It is the story of an unexpected journey both for members of C Company, United States Marine Corps Reserve, and for a nation at a most critical juncture in its history.

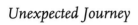

Unexpected Journey

1 *An Eddy on the Stream of Events*

In the late 1940s, on the eve of the Korean War, the nation as a whole continued to experience the incredible demographic and cultural transformations wrought by World War II. Two books in particular, both issued in 1948, reflected the cultural shifts with which America would soon struggle. Dr. Benjamin Spock's work, *The Common Sense Book of Baby and Child Care,* shaped an entire generation of parents. The book advised young mothers and fathers to disdain many traditional child-rearing practices and trust their intuition and common sense in raising their children. "You know more," Spock boldly declared to new parents, "than you think you do."[1] In the rather conservative Hoosier university town of Bloomington, Indiana, a respected academic was poised to drop some less-subtle information on the American people. Dr. Alfred Kinsey had quietly been compiling widespread research concerning American males' sexual habits for some time. In 1948, his *Sexual Behavior in the Human Male* hit bookstores like a bombshell. Kinsey's research seemed to explode once and for all "any hope Americans may have had of moral certainties."[2]

In the nation's heartland, during these turbulent times, moral leaders of the southwestern Indiana community of Evansville, despite what upstart experts were saying, continued to battle perceived attacks upon traditional morality. One local paper, in a curious but likely unintentional double entendre, printed that city clergy were greatly "aroused by [a] sex picture showing." The episode occurred at "a meeting of the Young Men's Republican Club formed sometime ago by [male] Evansville College students." The article further related that local ministers were "shocked that such a thing should happen in Evansville."[3]

The same year Evansville clergymen fought any falling away from local moral standards, Little David, "the 12-year-old boy preacher," carried on a series of religious meetings at the Evansville Coliseum. A local paper carried a large ad in which the boy wonder said he had "spent five hours in heaven. Jesus has sent me to preach," he said. "He tells me what to say." Thousands attended the week-long religious revival.[4] Another factor also lent hope that Evansville could somehow maintain its grip on values shaped by the past. Residents of this Hoosier city, in spite of the deep and disturbing changes unfolding all around them, could naïvely wish to find some escape from these great shifts through the area's geographic seclusion. Indeed, the physical and cultural remoteness that the Ohio River city had historically experienced led Hoosier journalist John Bartlow Martin in the late 1940s to surmise that "more than once its isolation has made Evansville an eddy on the stream of events."[5] The history of the community certainly lends support to Martin's observation.

Nestled on the Indiana side of an abrupt and rather picturesque bend of the Ohio River, Evansville got its start as a rugged frontier outpost serving as a jumping-off spot for settlers anxious to grab cheap land in the newly opened Northwest Territory. Behind the few "miserable" log huts that made up the struggling village, an early visitor found "an almost impassable road through a sickly swamp." The traveler also discovered more than one recent settler "regretting" he had left his previous home to settle here.[6] Over the years, the village would battle epidemics and international depressions, finally emerging as the dominant city in the region and eventually becoming, by the time of the Korean outbreak, the unofficial "capital of the tri-state area compromising the neglected tag ends of Indiana, Kentucky, and Illinois."[7]

Ironically, the event that most profoundly shaped Evansville would take place due to its very isolation. Located in the nation's heartland, safe from foreign attack, and located near the demographic center of the nation at that time, where a healthy and large labor force resided, Evansville unexpectedly found itself chosen for a number of industrial plants during World War II. The city's Chrysler Plymouth plant and Sunbeam Electric manufacturing company soon came under the control of the U.S. Army Corps of Engineers, producing small-arms ammunition. Before the war ended, this plant manufactured the majority of small-caliber ammunition for the U.S. war effort. Fearing that the East Coast was too vulnerable to attack, Republic Aviation Corporation also began in 1942 to produce P-47 fighters in a mammoth building along U.S. Highway 41 on the northern outskirts of the city. Yet by far the most jarring and exciting news came when the Navy Bureau of Ships decreed that Evansville would become the location for an LST (landing sea transport) shipyard.

At the height of production, sixty thousand people labored in the city during the war.[8] The cultural, physical, and financial landscape of Evansville and the region would forever be changed by this unexpected circumstance. "The boom," noted John Bartlow Martin, brought Evansville "everything you would expect—juvenile delinquency and girls and soldiers, saloons crowded with war workers, a housing shortage that drove new residents to refuge in basements and attics and trailers, tottering old men in Western Union uniforms, a swarm of prostitutes and gamblers, and all the bathroom anecdotes about the lady welder."[9] By 1944 the number of new laborers in Evansville equaled half the 1940 population.[10] Many of the new workers hailed from rural Kentucky, Tennessee, and Southern Illinois, creating a sudden dichotomy between the older Evansville population and the small-town and rural newcomers. One local historian noted the sudden friction: "While Philharmonic concerts drew sparse crowds, hillbilly music and wrestling matches [soon] packed the [Evansville] coliseum."[11]

After the war ended, Evansville hardly paused to take a breath. As did the rest of the nation between World War II and Korea, the city and the region found itself experiencing the great postwar boom. In 1948 major oil strikes began to dot the tristate area as well, causing one particularly astute observer to note that in Evansville's popular McCurdy Hotel lobby, "Hoosier politicians [now] mingled with Texans in ten gallon hats, and the talk at the circular bar of the Coral Room [was] more likely to be of wildcat wells than of crops."[12] At about this same time Republic Aviation sold its huge P-47 plant to International Harvester, which quickly turned to the manufacturing of refrigerators and air conditioners, fast-selling items in the postwar spending frenzy. Much of the new wealth that fueled consumer spending came as a result of the nation's dramatic and eventually costly shift from guns to butter. The demobilization of our once-powerful armed forces would occur at breakneck speed.

In hindsight, the massive demobilization of our military following the close of World War II seems almost criminal. At the time, however, the policy made some sense. In part, the weakening of our once-mighty military machine, built during the war, stemmed from the twin desires to bring the boys home as rapidly as possible and to get on with peacetime living. Further, the staggering problems that were likely to spring from twelve million soldiers demanding a discharge and a job loomed. The dual domestic evils of high inflation and unemployment suddenly appeared on the horizon as well, "at least until industry could again begin meeting the growing consumer demands and hiring the workers." Another twist to the problem involved President Harry Truman's commitment to New Deal programs. The economic situation, noted one historian, "brought fears that New Deal social programs might be sacked as the price of the new economic task." Truman's response, beginning in 1946, was the path of least resistance. The president "spent much of 1946 trying to delay such fears by cutting military spending rather than social programs."[13]

Trying to explain the lack of readiness at the outset of the Korean War, *Time* magazine related in a 1950 issue that after World War II, "the U.S. destroyed and left strewn around the globe billions of dollars worth of arms and equipment. It was too expensive to bring the stuff home; it would not be needed anyhow in the long years of peace which [supposedly] lay ahead." The article also pointed out that the call from citizens for an immediate peacetime posture "shook U.S. politicians to their shoes."[14] Demobilization fever brought staggering results. On V-J Day in 1945 the United States had a standing army of twelve million. A year later, in January of 1946, President Truman instructed the Pentagon to pare down the armed forces to two million. Congress, even more sensitive to the voter's cry to bring the boys home, set a limit of just over one million to be accomplished by 1 July 1947.

One way American leaders cut military costs while maintaining a psychological sense of military readiness was by stressing air power at the expense of ground forces. Our successes in bringing Germany and Japan to their knees through massive air strikes had convinced some leaders that a large standing army was likely obsolete anyway. Another factor that helped create a false sense of security during this downsizing period was our sole possession, until 1949, of the atomic bomb. Thus in early 1950, the United States possessed no long-range plans for a war requiring a substantial number of well-trained ground troops. This dangerous situation confronted the United States Marine Corps more profoundly than the other branches of the service.[15] The postwar mission of the Corps involved providing a trained force "to meet the requirements of a force in readiness in time of national emergency."[16] However, the fury of demobilization that occurred after the Japanese surrendered in 1945 dealt an especially hard blow to the marines and their unique mission.

Besides downsizing, the Corps also found itself threatened by a potential plan to unify the armed forces. Disturbing talk of cutting back wholesale on the Corps had drifted from the Pentagon since the war's end, so that its very identity seemed in jeopardy, and by 1946 the Corps' mission of being able to respond rapidly to threats anywhere in the world stood endangered. Marines feared that under a single Department of Defense "they would be devoured by the Army" or, at the very least, "lose their air arm to the Air Force."[17] At a hearing before the Senate Naval Affairs Committee, the Marine Corps commandant gave an especially powerful and emotional statement that soon became public: "The bended knee is not a tradition of our Corps. If the Marine as a fighting man has not made a case for himself after 170 years of service, he must go. But . . . he has earned the right to depart with dignity and honor."[18] Public outcry soon stifled any plans to disband the Marine Corps, though shrinking numbers due to cutbacks still threatened to be an insurmountable problem. Resourceful Marine Corps leaders, however, soon launched a plan to help compensate for Washington's dramatic cuts and keep the Corps in relative fighting form, estimated to be two full-strength divisions.[19]

Having had great success during World War II with a reserve system, the Corps decided once more to create a strong nonregular component that would serve to bring the Corps up to full strength in an emergency. Consequently, after World War II ended, Marine Corps planners allotted a major portion of the Corps' defense budget for training reserve units.[20] Altogether, twenty-one infantry battalions and a number of supporting-arms battalions, along with thirty fighter-bomber squadrons, would come to make up the nonregular portion of the Corps. The change, however, also called for the acceptance of a larger role for reserve members. Gen. Alexander Vandegrift, Marine Corps commandant, now sent out the word to regulars about this important development by noting that "during World War II, Marine Reserves, constituting the bulk of the Marine Corps, had a major share in its wartime achievements." Vandegrift then stressed to regulars that "all activities and personnel of the Marine Corps will share in the development and support of the Marine Corps Reserve. The objective for . . . both Regular and Reserve," further explained the commandant, "is the attainment of a mutual and cooperative appreciation to accompany a cautious program of military efficiency."[21] As it turned out, cooperation and respect between regular and reserve would not always be forthcoming.

More than 120 cities across the nation would eventually become sites for new Marine Corps Reserve companies. The Corps, realizing that filling the rosters was essential to the success of this endeavor, quickly went all out for recruiting. The Corps first sent out a plea to marine veterans of World War II, calling on the former marines "to wrestle a beachhead from the forces of indifference by volunteering for the reserve. We are calling," Commandant Vandegrift declared, "upon men whose courage helped smash the enemy at Guadalcanal, at Tarawa, at Iwo Jima" to help in the cause. Vandegrift went on to assert confidently that "if war should come, the men of the organized Reserves, trained in the latest tactics and techniques . . . will be ready to join their comrades . . . in manning the nation's first line of defense."[22]

To help ensure the success of the reserve recruitment plan, the Marine Corps League, roughly the Corps' version of the American Legion, also geared up to seek new recruits. One of the league's principal aims now became "to support a strong . . . Reserve."[23] All across America in the latter 1940s, marine recruiters, regulars, reservists, and veterans plunged headlong into the task of recruiting a large and effective reserve force. A motion picture produced by the Corps, *Centerville, U.S.A.,* opened in 1948, calling for patriots to join the Marine Corps Reserve system. It certainly did not hurt the recruiting cause either when *Sands of Iwo Jima,* starring John Wayne and glorifying the Marine Corps' efforts on that island in World War II, also came out in 1948. One ad for the movie in the popular Marine Corps magazine *Leatherneck* declared, in large bold letters, "Here it is mates, *Sands of Iwo Jima.* Just the way it was! . . . It's real, it's gutsy! It's the real McCoy!"[24] Marine recruiters claimed that enlistments in regular and reserve units shot up dramatically at the time of the movie's release.[25]

Regenerating some of the glory the marines had garnered in World War II, the Corps also speeded the delivery of medals and decorations to recently discharged troops, including reservists on inactive status.[26] To further attract high school recruits to join reserve units, the organized reserve purchased recreational and athletic equipment, and marine instructors for the reserve program were promptly told to employ up-to-date methods of instruction to ensure interesting presentations.[27] Sports served as an especially appealing hook for high schoolers. An advertisement in *Leatherneck* portrayed a youthful-looking baseball player swinging at a pitch. On the front of his shirt in bold letters were the words "Marine Reserve." The caption read "Join the home team."[28] Organized drills for reservists occurred weekly, supplemented by a two-week volunteer summer camp. Attendance at weekly volunteer sessions brought a reservist $7.50 for each effort. Every organized unit also obtained ornate blue uniforms for a unit band along with .22-caliber rifles and pistols for target training. Individual commanders of units received orders to make drills "fun," this to lure high school enlistees. Because they could offer plenty of "sea stories," a term marine veterans used to signify war stories, former marines who came into the new reserve system often made the best recruiters when it came to reaching the younger set.

Evansville, Indiana, had an ample number of World War II Marine Corps veterans, some of whom had witnessed considerable action in the Pacific. Most of these Evansville men belonged to the Marine Corps League, and it was this group that in early 1947 lobbied Col. Walker A. Reeves, director of the 9th Marine Corps Reserve District in Chicago, for an Evansville reserve company.[29] An indication of the success of their lobbying efforts appeared in a local newspaper article in September 1947: "Plans for the activation of a Marine Reserve unit to be attached to the 16th Infantry Battalion at Indianapolis were discussed at the Marine Corps League last night." The paper further reported that the new company was to meet at a temporary headquarters at the post office "until facilities are available at the Naval Armory, the former Marine Hospital," on Evansville's west side.[30]

In September 1947, Capt. William Chip, USMC, reached the river city as inspector-instructor of the new company and set about bringing aboard a group of men to begin the all-important recruitment process. The position of inspector-instructor was one the Corps did not take lightly. Other services used extended-active-duty reservists or special category noncombatants in this capacity, but the Corps almost always assigned the post to seasoned veterans, who spent several years out of their regular careers in this important work. Many of these men went on to obtain high officer rank in the Corps. William Chip eventually obtained the rank of general.[31]

C Company, 16th Infantry Battalion, was officially activated on 27 October 1947. The first locals to join the new unit had served in World War II and included, among others, Paul Torian, Roy Jolly, Don Savage, Sonny Hoepner, Garnet December, and Jerry Wilson. Donald Inkenbrandt also joined about this time and was the first nonveteran to enlist in the company. Paul Torian, who worked in his family's insurance business, was already a major in the Marine Corps Reserves and would soon find himself being considered for a leadership position in the new unit. As a marine captain, Torian had commanded a rifle company during some of the most furious fighting in the South Pacific theater. The tall, lanky former Dartmouth basketball star and Evansville native fought in the Bougainville and Guam campaigns and carried vivid memories of sleeping in standing water at nights while struggling to stay alive in inhospitable jungles.

Mostly forgotten today, the battle waged on Bougainville in many respects defies description. Marine veteran and historian William Manchester believed that the worst part of the struggle on that island involved the difficult terrain and weather. A "large mountainous island of spectacular volcanoes and trackless rain forests, Bougainville was a place where bulldozers can, and did, sink in the green porridge of swamp land without leaving a trace."[32] Torian, in that spirit-crunching struggle, won a Navy Cross, our nation's second highest military honor, "for extraordinary heroism as commanding officer of K Company, 3rd Regiment, 3rd Marine Division, against the Japanese . . . on November 24, 1943."[33] Torian also recalled that by his second series of combat experiences in Guam, he had lost much of his naïve enthusiasm for fighting. "The Marine Corps had you convinced you weren't a man until you killed a Jap," Torian remembered, "but by the time the Guam campaign rolled around, I had seen too much to buy into the typical marine line about killing."

In spite of his realistic attitude toward war, Torian understood the necessity of maintaining an effective fighting force and soon threw all his efforts in bringing in new recruits for the Evansville company. Roy Jolly, another Evansville marine veteran, also kept close contact with the Corps after World War II ended. Jolly, who noted he "always wanted to be a marine," had first joined the Corps on 8 January 1944, while still attending Reitz High School. Like Torian, Jolly had also witnessed the ferociousness and cruelty of war, having seen a number of young Marine Corps troops in the Pacific extracting gold teeth from Japanese soldiers, some of whom were still alive, with K-Bar Knives. These two World War II veterans, along with a number of other marines who served during the just completed war, would come to stand as important role models for the great majority of teenage C Company members.

When the Evansville reserve unit was officially activated in the early fall of 1947, Maj. Paul T. Torian found himself chosen as the commanding officer. At the ramshackle two-story Naval Reserve Armory, now also in use by the Marine Corps Reserve, Torian faced the unenviable task of filling a roster of about 240 men in a relatively short period of time. Fortunately, the sports-minded major quickly hit upon an effective plan of recruitment. In 1947 four high schools, Central, Bosse, Memorial, and Reitz, dotted the city. Torian contacted coaches in each school who were marine veterans to recruit their high school players. "There are four platoons in a rifle company, and I hit upon the idea of having a platoon to represent each high school in the city," Torian recalled. Jimmy Rausch, a coach at Reitz, found himself appointed lieutenant for the Reitz platoon; Marion "Tex" Graham from Central, now a lieutenant in C Company, headed the Central platoon;

coach Jimmy Graham of Bosse brought in his boys; and Hermie Will, coach at Memorial, led the Memorial platoon. At the time, these coaches felt they were doing their players a favor by encouraging them to join the reserve. The experience these boys would receive, their coaches believed, would be of great benefit to them in the future.

Limitations inherent in the reserve system soon placed tremendous pressure on reserve unit leaders. Enlistees maintained great latitude in staying or leaving this form of service, for they could be called up to active duty in time of peace only with their permission and had the right to be discharged "at [their] own request at any time when an emergency was not in effect."[34] Of course, no one at that time could fathom that any emergency would pop up and steal from reservists the option to walk away from reserve duty. Indeed, the opportunity to quit the reserve at any time was often emphasized by recruiters. High school–aged enlistees were told by recruiters "they could quit any time they wanted."[35] Another problem for reserve leaders, just as pressing as the retention dilemma, was the lack of training time. These two difficulties constantly loomed over reserve unit commanders, such as Major Torian, as they strove to create a viable Marine Corps Reserve component. "In just two hours a week, it was difficult to get much training done," Torian recalled. "On top of that, the emphasis, of course, had to be on making it interesting and fun because the young enlistees could quit anytime. Fortunately, in our case, the high school rivalry technique kept them interested and made them work harder."

Another surprise recruiting device turned out to be the success of C Company's softball team, fielded to play in Evansville's highly competitive industrial league. Roy Jolly, who played on the team, recalled that the regular marine staff in Chicago, realizing the public relations and recruiting opportunities a successful team would bring, requested that the Evansville unit field a team: "The company had two or three very good players at first, and they went out and encouraged their high school teammates to fill the ranks." In 1948 the C Company group won the City League Championship. "This," said Torian some years later, "was a great recruiting tool." Indeed, the marine softball team brought almost instant positive recognition in the sports-minded city.

One Evansville newspaper declared the marine reserve team "the team to beat in the Evansville Industrial Softball League." The article went on to note that "the Evansville Marine Corps Reserve team has clicked off eleven straight victories without defeat so far this season." Besides Roy Jolly, those who played on the team included, among others, Gill Pinkston, Sonny Hoepner, Bill Caulkins, Gene Koonce, Jimmy Rausch, Don Savage, and Bill Allgood. The local reserve paper bragged of the success of the company's softball endeavors and reported, "When the season finally ended, the Marines, as usual, had the situation well in hand as class B League Champions."[36] The company bowling team and basketball team also enjoyed good seasons in city league play. These and other recreational activities soon became an important drawing card for bringing young recruits into the fledgling company.

As a way of boosting its image even more, the reserve unit also carried out Operation Santa Claus Land in December 1948. An Evansville newspaper noted, "Twelve Marines in dress blues drove a parade of Yellow Taxi cabs carrying sixty orphans and underprivileged children through Evansville to Santa Claus, Indiana."[37] At the theme park in Santa Claus Land, the children were given presents and a meal by the Marine Corps drivers. A photograph of reservists Henry Maley, Robert Egan, Paul McDaniel, and William Mangrum with two of the underprivileged children appeared the next day in the local paper.

Many of the members who joined C Company in 1948, 1949, and 1950 were still in high school or had recently graduated. David Graham, a Bosse High School student when he joined the group, was perhaps typical of the many Evansville teenagers who soon made up a large portion of the local marine unit. Graham was a seventeen-year-old student when "the recruiters came to Bosse in full uniform and made their pitch." The glory of wearing a Marine Corps uniform, along with the extra money to be made from attending weekly drills and summer camp, acted as a powerful magnet to teenagers like Graham. Another Bosse High Schooler, Jess Thurman, had played football for the scarlet and gray. When Thurman graduated in 1947, he "was ready for the world." However, jobs that paid good money were hard to find. Luckily, Thurman's father helped his son get on at International Harvester. Thurman recalled "working many hours overtime and in a year saving enough money to pay cash for a new car." The young Bosse grad also needed cash for his hobby of racing stock cars, however, and the reserve offered just such a financial opportunity. Soon the resourceful Thurman purchased a used Ford and converted it into a stock car. "We raced on dirt tracks for fun and a little money," he recalled. The money the Evansville stock car driver made from attending weekly meetings at C Company drills, along with yearly summer camps, "helped pay the bills." Reitz graduate Bill Etheridge had two brothers in the Corps who often spoke about how great it was to wear a marine uniform. Etheridge's friend, Billy Grove, also told Etheridge how fun summer camps were, and these two factors convinced Etheridge to join the reserve in 1948 in order to "travel, see things, and make a few bucks."

Sometime in the fall of 1947, eighteen-year-old Charlie Deffendall, who had dropped out of school in order to go to work and bring in some desperately needed income for his family, spied a Marine Corps Reserve recruiting poster placed in the window of a temporary recruiting office in downtown Evansville: "Captain Chip came out and asked me if I was going to 'just stand there reading or do something about it.' I said 'Let's do something about it.'" Deffendall quickly joined, finding the meetings a good place to make up for the camaraderie he had missed by dropping out of school. The young man became one of the most loyal of the reservists, hardly missing a weekly meeting and making both summer camps.

Henry Orth Jr. was another Evansville native who had dropped out of high school and discovered the reserves offered some solace for not having finished schooling: "I went right to work at Stocker Body Company when I was sixteen. I always liked cars—I had been driving since I was thirteen." Orth and his best friend had joined the reserves together in 1948. "Richard Whitfield's coach at Central High School talked Whitfield into signing up; then Whitfield convinced me to join," Orth recalled. "We signed in the living room of Whitfield's mother's house." Orth remembered going to a few of the meetings at first and "playing soldier," but the hard working Evansville man soon grew tired of the routine at the Reserve Headquarters and mostly stopped attending meetings. Still, there were perks in attending. "The best thing about the deal was you could go into a tavern and be served as long as you were in uniform—underaged or not. We'd go to Bert Lehr's [a local tavern] or pick up girls when we were coming back from meetings—while we still had our uniforms on."

Local veterans of World War II soon flocked to the Evansville reserve as well. Paul McDaniel, who along with several other members of the Evansville chapter of the Marine Corps League had first requested a reserve company for Evansville, joined after his boss, who had come aboard the week before, "thought I ought to go out there and join too." Bill Wright, a Virginia native who at seventeen had escaped the coal fields by joining the marines during World War II, found himself in Evansville, Indiana, in 1946 working for a local phone company. Having enjoyed his Marine Corps experiences during the previous war, Wright soon enlisted in the Evansville unit. About one-fourth of the unit's members were, like Wright, veterans, and it was "comforting" for the Virginia native "to go back and see familiar things."

Twenty-two-year-old veteran Robert Egan was at the end of his freshmen year at Evansville College, going to that school on the GI Bill, when he joined the marine unit in the early summer of 1950. Fellow Evansville college student and World War II veteran Gene Koonce had joined in 1947. Koonce was just a teenager when he participated in heavy fighting on Guam and Okinawa. On the latter island he became engaged in some of the most hellish action in the Pacific theater. Fighting on Sugarloaf Hill, Koonce recalled the horrors of an Japanese artillery attack. "If you never prayed before, you did under one of those Japanese bombardments," he said. "The shells would just come in screaming." Koonce's battlefield experiences would later make the difference between life and death for many of the reservists at the Chosin Reservoir.

Over in Poseyville, Indiana, veteran Raleigh McGary listened to some of his friends as they badgered him to join the reserves with them. "We'll sit around after meetings and have a couple of beers and have a lot of fun," they told McGary. The Poseyville man had just finished his junior year at Evansville College and worked at Servel in Evansville during the summer between college semesters. Ironically, by the time the reserves were called up, McGary's friends had resigned, leaving McGary to receive a free trip to Korea. Another World War II veteran, Richard Eberle, became a part of the reserve without his knowledge when an overeager officer of C Company, who was trying to help fill the roster, swore the sleeping Eberle into the reserve while the former marine lay dozing on his cot at the local YMCA. When the Evansville reserve company was suddenly activated shortly after the war began, the stunned Eberle discovered that he was a part of the unit when an MP delivered a notice of activation. To his shock, Eberle also discovered that his lack of participation in reserve training did not exempt him from being called up. The Evansville native was not alone in his belief that a lack of attendance at reserve meetings would exclude him from any call up. Many reservists across the country who had not taken part in drills or summer camps mistakenly believed they were no longer in the service because of their lack of involvement.

It was not unusual for reserve companies to battle with the problem of members not showing up. The Evansville unit apparently was struggling with this problem by the spring of 1950, for the company's monthly monogram declared that "the members of C company should keep the goal of the Organized Marine Corps Reserve in mind, and, regardless of their own reasons for joining . . . make every effort to accomplish its goals. That means starting here in C Company with Better Attendance, More Cooperation, and Better Military Bearing."[38] In early 1950 the national reserve publication, the *Reserve Marine,* also stressed the need for improvement in attendance among nonregular marine members. Reservists were urged to go to summer camp and were further cautioned that "glamour was not part of the summer camp training." The *Reserve Marine* went on to declare, "Be prepared upon your return to answer affirmatively the question— 'Could I now better serve my country in the event of mobilization?'"[39]

Evansville was not the only area community caught up in "Marine Corps Fever" during the latter portion of the 1940s. When Lt. Mason Wiers, dressed in his blues, came and spoke at nearby Boonville and Tennyson High Schools, several area juniors and seniors came forward and joined. Their interest in enlisting was not surprising. Boonville sits at the center of Warrick County and serves as the county seat. Several large coal-stripping operations dotted the area in the late 1940s, where monstrous drag lines pulled tons of dirt from rich coal seams. Teenagers of the area were expected to take their places alongside their coal mining fathers when they graduated from high school. The reserve unit at Evansville now offered occasional relief from the vocational world these young men would be expected to join. "We were looking for some excitement, and they threw a little money into the mix," recalled one former Boonville high schooler, Carl Barnett. Many, like Charles Gottman, were so young that a parent, in Gottman's case his mother, had to sign a release before they could actually join.

Having something to look forward to, to break the monotony of small-town life, ultimately induced several Warrick County boys to sign. "World War II was over," remembered Gottman, "and we were at peace—it looked like it would last forever, so joining the reserve offered a summer of fun and some extra money." Several Boonville area men and boys would join C Company, including Bill Hester, George France, Albert Ashley, Bill Gordon, Charles Gottman, Carl Barnett, George Middleton, and Ralph Hargrave. Hargrave worked as a mechanic in Boonville and had seen action in World War II at Bougainville, Guam, and Okinawa. In the spring of 1948 the twenty-seven year old decided he needed the extra money that attending reserve meetings provided. Getting his corporal rank back, the Boonville native soon noticed that many of the Evansville unit members were either just out of high school or still in their junior and senior years of school, a knowledge that brought him a vague sense of déjà vu, as he was suddenly reminded how young and naïve he and his comrades had been when they were shipped off to fight the Japanese. Hargrave was glad that these young men would not have to experience the horrors of combat, or so he believed at the time.

Another nearby small community, Oakland City, a quiet college town thirty miles north of Evansville, would also offer up some of its best young citizens to the Marine Corps Reserve. Charles "Barney" Barnard had been the first Oakland City native to join C Company, and in this town where nothing ever seemed to happen, word spread rapidly of how much fun reserve meetings were. Barnard sought out his Boy Scout companions, Albert Dickson and Gordon Greene, telling them of the extra money and adventure the Marine Corps Reserve offered. The six-foot-four Dickson, who was a popular basketball star and Boy Scout leader, influenced still others to enlist.

Gordon Greene, labeled the "happiest student" in his senior class yearbook, carried the reputation of class cutup and jokester. Greene constantly encouraged all those around him to have fun. Photographs of Greene at this age often show the young teenager making funny faces at the camera. Greene's persona, however, masked a difficult early life. Abandoned by his father when young, Greene would come to live with a large, extended family who resided in rural Pike County, Indiana. Surrounded by a number of older siblings, the young boy often found himself walking forlornly to and from a one-room school and later recalled how in winter the wind chilled him to the bone on his lonely sojourns. When World War II broke, Greene's brothers went into the service, forcing Greene's mother to move to nearby Oakland City. Once again, the sensitive young boy faced a new and difficult environment.

While poorer than many of the other boys in Oakland City, Greene quickly befriended three of the more popular kids in the community: Albert Dickson, Barney Barnard, and Robert "Bud" Fitch. Together, the four boys shared the bonding adventures typical of American males in that time and place. Some early experiences, however, were traumatic. In 1944, Greene and some other boys had been playing along the street curbs after a particularly heavy summer storm. Suddenly, a boy slipped, and the raging waters carried him into a storm drain, where he drowned. Oddly, Greene felt a great deal of guilt over this event: "I don't believe that the parents ever recovered from his loss. As the years passed and I grew older, I would make conversation with the mother, but I always felt uncomfortable around her. It was as if I had a guilt feeling about surviving."[40] Many years later, another death of a childhood friend in Korea would elicit the same kind of guilt from Greene. It would be a feeling Greene would wrestle with the rest of his life.

Bud Fitch was perhaps the brightest of the exceptional group of young men from Oakland City who joined the reserves. The oldest son of the local Blackfoot Coal Mine superintendent, Bud had been chosen the most talkative and wittiest boy in his senior class. Smart and well liked, Bud possessed a terrific sense of humor that could sometimes turn sharp. The thick glasses he wore added an extra air of intelligence to his demeanor. Like most high school males of that day, young Fitch dreamed of success in sports, and although not the most athletic boy in the class of 1950, he worked hard on this dream, going out for both the Oakland City High School baseball and football teams. This effort had paid off by his senior year. Voted captain of the Oakland City Acorns' football team, Bud Fitch also made the honorable mention all-conference team at the position of center.[41] Boy Scout meetings (many of the young men in this group became Eagle Scouts) and a paper route also took up much of Fitch's and the other Oakland City boys' time; yet something was missing for these boys—an element of excitement for which teenage males often long. The Marine Corps Reserve seemed to be just the thing to bring some excitement into their lives. Bud Fitch, however, like several other of the Oakland City boys who came to join C Company, was underage that summer of 1949, the summer before his senior year. It seemed good fortune at the time when Bud's mother, Garnet, signed a release for him so that he could wear a marine uniform.

The same summer Bud Fitch enlisted in the reserves, sixteen-year-old William Marshall, while swimming one day at Enos Lake east of Oakland City, listened to three older boys, Albert Dickson, Gordon Greene, and William Cunningham, chatter excitedly about their experiences at a Marine Corps Reserve summer camp. Kenny Dougan, another sixteen year old, also heard the same talk that summer. The next spring, in May 1950, Marshall and Dougan joined the C Company unit. Both boys still had a year of high school to complete. Marshall and Dougan, like Fitch, were underage, but Marshall got his grandfather, with whom he lived, to sign for him, and Dougan charmed his mother into doing the same, much to his father's distress. The trauma caused by one parent signing a release while the other fretted over the potential repercussions would be repeated often during the reserve enlistment drive prior to the Korean War. When the war did fall upon these families, those who lost sons were often shattered by the fact that a family member had signed a release for their underage son.

Besides the prestige a marine uniform brought, other motives no doubt drove Bud Fitch and several other teenagers from Oakland City to become Marine Corps reservists. In the summer of 1949 memories of World War II still flourished in the minds of most Oakland City natives, continuing a spirit of patriotism. The nation as a whole had thrown itself totally into the recent war effort, causing the country to experience a unity of purpose unsurpassed in its history. In Indiana the latest news of the war created the kind of excitement previously generated only by the state basketball tournament. People in communities such as Oakland City often bought large maps to follow the war effort and discussed the latest battle reports as if they were sporting events. During that war, troop trains had sometimes rolled through town, packed full of noisy GIs. Occasionally, one of these trains would unexpectedly stop, blocking the crossings and giving younger Oakland City boys an exciting opportunity to converse with real soldiers through the train car windows. In one instance, Gordon Greene remembered loping alongside a line of cars just starting to move, imploring anyone who might happen to end up in Sicily to tell his brother hello for him. "He is an army engineer," Greene shouted to anyone who might have happened to listen in the rapidly accelerating cars.[42] Like most communities during World War II, Oakland City also had a large "Roll of Honor" board placed downtown on which the names of those who were serving in the war could be seen by the entire community. Those who lost their lives while serving their country had a gold star placed beside their name. As Boy Scouts, during the war, all of the boys from Oakland City who would come to join the Marine Corps Reserve unit had worked closely together for the war effort through scrap and paper drives.[43]

West of town, near the house in which Bud Fitch lived, Oakland City boys spent endless hours playing soldier during World War II, fighting "our own war, Americans against Germans." Elaborate trenches were constructed in the loose brown soil and "the woods was soon honeycombed with bunkers."[44] Albert Dickson recalled that, when unable to go outside, the boys "gathered inside to play with toy soldiers." Bloody battles that raged overseas were eagerly reenacted by this innocent band of boys who dreamed of one day achieving the ultimate glory they believed came from combat. Garold Sheetz also remembered staying overnight in the Fitch home where he and Bud worked on a "secret invention which would end the war." Occasionally, the brutality of war would intrude upon the world of these young men. Oakland City gave up several of its citizens to the war effort, and Gordon Greene even sent his dog Buster to the army K-9 Corps, where the animal died while in that service.

Perhaps the most influencing force that eventually brought Fitch, Greene, Sheetz, Marshall, and the other Oakland City boys to join the Marine Corps Reserves were all the stories they had heard from veterans of World War II. To these teenagers, war looked to be the most exciting adventure a person could possibly experience. Gordon Greene, who had two brothers in the war, especially longed to experience combat and return with "sea stories" to tell to admiring friends in Oakland City. With the reserve system in place by 1947, teenagers all across the nation could now fulfill fantasies stirred by the recent memories of World War II. By May 1950, eleven Oakland City boys were serving in C Company: Barney Barnard, Albert Dickson, Gordon Greene, William Cunningham, Forrest Miller, Bud Fitch, Garold Sheetz, Donald Cochren, Donald Corn, Kenneth Dougan, and William Marshall.

Although younger reservists from Evansville would probably not have found going to meetings as exciting as the teenagers from the smaller outlying towns, they still could look forward to having something to do. David Graham, the Bosse High School student who had joined in 1947, remembered the two-hour sessions at the reserve center as including close-order drills, lectures, firing .22-caliber rifles on a small inside firing range, and carrying out "field problems" in a nearby grove of woods. Sometimes, Graham recollected, the lecturer attempted to add some color and reality to the training. In one instance a speaker held a "live" grenade in front of his young audience, pulled the pin, then "accidentally" dropped it. The grenade rolled on the floor while the speaker ducked for cover. The startled reservists hit the deck, but not before one resourceful teenager picked up the grenade and hurled it through a closed window, shattering the glass. When the fake grenade failed to explode, the instructor nonchalantly walked back into the room and complimented the fast-reacting young man who had thrown the grenade through the window. The young man's reactions "demonstrated," said the instructor, "true marine-like composure."

Often the younger enlistees had difficulty understanding exactly what their instructors wanted. Bill Etheridge, another teenage recruit who would soon participate in some of the most brutal fighting of the Korean War, remembered being told by a lieutenant at one of the Evansville drills that he would "never shape up to be a marine." Despite the lieutenant's opinion, Etheridge served with great distinction in combat. Although many teenage reservists struggled with learning true marine-like composure, the younger men could look up to twenty-year-old John Elliott, who had just finished his sophomore year at Evansville College in the spring of 1950 and had previously attended a military school in Chattanooga, Tennessee. The popular Elliott seemed to understand the military lifestyle better than any of the younger members of C Company and so was looked upon as a model of how to be a marine.

Veterans seemed to get more out of the training at the Evansville meetings than the younger members of the reserve group. Paul McDaniel recalled that the training in Evansville included rifle assembly, squad performance, hand signaling, and general field hygiene. Bill Wright, another "older" member of the unit, also believed the training proved to be "top notched." Although such brief instruction time may have helped veterans brush up, it likely did little to prepare the vast majority of the group of younger men who had their minds on things other than training. A lack of proper equipment only added to the problem. The unit would not actually handle M1 rifles until about two weeks before they left Evansville for Camp Pendleton.

This lack of experience with weapons, especially on the part of the younger reservists, became dramatically apparent at one reservist gathering held as a send-off for the Evansville group. Teenagers Arthur Hart Jr. and William Ginger were standing around inside the Marine Corps Reserve Headquarters when they spied a reservist carrying a .45 automatic pistol. The two marines casually asked the fellow reservist if his gun was loaded. "The guy said it wasn't, and we jokingly asked him if he was sure," Hart recalled. "'I'll show you' he told us. So he pulled out the .45, aimed it at Ginger's chest, and pulled the trigger." A loud explosion told the three young men that the gun owner had been terribly wrong. Ginger was rushed by ambulance to a nearby hospital, where doctors discovered that the bullet had traveled through Ginger's body without hitting any vital organs. The lucky marine reservist recovered quickly and, in fact, was able to rejoin his company members for combat training.

If the weekly volunteer meetings at sites such as Evansville failed to prepare reservists for handling weapons and for unexpected combat, it was hoped by Marine Corps top brass that the two-week volunteer summer camps would fill the void. Indeed, the national director of the reserves boldly declared in 1948 that the military efficiency of the reserve as a potential fighting force, able to take its place alongside the regular service, "increased 100 percent over 1947" because of summer camp training.[45] Contrary to this assessment, summer camp participation, which was voluntary, fell off from 54 percent in 1948 to 41 percent in the summer of 1949.[46]

In reality, both weekly sessions and summer camps probably failed to prepare reservists for the rigors of actual combat. As one historian of Marine Corps history noted, "Once-a-week nighttime drills inhibited training, and summer camps were not well attended. More significantly, new recruits did not attend boot camp or receive advanced training." The reservists were "largely untrained and many [had] joined for social and athletic reasons." The result of these circumstances was "a Reserve unprepared for war."[47] Some reservists' experiences in the training process led them to believe that the drills and camps were a monumental waste as well. Said one disgruntled reservist of his experiences, "I witnessed nothing but confusion, disorder, overspending, . . . and everything but sound constructive training."[48]

Regardless of the criticisms, most Marine Corps leaders still considered the reserve training process as viable and the two-week summer camps as the most important piece of instruction for reserve members. Addressing a letter to "Mr. Volunteer Marine Reservist, Everywhere U.S.A.," in the spring of 1950, the national director of reserves, Maj. Gen. Merwin H. Silverthorn, strongly encouraged every reservist to attend: "Marines are noted for their constant improvements in modern warfare. It is essential that you as a member of the Volunteer Reserve be thoroughly familiar with those improvements so that, should an emergency arise, you will be fully prepared for active duties."[49]

Despite hopes of what might be accomplished at these camps, the results were often spotty for those who attended, as evidenced by the experiences of the Evansville group. Summer camps were billed in the Evansville reserve publication, *Devil Dog,* as "the most important single training place, providing," the publication claimed, "an excellent opportunity for officers to evaluate [a] unit's performance." The camps also offered the enlistee the possibility "of evaluat[ing] himself, to find out how he stacks up." Camps were voluntary, so they were often touted for the adventure they provided and for the escape from familiar surroundings they offered. "Two weeks at Summer Camp spells travel and adventure," proclaimed one reservist publication. "It is a chance to see NEW SIGHTS and live away from home." This same publication also noted, "There will be plenty of time and equipment for recreation."[50] These activities included softball, baseball, golf, swimming, boating, fishing, tennis, and bowling.

On 30 June 1948, the Evansville unit received their first orders to report "for annual field training duty . . . at the Marine Barracks, Camp Lejeune."[51] Here the younger Evansville reserves would be immersed in Marine Corps culture, learning the idioms that all marines were expected to use: scuttlebutt, pogey bait, slopchute, skivvies, and so on. Assigned sixty-six lower and sixty-six upper tourist berths in Pullman cars, those who volunteered for camp began their journey on a hot August day. Although the younger members of C Company looked forward to the experience, the older veterans, especially those with families, dreaded the hot, smoky, coal-fired train ride that lay before them. Opening a Pullman window to get a little air, Evansville marines would "be hit with a hot blast of sooty smoke."

Despite the opportunity to experience instruction from regular marines, only about half of the Evansville reservists took part in "eight mile hikes and small arms instructions in the 1948 camp."[52] Arriving back in Evansville some days later, the C Company group was interviewed by a local newspaper, and their remarks suggested the camp's lack of difficulty. "Upon leaving the train," the paper read, "the majority of the men agreed the two weeks had been fun. Talking the marine lingo, they said the chow had been good and many expressed desire to go back next year." Many of the participants were teenagers who had their first experience "swimming in the ocean."[53] At the 1948 camp, Evansville reservist and World War II veteran Roy Jolly set a new camp target-shooting record with a Browning automatic rifle. His brilliant effort also tied the world's record.

The next year, on 18 June 1949, C Company left once more for summer training, this time traveling to the Naval Amphibious Base at Little Creek,

Virginia. Oakland City native Gordon Greene, who was seventeen at the time, wrote his mother about the long, uncomfortable train ride to the 1949 camp: "We arrived here Sunday afternoon about 5:30 o'clock. Our trip was marred by rain and fog. The Pullman we came over on was an old dilapidated one. There was no air conditioning but only two small fans in each end. Coal dust was continually coming in and as a result all the seats and bunks were covered with soot." The trip was Greene's first adventure away from southwest Indiana, and the young Hoosier excitedly reported to his mother that he saw "twenty aircraft carriers in the harbor and many Navy and Marine Corps planes." Greene's childhood wish to be a real soldier had partially come true.

Despite the excitement the camps may have generated among teenage reservists, training procedures did not always go smoothly during summer camp exercises. Younger reservists discovered, for example, that marine instructors sometimes had their own agendas. During the 1949 camp, the Evansville group took part in landing on a simulated defended beach. Tossed by ten-foot waves and whipped by a hot wind, the Evansville men "clung grimly to slick and wet cargo nets as they made their way" into the small landing boats.[54] Bill Etheridge found the going especially rough when one C Company platoon lieutenant, who had coached against Etheridge when the powerfully built athlete played football for Reitz, made Etheridge go down the dangerous rope ladder first to hold down the net for the others. "Why do I have to go first?" the puzzled and scared Etheridge asked. "Because you played football for Reitz . . . and I don't want to get my players hurt," answered the lieutenant.

Another Evansville member's experiences also indicated the lack of discipline present at these camps. Reservist Jess Thurman was told to report to his sergeant before they were to leave on an evening march. "Sergeant Poole unloaded my pack and filled it up with cans of beer," Thurman recalled. "Later on in the field he would yell at me to report to him. Each time he would chew me out and take out a couple of beers, then he would yell at me to take my position and keep alert. If I had been caught, I would have been the one in trouble." Other circumstances, besides uneven instruction, also made summer training difficult and sometimes ineffective for the younger participants. One Evansville reservist talked of the dust and heat that summer and how "it had hardly rained at all here and the temperature is always around a hundred degrees."[55] Summing up the summer camp experiences just prior to the outbreak of the Korean War, Major Torian observed, "None of these men, veterans or teenagers, ever imagined they would end up in a place like Korea. Had they known this, they likely would have paid much more attention to their instructors."

Another major problem for the reserve program, which became evident during these summer camps, was the negative attitude regular marines often had toward reservists. "It was hard to make friends with the regulars," feisty Evansville reservist and World War II veteran Roy Jolly remembered. "They called us weekend warriors." What galled Jolly in particular was that he set a new record with the BAR rifle at the 1948 summer camp and yet was still looked down upon by regular marines. (The BAR was dropped from our nation's weapon arsenal after the Korean War, leaving Jolly's record to stand permanently.) After Jolly broke the record for Camp Lejeune by hitting 123 out of 125 targets, a regular presented Jolly with the trophy. "He was one who kind of came over to our side," the Evansville native noted, "but I later witnessed several regulars confront one of our boys at that same summer camp." A few of the Evansville reserves had just taken seats at a "slopchute" when some regulars came up to them and said, "Weekend warriors. We can tell that by looking." Jolly then recalled how the regulars began to pick on John Hirsch, an Evansville reservist at the time: "Hirsch had training in the martial arts. He tried to avoid a fight, but one regular pushed him down, and when Hirsch got up another pushed him down again. Finally they took it outside, and Hirsch whipped both of the regulars."

Gene Koonce recalled that the regulars who were most vocal about their dislike of the reservists were those who had come into the Corps after World War II: "What made the situation so odd was that reservists like myself who had participated in actual combat were being talked down to by younger men who had not even been there." Evansville reservist Wayne Poole, however, had a unique answer to the problem. When he and another reservist, David Schellhase, went into a local bar during summer training, Schellhase remembered Poole telling him, "Whatever you do, don't tell anyone you're a reservist."

The putdowns from regulars the Evansville reservists experienced in summer camp training were just part of a much larger and potentially more damaging problem. The controversy, which had heated up in the late 1940s as the Corps aggressively pursued building up a large reserve component, had first appeared during World War II when "early Regulars, contemptuous of the high-spirited new-comers, attempted to preserve their 'old boys club.'" One of the most renowned jungle fighters of the "Banana Wars" and, later, Guadalcanal, Merritt "Red Mike" Edson, "actually sought to replace the Reserve officers in his new raider battalion with Regulars." The prejudice never went away. Battalion monthly muster rolls, for example, "continued to report Regular members first, from colonel to private, then separately, the reserves."[56]

The ongoing conflict was clearly reflected in letters written in the late 1940s to the editors of two popular Marine Corps magazines, *Leatherneck* and the *Marine Corps Gazette*. In 1947 one regular complained in a letter to *Leatherneck* that "when a Marine goes back to his hometown and finds a lot of people living there who parade around at night in a Marine uniform, it's about time someone did a little gumbeating." The regular went on to note that reservists "wear civilian clothes during the day . . . and change into uniforms at night."[57] Officially, inactive reserve members such as the Evansville group were allowed to wear their uniforms "only while at drill, while taking part in appropriate ceremonies, . . . at memorial services, or while performing . . . active duty or training."[58] However, the practice of wearing uniforms at inappropriate times seemed to be universal. Another regular lamented that even though the Marine Corps manual restricted the wearing of uniforms by reservists, "Who is seeing that these regulations are being adhered to?" The writer added, "I have run into more than one of these 'big time Joes' in my hometown and elsewhere complete with a snow job for the unwary citizen. Their overall scroungy appearance would make one shudder." Finally, the regular pointed out that he believed it was primarily "high school, just out of high school, and the non-military component of the Reserve that are creating this lowered opinion of the Marine Corps by wearing uniforms at improper times."[59]

In an attempt to bridge the gap between the reserve and the regular, *Leatherneck* magazine soon began to carry at least one article per issue that focused solely on the reserves' part in the larger picture of the Marine Corps mission. The response of regulars to these articles was for the most part negative. One letter complained, "We would like to know why the Reserves rate more space in the magazine than the Regulars? Is their work more important than the job of the Regulars who are sweating out their overseas time in places like Guam?"[60] This complaint quickly drew a counterresponse from a reservist who was also a marine veteran from World War II: "We don't want more space than the Regulars but it's good to print a few pages of what the Reserves are doing, to show the Regulars . . . that they have someone to count on in case anything should happen." He added, "There are quite a few Marine veterans in the Reserve. I am a Marine veteran, myself, with two campaigns to my credit." Broaching the tension between regulars and reserves, the vet continued, "I'm not going to say that the Reserves are better than the Regulars but why don't they quit knocking us down? Don't forget, as I said before, there are quite a few Marine vets in the Reserve; what they learned during the war some of the present-day Marine Regulars will never learn. . . . Give us Reserves a break. Don't forget, we know what the score is, too."[61]

Tension between the two marine components showed up in the *Marine Corps Gazette* as well. One reserve sergeant suggested in 1948 that since most reservists had spent "two weeks of strenuous training" and had taken part "in local parades, civic functions, celebrations . . . all on their own time" that they be exempt from boot camp and be given their grade if they transferred to the regular marines.[62] The response to the sergeant's suggestion was swift and cutting: "It just burns me up," countered a regular, "to see someone who has been in the Organized Reserve for 'a year or more' and who has undergone two weeks of *strenuous training* at Camp Pendleton and who was probably handed a Reserve sergeant's rate because there just didn't happen to be any one else to give it to say that he wants to be a sergeant in the Regulars for those reasons. . . . If he wants to be a Marine sergeant let him come in as a private and earn his rate by a lot of hard work like the rest of us have."[63] Some who sent letters to the editor, usually officers, called for peace on the matter. One wrote, "I think it is no accident that, of all the Armed Services, the Marine Corps alone can say with confidence, that among its Reservists and other alumni, there are no soreheads. The main reason for this, as I see it, is that everyone who wears the Marine Corps emblem is a Marine. . . . Every measure must be taken to keep this concept alive." The officer ended the letter by restating that the important thing to remember was that "every one of us is a Marine."[64]

Like *Leatherneck,* the *Marine Corps Gazette* also began to emphasize the importance of the reserve component after the recruiting drive for new reserve members began full blast in 1947. "Reserve Duty Is No Frolic" was the title of one October 1948 article. This piece noted that "the Reserve is now charged with grim and intense realism" and warned that inspector-instructors who are placed in charge of a reserve unit had better forget their "dreams about a rest cure and prepare . . . for two or more years of hard work."[65] In another article printed in 1949, the *Gazette* emphasized the sobering fact that "the global wars featured in this century call upon the Reserves to do most of the fighting and dying. This is not due to the surpassing bravery every Reserve hides beneath his civilian vest. It is just that, like the Lord's poor people, there are so many of them." The article went on to declare that it was of utmost importance that the reservist be instilled with the esprit de corps of the marines so that "in a national emergency . . . , he has acquired the feeling of being a Marine . . . it will carry him through situations he could not tolerate in a civilian state of mind."[66]

Marine Corps leadership finally realized that the animosity between the regulars and reserves lay at the feet of both groups. "Too many Regulars consider Reservists as outsiders," noted one Corps leader, "trying to 'muscle in' as rank seekers and parasites on their appropriations." Conversely, "many Reservists have a chip on their shoulders and too frequently take the attitude that all Regulars are 'interested only in holding down the Reserves.'"[67] Despite pleas from the top for both parties to seek "unity and loyalty," the dichotomy between the two groups would continue to simmer with some marines, even throughout the Korean War.

In the months before the shocking news of Korea broke, nothing was likely more remote from the thoughts of the American people than the notion of war in Asia. The week prior to the war's outbreak witnessed the end of the most prosperous six-month period for the nation since the end of World War II. Customers, for example, purchased "so many automobiles and television sets . . . that the food and clothing industries were preparing a campaign to lure people away from auto and TV showrooms by reducing prices."[68] Yet not everything was perceived as rosy at this time. In the spring of 1950, in a poll of fifty-one of the nation's leading newspapers, *Argosy* magazine asked editors what headlines their readers would most like to see. Three themes dominated: the end of Russia's threat to world peace (including a decline in danger from atomic weapons), a cure for cancer, and proof of personal immortality. Perhaps due to the overshadowing atomic threat and growing fear of cancer, "church membership in all faiths of the United States took an upward swoop of 2,426,723 during the year of 1949 . . . [to] an all-time high of 81,862,328."[69] Most events, however, presented by the news media in the first half of 1950 suggested a nation thinking of anything but war. Happenings reported in newspapers and magazines that first week of summer underscored the peaceful times in which America and the Evansville region had settled.

Time magazine noted that summer, "Americans were simply engaged in history's biggest vacation travel spree."[70] President Harry Truman participated by taking a leisurely overnight cruise down the Potomac in the presidential yacht *Williamsburg.* "The taxpayers," Truman said with a grin, "are working me too hard."[71] Ads in Evansville's Sunday *Courier and Press* touted Havana, Cuba, and Tampa, Florida, as popular vacation destinations. Eastern Airlines promised to deliver vacationers from Evansville to St. Louis in seventy-five minutes, and railroad ads stressed being able to *see* the countryside while traveling. Local front-page news featured the crowning of Miss Betty Sue Kemmerling as queen of New Harmony's Golden Raintree Festival. Also appearing in the paper in a feature story, a former Bosse High School teacher who was home on visit from Hong Kong, Mrs. Reginald G. Parsons, confidently declared that "the reverence of family in China would doom communism to an early end there." Local ads, like their national big brothers, offered folks of the tristate the latest deals. The 18 June paper declared the next day to be "Evansville Day" for area shoppers, and merchants filled page after page with advertisements of the bargains available. Salm's offered $2.99 dresses on sale for $1.88, and men's dress shirts were on sale at Sater's for $1.65. Kresge's plugged "sun-back cottons for tan or for town" at $1.98, and DeJong's offered

"Microfilm No-Seam Nylons" for 69 cents. Finke's promoted a "Suntan Lounge" for $29.95.[72]

Along with news and advertisements, the local paper offered possibilities for filling leisure hours. Readers could find their favorite comics, such as *Ally Oop, L'il Abner, Wash Tubb,* and *Steve Canyon,* among others. The "Books Readers Like Best" column showcased *I Leap Over the Wall,* Monica Baldwin's account of the return to the secular world after twenty-eight years in a convent. Ironically, the book review column also discussed *The Wisdom of America,* by Chinese philosopher Lin Yutang. Local radio programming the week of 18 June included *Your Hit Parade* and *Dennis Day* on WGBF, *Stop the Music* and *Harry Wismer Sports* on WJPS, and *The Gene Autry Show* on WEOA. Television fans could settle in to watch *The Gary Moore Show, Studio One,* or *Meet the Press.* Moviegoers had several choices, such as Shirley Temple and David Niven in *A Kiss for Corliss* at the Carlton, *In the Good Old Summertime* with Judy Garland and Van Johnson at the Alhambra, and opening at the Ross: *Johnny Holiday,* a story of juvenile delinquency filmed at the Plainfield Indiana's Boys' School. Fans were eagerly anticipating Spencer Tracy and Elizabeth Taylor in *Father of the Bride,* which would open soon at Loews. The Family Drive-in Theater, where many of the younger C Company members took dates, was showing *So Dear to My Heart.* Live entertainment in the area included Woody Herman and his orchestra at the Coliseum, Jan Garber and his orchestra at the Club Trocadero, and a nighttime dance at Burdette Park. Baseball and golf produced the sports headlines that final week of tranquility, both on a national and local level. Headlines proclaimed "Musial's .366 Tops National" and "Detroit Increases Lead with 2-1 Win Over Boston." Local baseball league statistics filled columns of copy. In the city golf meet, Jack Schaff led Earl Greenwelle by a stroke.[73]

The week of 18 June 1950, just a week before the war fell, found a few C Company men and their families in complete sync with the rest of the "vacation happy" country. Bill and Evelyn Wright hid away in sunny Daytona Beach, Florida, and platoon leader Tex Graham, between classes at Indiana State University, stayed at McCormick Creek State Park, where his wife Joan held a summer job as a waitress. Many of the unit members found themselves working during that summer. Raleigh McGary labored in an Evansville factory between college semesters. Some just-graduated high school students, such as Bud Fitch of Oakland City, drove to Evansville each day to work at the International Harvester Plant to save money for college. Bud's friend Gordon Greene, who had so eagerly encouraged Bud to join the reserves, also labored at International Harvester that summer. Another Oakland City resident, seventeen-year-old Bill Marshall, who still had another year of high school, prepared that summer to play American Legion baseball. He dreamed of one day signing a major league contract just like his neighbor, former major league player Edd Roush. In the mornings the enterprising Marshall rose at 4:00 A.M. to deliver the *Evansville Courier* along the dark, tree-lined streets of Oakland City. Ralph Hargrave toiled in a broiling hot Boonville garage that same early summer as a mechanic. Paul Torian was just getting a good start in his fledgling insurance business. Blissfully lacking knowledge as to where a place called Korea appeared on the globe, honeymooners Jess and Nina Thurman set up housekeeping and looked forward to all the future had to offer them. All in all, life looked to be occasionally difficult but certainly uncomplicated for the members and families of C Company in that summer of 1950. If only one could go back.

Soon after the Korean War broke out, geography would play a trick on the city at the great bend of the Ohio River. On the outbreak of hostilities, someone in Evansville noted that the town straddled the thirty-eighth latitude line. Perhaps the members of C Company, 16th Infantry Battalion, Marine Corps Reserve should have taken this fact as an omen of things to come.

2   *Like Lightning Out of a Clear Sky*

For those few unfortunate GIs who pulled guard duty in occupied Japan on the weekend of 24–25 June 1950, the assignment meant missing the ample opportunities for weekend pleasures afforded by the soft garrison duty in Japan. One soldier described military life in that era as "heaven."[1] During the early morning hours of Sunday, 25 June, most military personnel were sleeping soundly, and those on duty could relax in the knowledge that all was seemingly well in their corner of the world. However, just a few hundred miles away, in the muggy predawn darkness of what would become a steamy summer day, hundreds of truck and tank engines roared to life. Soon innumerable columns of men and machines began to roll southward. By the time the sun rose, the juggernaut was rumbling past quiet, terraced hills, green with freshly planted rice. As the day progressed, artillery boomed more and more frequently, the blasts punctuated by an occasional fighter plane tearing south through the gray skies. Fresh soldiers coming upon those who had gone before them found their comrades weary but smiling: things were going even better than expected. The attack came as a total surprise. On the other side of the International Dateline it was Saturday, and well into the afternoon before Americans back home began to hear the breaking news about a war in some strange place called Korea.

Unlike during World War II, when there was an interval of time between Hitler's invasion of Poland and Japan's attack on Pearl Harbor to psychologically prepare Americans for war, absolutely no one's crystal ball saw the Korean conflict coming. Major national news magazines of the day fretted primarily over a possible military confrontation with Russia in Western Europe. Concerns in Asia revolved around the recent fall of China to Mao's forces and the coming showdown on the island of Formosa, where Chiang Kai-shek's army had taken refuge. Of secondary concern were deteriorating conditions in Indochina and the Philippines. Korea was almost never mentioned.

Official U.S. commitment regarding the defense of Korea seemed lacking as well. A major policy address by Secretary of State Dean Acheson in January 1950, for example, left Korea completely off the list of Asian countries that America would automatically protect. Further, Acheson's remarks strongly indicated that the United States would not necessarily intervene in an Asian conflict. Speaking of a possible attack of a Communist nation on an American ally in Asia, the secretary of state said, "Should such an attack occur, the initial reliance must be on the people attacked to resist it. . . . It is a mistake for America," argued Acheson, "to become obsessed with military considerations."[2] Acheson's policy ideas stemmed from the Defense Department, which had struggled in the first months of 1947 to develop a plan for deploying the shrinking numbers of U.S. servicemen and women. The department's first priority by far was Europe, where Russia was thought to be showing signs of "moving against weakened France and Italy." In a key memorandum, the Joint Chiefs of Staff concluded that given America's limited military resources, the United States would have "little strategic interest" in keeping bases and troops in Korea. Secretary of Defense James Forrestal agreed, noting that even "in the event of hostilities in the Far East our present forces in Korea would be a military liability."[3]

A narrow majority of politicians agreed with Acheson and the Defense Department. When the Korean War Aid Bill went before the House of Representatives in May, it was defeated by a margin of one vote. Sen. Tom Connally, a Texas Democrat, bemoaned the lack of support for Korea. When asked about the possible abandonment of the small Asian nation,

Connally replied, "I am afraid it is going to be seriously considered. . . . South Korea is cut right across by this line—North of it are Communists with access to the mainland—and Russia is over there on the mainland." Regardless of Connally's concern, South Korean president Syngman Rhee believed the Texan's remarks stood as an open invitation for the North to invade.[4]

Whatever political squabblings there were over foreign affairs, in early 1950 Americans were being told that major global trouble was unlikely. *U.S. News and World Report,* for example, boldly asserted in its first issue of the new decade that "things are to be more nearly normal in 1950 than at any other time in ten years. Alarms," the magazine confidently announced, "will be fewer, excitement less." The issue further speculated that "business is to be good. . . . Most people will be better off than ever. . . . There will be a feeling of stability that hasn't been present before." Most optimistic of all, the magazine predicted, "War scares are to fade."[5] One of the few pieces in a national magazine suggesting possible trouble in Korea, however, proved to be eerily prophetic. "It can't be officially admitted," the brief article reported, "but the U.S. is trapped in South Korea."[6]

Psychological preparedness for war was not the only thing Americans lacked in the early part of 1950. Because of the spectacular military demobilization that followed World War II, America in the beginning of that year stood woefully unprepared for military action. When the war came, one requiring a large number of just plain old infantry, it occurred in such an abrupt and ferocious manner that the nation, civilians and military leaders alike, simply stood dumbfounded. "The news hit the United States like lightning out of a clear sky," declared a stunned *Newsweek* in its 3 July 1950 issue.[7]

The lightning of which *Newsweek* spoke took the specific form of some 135,000 heavily trained and highly motivated North Korean soldiers who came hurtling south across the thirty-eighth parallel on that steamy morning in June 1950. The onslaught included 150 Russian-built T-34 tanks, heavy artillery, and planes against an opposing army of 95,000 mostly ill-trained South Koreans who possessed few planes or heavy guns and no tanks. The T-34 tanks proved especially effective in speeding the North

Korean charge. Obsolete American antitank weapons employed by the South Koreans and later by U.S. troops fired missiles that most often bounced off the T-34's heavy armor like "ping-pong balls."[8] Soon most South Korean soldiers were fleeing in terror at the sight of the giant metal monsters, though some bravely stood and died trying to stop the invaders. America, for her part, had not spent a great amount of time or effort in training or arming her South Korean allies, fearing that radical South Korean president Syngman Rhee would himself call for an invasion of the North in an attempt to reunite the two countries. So stood matters in Korea in the early morning hours of 25 June.

Back in the United States, President Truman traveled on *Air Force One* to his home in Missouri for a weekend with family and friends. He had planned that weekend to "oversee some fence building—not political, order a new roof on the farmhouse and tell some politicians to go to hell." All in all, "a grand visit," he hoped.[9] Ironically, the president had, just before leaving the East Coast, dedicated a new airport near Baltimore "to the cause of peace in the world."[10] Arriving at the municipal airport at Kansas City, Missouri, around 2:00 in the afternoon, the president hastened off the plane and into a sauna-like Midwest summer. But the 100-degree-plus temperature that greeted him would not hit the sixty-six-year-old president nearly as hard as the news about Korea. Cautioning news reporters to go easy on the story lest a national panic occur, the president soon found himself standing in the most lonely situation imaginable. Ultimately, he would have to decide in short order what our nation's response to the Korean situation would be. Like his decision on using the atomic bomb, many thousands of lives would be affected. His first official pronouncement about the crisis suggested the direction the president was leaning. On Monday, at 11:30, he issued through his press secretary a formal statement: "Those responsible for this act of aggression must realize how seriously the government of the United States views such threats to the peace of the world. Willful disregard of the obligation to keep the peace cannot be tolerated by nations that support the United Nations Charter."[11]

Truman moved rapidly toward the decision to bring America into the war. His decisiveness was captured by his first remark to Dean Acheson after hearing that South Korea had been attacked: "We've got to stop the sons of bitches no matter what."[12] Truman's thoughts and later actions heralded a dramatic shift in policy regarding the defense of South Korea and occurred for reasons other than practical. Although Korea possessed little strategic value, our quick response to the invasion seemed the appropriate move to counter perceived Communist growth in general and Soviet expansion in particular.[13] The new reasoning regarding the sudden change in policy ran something like this: Had the United States stood by and let South Korea fall, the Soviets, who had armed and trained the North Koreans, would have achieved an indirect but nevertheless devastating victory. *U.S. News and World Report* pointed out at the time that the defense of Korea was now "psychologically important."[14] Brother columnists Joseph and Stewart Alsop concurred, asserting, "The whole momentous meaning of President Truman's decision . . . can only be grasped in light of what surely would have happened if he had decided otherwise. . . . There can be no doubt," the Alsops added, that the invasion of South Korea was "the first of a whole series of demonstrations of Russian strength . . . designed to lead to the crumbling of the western will to resist."[15]

Many of the first responses to the invasion were garbed in religious imagery. John Foster Dulles, for example, called for America "to act quickly . . . to translate their freedom into strength of moral purpose" so that America "may yet save humanity from the deep abyss."[16] Barbara Ward, in the same magazine, called for a "crusading faith to counter communism."[17] One also heard national leaders suddenly speak of the dangers of appeasement and how earlier Hitler initially seized so much real estate without being challenged. The free world, it was felt, should not let this happen again in Korea. "Whether the attack on Korea be called the Austria, the Ethiopia, or the Czechoslovakia of the third world war, its meaning is comparable to those preliminary axis aggressions,"[18] warned one national magazine editorial.

Some years later, Truman, who prided himself on being an amateur student of history, gave his own account of what moved him to change his mind so abruptly about defending Korea. Speaking of the time period from when his plane left Missouri to when it landed at the nation's capital on the fateful day of the invasion, Truman related how he remembered that "in my generation, this was not the first occasion when the strong had attacked the weak. I recalled some earlier instances: Manchuria, Ethiopia, Austria. I remembered how each time that the democracies failed to act it had encouraged the aggressors to keep going ahead. I felt certain that if South Korea was allowed to fall, Communist leaders would be emboldened to override nations closer to our own shores."[19] Truman's reasoning seems to have been the most common rationalization for America's intervention in Korea.

When the president ordered United States ground troops into the war on 30 June, just five days after the North's invasion, the die was cast. Now bold declarations of support for the South Korean government would soon have to be backed up with action. The first U.S. troops rushed to Korea came from garrison duty in Japan. However, like their fellow Americans back in the states, they too were psychologically unprepared for war. When first told of the invasion in Korea, many American soldiers stationed in Japan assumed we would not fight. One corporal serving in a medical company observed that "among the majority of the men there was absolutely no fear or thought that the United States would become involved in the war."[20] C. W. "Bill" Menniger, another member of the garrison force in Japan, heard of the invasion that same Sunday and also gave little or no thought to the notion that he or other Americans might soon become involved. "I was reading a book and nursing a drink when the call came for me to report at once to Headquarters," he said. "The wife wanted to know what the call was about. 'Something must be wrong,' I answered, 'with next week's training schedule.'" Menniger would not see his wife for another eleven months.[21]

Another problem these first American troops faced concerned a lack of military readiness. Remarks by the army's surgeon general on the day of the invasion vividly demonstrated the army leadership's surprise and shock at North Korea's actions: "Just a week or so ago G-2 made the statement that we would be alerted perhaps 6 months before any [Communist] invasion and *at least* 10 days. We had not a moment's notice regarding Korea."[22] It is not surprising, then, that the regular GIs, such as those in Japan, were even less ready for war. Occupation duty had brought on a state of lethargy. In those easygoing days in Japan, before the dark times in Korea, one army corporal found himself "playing on the regimental softball team, but really just goofing off."²³ Another soldier, a private first class, declared, "Occupation duty was heaven. . . . My unit did very little military training. Life . . . consisted mostly of athletics, clubs, night dances, theater and Japanese girls."²⁴ "Even the lowest ranking private," observed another corporal, "could afford a steady 'shack gal' and all the beer he could drink."²⁵ These good times and lack of conditioning spelled tragedy for many of the early troops; for them Korea became the most extreme kind of on-the-job training. Previously pampered soldiers quickly had to learn the art and science of fighting or end up dead, wounded, or captured. Heavily outnumbered and outgunned, these untested men soon found themselves struggling in tropical-like heat against a well-trained, well-conditioned army. To make matters worse, help would have to arrive soon; while our troops learned the tough lessons of fighting firsthand, their defensive perimeter shrank daily, quickly becoming centered around the southeast seaport of Pusan.

As our soldiers were experiencing on-the-job, life-or-death training in Korea, Americans back home struggled to get some kind of handle on this unexpected and unwanted war. Few Americans even knew of the Asian peninsular country prior to June 1950. The day the war broke out, a Dallas citizen immediately called his local newspaper demanding to know "where Korea was anyway, . . . and were the people Indians or Japanese?"²⁶ Evansville, Indiana, area residents were no less ignorant of history and geography when it came to Korea. Marine C Company member Roy Jolly's response when he heard of the hostilities was typical. "Where's Korea?" he asked fellow reservists. Some of the younger C Company members, teenagers who had the normal concerns of people that age, were not even aware for several days that a war had started. "This was before television," Charles Gottman noted, "and some of us didn't know fighting had begun."

World War II veteran and Marine Corps Reservist Bill Wright was basking in the sun at Daytona Beach, Florida, with his wife Evelyn and his brother's family when he heard of the invasion. Wright had a sinking feeling at the time that he would be going there to fight. The Wrights had been married for only three months. Paul McDaniel, another veteran of World War II, had stopped at a filling station in the tiny town of Hatfield, Indiana, when he heard the news. McDaniel, traveling with his uncle to visit a friend at a nearby army camp, thought the news disturbing but did not foresee the reserves being called up. "We figured it would be over in no time, kind of like a brush fire," he recalled. One of the most concerned groups of all in the Evansville area were the parents and guardians, such as Mr. and Mrs. Henry Fitch of Oakland City, who had initially signed for their teenage sons to join the Marine Corps Reserve. They could only hope, like McDaniel, that the war would be over almost as soon as it had started.

Despite Americans' lack of geographical knowledge regarding Korea, Truman's initial decision to involve United States ground forces gained surprisingly wide support. Suspicion of Russian involvement in the invasion apparently helped bring many Americans to Truman's side. One Illinois farmer believed "we did the right thing; we had . . . to take some kind of action against the Russians."[27] In the Republican stronghold of Warren County, Iowa, where isolationist opinion usually held sway, another citizen chimed, "We don't know who told [the president] to do it, but for once he made the right decision."[28]

Many Americans actually seemed relieved that we were at last confronting Communist aggression with force. A headline in one national news magazine announced, "Truman's Stand Electrifies Nation." The article's opening lines clearly reflected how profound the nation's support stood for the president: "A clear wind moved across the nation last week. Tired of murky defeats, inconclusive victories, and faulty diplomatic footwork, Americans were relieved by Harry S. Truman's immediate counterpunch against the communists in East Asia."[29] A lead article on 30 June in the *New York Times* proclaimed, "Democracy Takes a Stand." Joseph C. Harsch, Washington correspondent for the *Christian Science Monitor*, probably best summed up the nation's sense of this relief when he reported, "I have lived and worked in and out of this city for twenty years. Never before in that time have I felt such a sense of relief and unity pass through this city."[30] Support for the Democrat Truman in these heady days even witnessed Republicans hurriedly climbing on the go-to-war bandwagon. Noted *Time*, "Republicans were tripping over Democrats in their eagerness to give President Truman what they thought he needed to win in Korea."[31]

While most Americans were quickly lining up in favor of America's involvement in Asia in these first foggy days of war, the West Virginia family of Theodore Shadrick received shocking news about their son, Kenneth. In early July, while serving with the first U.S. troops to confront the North Koreans, the nineteen-year-old high school dropout had raised his head up from a firing pit to see if the bazooka round he had just fired at a T-34 Russian built tank had hit its mark. The antitank shell simply glanced off the tank's side and the tank's machine gun turned to rake Shadrick's position. Kenneth Shadrick would become one of the first of more than fifty-four thousand Americans who would die in that place of which few Americans had heard.[32]

Perhaps no other war in our history turned sour so quickly for American leaders and private citizens alike. Articles and headlines in Evansville's two newspapers during the tense early days of the war captured the sinking feeling that soon settled upon the nation. The 26 July edition of the *Evansville Courier* warned, "Enemy Guerrillas Operating Close to Our Last Seaport." The next day the same paper reported the city's first casualty. On 28 July the headlines reported that a decisive battle raged all along the Korean front and that American troops faced the real possibility of being pushed off the peninsula. That same month the *Evansville Press* carried a small article on the front page noting that all Marine Corps Reserve units had been alerted: "The Marine Corps today advises all its organized reserve ground units to be prepared to go on active duty on ten days' notice."[33] The article also pointed out that 75 percent of the Evansville reservists were not even veterans, the bulk of these nonveterans being teenagers. Like Evansville, the rest of the country agonized over the dismal early reports pouring in from Korea and held its breath at the thought of which of their sons might be called to fight.

By the end of July, when the military situation had reached the point of desperation, Americans began to fear the worst. Evangelist Billy Graham, "agleam in a pistachio-colored suit and white shoes," hastily met with the president and declared that Americans were "gripped by a fear you could almost call hysteria." Graham strongly recommended that the president proclaim a national day of prayer and humiliation.[34] The president, however, did not act upon Graham's suggestion. Graham's concern, though, likely captured the feelings of most Americans by the end of July and the beginning of August. "Why are U.S. troops being pushed around in Korea?" lamented *Newsweek* in late July.[35] *Life* magazine demanded to know why we were "taking a beating" and suggested that our problems in Korea stemmed from a lack of appropriate equipment and manpower.[36] A month later the same magazine predicted that fighting in Korea was nearing a "bloody crisis."[37] Many citizens raised the possibility of using the atom bomb. One Indiana school teacher reasoned, "What's the use of having those atom bombs if they're not to be used? What we ought to do is notify the Russians that if they don't get back North of the 38th parallel by a certain date, we'll drop the bomb on them."[38]

Some military leaders were also suggesting the unthinkable. Maj. Gen. James M. Gavin believed the bomb could be used effectively in Korea at this juncture. Noting that the enemy would be "forced to mass his means . . . because of our defense and his own lack of mobility . . . the atomic bomb [would be] the tactical answer."[39] In mid-July, MacArthur and the army chief of staff, Gen. Joseph Collins, seriously discussed the use of atomic weapons in Korea: "MacArthur's idea was to use the bomb to strike a 'blocking blow' which would cut North Korean supply lines."[40] Fortunately things never progressed that far. One was suddenly reminded of the bleakest days of World War II. There was a feeling, reported one national magazine, that for the first time in living memory "much of the U.S. might be devastated in an all-out war."[41] *U.S. News and World Report* guessed that another world war could possibly start in "8 weeks or less."[42]

Evansville and the nation as a whole at this time were also particularly frustrated by the lack of any military successes in Korea. The army that had so recently taken on and defeated Hitler and Tojo now found itself halted by some unknown upstart. "How had the once mighty U.S.A. been put into a position where it could be licked . . . by a country called North Korea?" demanded *Newsweek*.[43] Oddly, in those first several months of the war, news reports were not usually censored and information coming back from the front was desperately discouraging. One officer, battling in the stifling heat of that Korean summer, lamented, "It was a slaughterhouse. They [the North Koreans] mounted machine guns on hills above us and swept us clean."[44] Another officer railed, "You don't fight two, tank-equipped divisions with .30 caliber carbines. I never saw such a useless damned war in all my life."[45] Our nation's unpreparedness would become an especially hot political issue in the Evansville region when Herman McCray, Republican challenger for that year's congressional seat, accused his opponent Winfield K. Denton and other congressional Democrats of letting the nation's military readiness deteriorate. The American people, claimed McCray, "demand that the American leadership be changed so that never again will Americans be caught in such a miserable state of unpreparedness."[46]

Political maneuvering aside, the nation's early experiences in the Korean War were psychologically jolting. When comparing the early days of the Korean struggle with their experiences in World War II, many World War II veterans who also fought in Korea found the Korean War an even more difficult struggle. An army engineer, Maj. Russell Wilson, who had served in the Pacific theater, noted, "In the jungle in the last war, the engineers' biggest problem was road construction. [Engineers] had no missions for delaying tactics, such as roadblocks or antitank mine fields. In this war, on the Naktong River front alone, the division engineers laid 10,000 yards of wire and 18,000 anti-personnel and anti-tank mines." Wilson further pointed out that even though engineers had done some fighting in the previous wars, "they were never committed as infantry." This, however, often occurred in those early overwhelming days of fighting in Korea. During this time, Wilson witnessed engineers being used as regular infantry "in the thick of fighting on eleven different occasions for periods of three to seven days."[47] An infantry man, Sgt. Cornelius Kopper, tendered an opinion from the foot soldier's point of view. "The way it [is] worse in this war," Kopper argued, "is that leaders say '. . . go take this hill.' We'd go and take it and stay all night and the next day. And then they'd give us the order to pull back. It just ain't good to go backwards. . . . It's easier to move up the way we did in the Pacific. . . . Get your positions and keep going."[48]

One of the cruelest episodes of the early war involved the disaster that befell the 3d Battalion of the army's 29th Infantry Regiment, "the destruction of which was stomach-turning evidence of what can happen when sending untrained, ill-armed soldiers into combat."[49] Made up of unprepared garrison soldiers from Okinawa who had performed clerical and security duty, many knew little of the army's basic weapon, the M1 rifle. Sent almost immediately into the jaws of battle, the group was ambushed on 26 July, just a few short hours after coming on line. One survivor told how the North Koreans "hunted us down like they were shooting rabbits fleeing a brush fire."[50] So critical had the circumstances grown by late July and early August that many Americans, including some military leaders, came to believe U.S. troops might actually be forced to abandon Korea. Perhaps the most devastating, psychological blow at this juncture was the loss of Gen. William Dean, reported missing in action in July. Last seen personally leading a small party of men with a bazooka in a last-ditch stand against several North Korean tanks, Dean would not be heard of until almost a year later when he turned up in a prisoner of war camp. In those dismal days of July 1950, most gave him up for dead.

Back in American towns, such as Oakland City, Indiana, during those first sweltering days of early summer, Bud Fitch and other young men of the marine reserve cast a wary yet excited glance westward at events unfolding in a place of which most of them had never heard prior to that summer. Bud continued in his job at the International Harvester plant in Evansville, driving down Highway 57 every day to work. Other important news also came that summer. Fitch had been accepted into the electrical engineering program at Purdue University for the fall semester. Don Cochren also prepared to enroll at Purdue, and the two friends looked forward to the adventures that awaited them on that Big Ten campus. Meanwhile, with a mixture of joy and sadness, Bud's mother busied herself that summer purchasing and packing away new items of clothing for her eighteen-year-old son's fall semester at West Lafayette. Fate, however, intervened in July for Bud Fitch and thousands of young men across America.

The primary crisis during the earliest months of the Korean War concerned a sheer lack of manpower. The military first responded by mobilizing four National Guard divisions and two regimental combat teams in late July. Then, while Reverend Billy Graham called for national contrition and others clamored to drop the bomb or get out of Korea altogether, President Truman, in these seemingly hopeless hours, played another of his few remaining cards. General MacArthur had been particularly adamant in his request for help in the form of an entire marine division. Earlier he had been given the 1st Provisional Marine Brigade, but his first request for an entire division had been denied. In mid-July MacArthur sent this message to the Joint Chiefs of Staff: "I strongly request reconsideration of my need for a Marine division. Its availability is absolutely necessary."[51] The Joint Chiefs agreed to this second request. It was impossible, however, to get the 1st Marine Division up to strength without calling up the reserves. Thus on 19 July the call-up was approved by Congress, and President Harry Truman officially activated the Marine Corps Reserve.[52] The strength of the reserve at this crucial hour totaled 128,962 men and women, almost 40,000 of whom were a part of the organized reserve system.[53]

The activation seemed a wise move. The Corps had long occupied a special place in the American psyche; when all else failed, we could always send in the marines. As one national magazine noted, "The traditional job of the Marines is to be a hard hitting force, to take and hold ground until other services can bring up reinforcements." The article went on to point out that "as Reservists, many have had periodic peacetime training, only a short time . . . will be needed to prepare them for combat." Americans "got a heartening lift" when they heard the marines were about to land once more.[54] The enemy apparently feared the prowess of the marines as well. When the Chinese came into the war in November 1950, many carried a pamphlet warning them of the ferociousness of marines in combat. "U.S. Marine units have been trained more than any other type of American force for waging . . . war," the pamphlet warned.[55] What was not understood by the American general public at the time of the call-up, however, was the profound difference between marine regulars and marine reservists.

An Evansville paper reported on 28 July that "Evansville Marine Reservists have got the word" that they had been activated.[56] Despite the ongoing war, however, most of the Evansville men found themselves stunned by the unexpected call-up. "Wow, such a surprise," remembered the C Company commander, Paul Torian. "We didn't see it coming even after the war started." The activation "was shocking," he said. "We were just staggered." Torian and the older members of C Company felt especially concerned because they had convinced so many high school–aged kids to join. These teenagers, like all reservists who joined in the late 1940s and early 1950s, had been told they could quit anytime they wanted. That promise, however, no longer counted after President Truman issued the call-up. Coming to a reserve meeting on the eve of their summer camp departure in 1950, young David Graham recalled, "We met as usual down at the headquarters, and they called us into formation to read a letter. I thought the letter was going to be about where we were going to summer camp." Major Torian began to read in his deep somber voice, and Graham couldn't believe what he was hearing. "Our orders for summer camp had been canceled, and we were being activated. They gave us a few weeks to get ready[,] . . . talk to our bosses and so forth." Reservists, since they were now on alert, were told, "You will attend the meetings or we will send the MPs."

Suddenly members of C Company were given M1 rifles for the first time and told they had better learn how to break down their weapon because they were "going to be using it soon."[57] More than a few members on C Company's roster had neglected to come to a single meeting and, consequently, believed they were no longer in the reserves. Notices came to them regardless. Raleigh McGary, vacationing in the rural wilds of Michigan, watched a beat-up pickup truck slowly approaching his wife's family's farm. A man stepped out and asked for McGary. When the Poseyville, Indiana, native responded, the driver gave McGary the notice that he was to report back to his unit in Evansville. "How did they find me way out here?" McGary wondered as he reread the shocking letter for the second time. Strangest of all the call-up orders, however, was that to Richard Eberle. When an MP delivered the notice, Eberle could only scratch his head at the mistake. He did not know he'd been sworn in while sleeping at the YMCA back in 1948 and his name included on the roster. Eberle, like several men whose name had filled the C Company rolls, had never trained with the company.

Many parents and guardians of teenagers across the nation who had initially signed releases for their sons to join the reserves now scrambled to try to keep their sons out of the war. Several, like Charlie Gottman's mother, wrote their congressmen. Mrs. Gottman had signed for her son to join, never believing a war would erupt and that the reserves might be called upon to fight. "She never thought I'd come back alive," Gottman remembered. Oakland City teenager Kenny Dougan had watched his mother and father feud over his initial joining. The mother had signed for Dougan against the father's protests back in the spring of 1950, causing them not to speak to each other for some time. In late July, Mrs. Dougan, like so many parents, also desperately wrote her congressman in a failed attempt to at least get her son a deferment so he could finish his senior year of high school.

Kenny Dougan's classmate, William Marshall, had also been too young to sign for himself that spring, but the clever Marshall had convinced his grandfather to sign the release form. When Marshall's mother discovered that her son was being activated with the marine reserves, she panicked. Harry Black, a local Oakland City grocer, did not help matters any when he loudly teased Marshall in his mother's presence that the Oakland City lad would soon become cannon fodder. A few days before the reserves departed, and without Marshall's knowledge, his mother hurried down to the Reserve Headquarters in Evansville to try to pull her son out of the group. Alva Cato, Bill Marshall's high school basketball coach, went with her to help argue that her son should be allowed to finish high school. The marine officials, however, would not relent, and Marshall's mother finally had to accept her son's fate. Even so, Marshall's aunt, Mrs. Homer H. McAtee, would not let the matter die. She first wrote a strong letter of protest to U.S. senator Margaret Chase Smith of Maine in early September to try to stop the activation of the young Oakland City boys. Smith had recently talked of being disturbed by the call-up of reservists, so it was likely, Mrs. McAtee thought, that she would have a sympathetic ally. Her letter was typical of the thousands written to legislators at this time:

> I am writing you asking that you use your influence to keep these half-trained (in some cases "no" trained) boys from being sent overseas to be slaughtered. Ten boys from our community which is only about thirty miles from Evansville, Indiana, were sent with the Marine Reserves August 28th to Camp Pendleton, California. My seventeen-year-old nephew was among them. He persuaded my father who is old, sick and a paralytic to sign the papers giving consent for him to join. Other high school boys were going to the meetings four hours each week and he

thought the two weeks of training each summer would be fun. They were told if they grew tired of coming to the Marine base just "turn in their suits." But when this boy's mother came home (she teaches in the northern part of our state to support several children) and tried to explain that my father had no legal right to give his consent and that he was sick and had not even read the papers which he signed—do you think she could get the boy out? NO! She could not even get him deferred to finish high school. . . . Mrs. Smith are our leaders in this country going mad?

Mrs. McAtee's letter would stir up a beehive of responses. Senator Smith, perhaps realizing the volatility of the issue, quickly passed on the letter like a hot potato. "I appreciate your generous remarks and the confidence you have shown me as you have concerning your nephew and other cases like his," Smith wrote McAtee. "*However,* I am taking the liberty of forwarding your letter to Senator Homer E. Capehart, the senior senator from Indiana." Senator Smith closed by asserting, "I am sure that he will do all that he possibly can for you." A day after the Smith letter arrived, Mrs. McAtee received a full two-page letter from Capehart's administrative assistant (the senior Indiana senator was out of town for a speaking engagement). "The senator," wrote the assistant, "shares your views fully. . . . Just a few days ago, Senator Capehart received assurances [from the secretary of defense] that not one of our boys would be sent overseas until he had received necessary training which will probably be of about thirteen weeks duration." Regarding Mrs. McAtee's nephew, Capehart's office stated:

I assume that your nephew has only one more year of high school remaining. If so, and provided that his high school has adopted the policy placed into effect by many high schools of permitting the completion of the remaining year in one semester, he can on his own application receive deferment for this period of time. He will then be permitted to finish his schooling, either in the Marine Corps, or will be permitted to return home to complete one semester. Furthermore, since your nephew is under the age limit, and since his legal guardian did not consent to his going in the service, I believe his release could be obtained on that basis. However, he would be subject to the draft when he reaches his 18th birthday.

William E. Jenner, Indiana's ultraconservative and isolationist senator, had received a letter earlier in August from the Oakland City woman as well. Oddly, the antiadministration Jenner was the least supportive of all the representatives contacted concerning the reservists' cause. "It is unfortunate the situation exists," Jenner explained, "and I only wish there was something I could do. However, all authority is in the hands of the Department of Defense and the Selective Service Board, over which I have no jurisdiction." Jenner did add a sympathetic afterthought: "I agree with you this matter of taking young boys and sacrificing them on the battlefield to cover up the bungling foreign policy we are shouldered with, is a blot on our history, and you may be sure that if there is anything I can do to change the situation, I shall do it."

William Marshall's mother, Dorothy Michael, also hurriedly wrote her congressman, James E. Noland, about the matter. Noland was also less than optimistic about the problem, noting, "If the Marine Corps holds firm to their policy, it is doubtful if we will be successful." However, Noland quickly contacted Congressman Carl Vinson, who chaired the Committee on Armed Services. Vinson then personally phoned Gen. C. B. Cates, commandant of the Marine Corps, to discuss the matter. Cates issued a quick and curt response and went on to explain that "a very large number of Marine Reservists are in the high school age group. It becomes apparent that should all of these young men be deferred, the strength of the Reserves available for call to active duty would be considerably reduced."

Gadfly columnist Drew Pearson, who had written an earlier story about the marines in Korea, also wrote a sympathetic letter to William Marshall's aunt, saying, "I feel the families of our soldiers should at least have the assurance that their sons who go forth to battle are adequately prepared, and I shall do all in my power to see that the present situation is corrected." Marine Corps Headquarters received such a large volume of congressional mail regarding letters such as Mrs. McAtee's that the Corps released a bulletin to its regular and reserve components: "Since the mobilization of reserves the amount of congressional mail reaching this Headquarters has increased to the point where it has become a detrimental burden. . . . While the Headquarters does not desire to take issue with the fundamental right of an American citizen to correspond with his congressional representatives, it does desire to eliminate unnecessary, expensive, time-consuming letters to members of Congress." The bulletin asserted that such letters did little or nothing to change the outcome of an individual reservist being called up: "Contrary to what appears to be a general impression, correspondence with a Congressman or Senator does not result in favorable action where favorable action is not otherwise to be expected nor does it expedite action. Each individual's letter to the Commandant of the Marine Corps is fully and fairly considered *on the merits of the case alone.*"[58] Despite volumes of letters from relatives of young reservists to congressmen, the Marine Corps did not change its stance one bit.

Great bitterness would eventually surface over the "not to be called except in time of national emergencies clause." One recruiter vented a particularly strong dose of anger at the Corps after the war started in a letter to the editor of *Leatherneck:* "In 1947 . . . I, under direct instructions from the main office, delivered into the Corps a number of these unsuspecting Reserves with the same phrase 'You will not be called except in time of war or national emergency.'" The recruiter went on to explain how he too joined the reserves: "Come time for my discharge and I believed the 'not-being-called clause,' so I enlisted myself in the inactive Reserves." That was, said the recruiter, "my fatal mistake because came Korea (a United Nations POLICE Action) no war or national emergency is declared but the Marine Corps doesn't pay any attention to that, they call us anyway. Now I am suffering the same fate as my former clientele." Ending the letter, the marine declared, "And when I get out this time I will never ever believe my own stories about the Marine Corps or the Marine Corps Reserve. It's taken me eight years to learn the meaning of Semper Fidelis."[59]

Another angry reservist who signed before the war began also blasted what he perceived to be the deceptiveness of marine recruiters: "Once I obtain a discharge, no recruiter will ever talk me into taking a chance on my ignorance again. If I sound bitter, believe me, I am." In spite of his anger, the marine reservist was "thankful that freedom of speech still exists in these United States. Behind the Iron Curtain, a man would be shot for even thinking the things I voiced against the Marine Corps and all other branches of service since last July."[60] A former marine wrote to

Leatherneck and explained how he barely escaped the fate of the reservists: "My last Commanding Officer called me into his office on the day of my discharge and said that I could join the Reserves with my present rank . . . and that I would only be called to active duty in case of a National Emergency by an Act of Congress. I see by the papers that over-night the inactives became volunteer Reserves." He ended by saying, "When I think of the misleading facts I was presented with I am thankful I kept my head and said to just give me my discharge."[61]

Not every reservist recruit agreed with the notion that they had somehow been deceived. Wrote one, "I left a very well-paid job at home, plus my dear wife and two-year-old child. So I'm in the same boat with many others." This letter, however, went on to emphasize what a privilege it was to live in the United States and how such a privilege demanded sacrifice: "So far this country has given me an education in my childhood, a chance to choose my own trade, place to live, a place to demand my rights as a citizen, and my own choice of whom I want to serve in *my* government. It has given me nearly all I want, and now it's my turn to reciprocate."[62] Another proud reservist added, "I don't want anyone to feel sorry for me. . . . I knew what I was doing when I signed the enlistment papers. I was volunteering my services to fight for my country. That may sound like a lot of mushy patriotism to a lot of people but my peacetime freedom is worth fighting for when the shooting starts."[63] A regular marine tore into reservists' complaints by asking, "Was it just the Reserves who were given short notice? How about the Regulars who were sent to the West Coast from the East to bring up the First Division?" The writer added that "everyone was inconvenienced. It wasn't just the Reserves." Speaking of the complaint about the national emergency clause, this marine pointed out, "A man doesn't have to have brain one to realize that the Marine Corps wasn't spending money on its Reserve Program because it had money to spend and didn't know where to spend it. It was maintaining a military force with the least possible expense."[64]

Another group of marines who suffered in the initial call-up were the older reservists, many of whom were veterans of World War II. Most were married and had just gotten their vocational careers fully started when they were activated. Often they were referred to as "retreads" or "two-time losers," and in many cases they left behind heartbroken young wives and children. One sympathetic national magazine noted that active duty for these men meant real hardships: "A 'lost generation' of young men, in their late 20s and 30s, is being built in this country. . . . These are men who have already given years of military service to their country. In each case, they are men who have broken their civilian ties once, left their jobs, their schooling, their families to go to war." Now, the article noted, "they are recalled again later in life, giving up business enterprises, professions, civilian careers that are often just starting, breaking the ties once more." What really bothered many reservists in this situation was that they saw "others with equal ability and often without prior service, safe from call by the armed forces." As the article observed, these nonreservists "who are not on military lists of available men, can go ahead in their civilian lines, get the breaks, while those called back into military service sacrifice more years of progress in their chosen fields."[65] This problem, however, along with the plight of those younger men who had begged their parents to sign for them to join the reserve, believing they could quit at any time, did not go away despite the volume of mail sent to scores of congressmen and senators and despite sympathetic media.

By August, the reality that the group would be shipping out to Camp Pendleton, California, for training descended upon Evansville's C Company like a darkening cloud. Not all the men, however, completely dreaded the possibility of going to war. Bud Fitch and Gordon Greene, for example, spent much of their remaining time after the call-up riding double through the Gibson County countryside on Bud's motorcycle, stopping occasionally to ponder whether they would have the courage to stand up to actual combat.[66] Before they and the other Oakland City boys left, their mothers gave them a going-away dinner at a little restaurant on South Jackson Street called Sharkey's. The most startling thing about the snapshots taken that day was how young but serious the boys all looked as they gazed into the camera. The mothers' faces can best be described as stoic. About this time, high school junior Bill Marshall promised his mother that when he returned to Oakland City he would finish his secondary education. She, however, harbored a sorrowful doubt about her son's chances of being able to keep his pledge.

The rest of C Company also prepared to leave. Many of the older veterans had to work out plans with their bosses. A few, such as Tex Graham, taught and coached in the public high schools. Luckily for the teachers, the Evansville schools made arrangements for the reservists' absences. Some were not so fortunate. Paul McDaniel, who had thought himself lucky to be in the reserves "drawing money every month," now suddenly found himself "married, with a family, and having to give my boss and creditors notice I was leaving." Some Evansville businesses, in the spirit of the last war, highlighted in company publications employees who had been called to serve. Noted one company pamphlet: "Last Saturday the Korean War became more than newspaper headlines and radio reports to all Orr Iron Company people. It became a symbol of stern reality, as one by one they took Walter 'Sonny' Hoepner's hand, gave him a pat on the back, and wished him luck."[67] Most often the Corps cut reservists little slack regarding job notification. One national magazine observed wryly, "In Longview, Washington, Marine Reservist Thomas B. Meyers, ordered to report to active duty by 8 am August 5, wired for an extension so he could train a replacement for his job. He was granted until 9 am August 5."[68]

Throughout late July and August, C Company members faithfully participated in the weekly drills and paid close attention to instructions. A new and more serious spirit now possessed these men. Joking, jostling, and general clowning around disappeared entirely, even among the younger marines. A reporter for the *Evansville Press,* Guy Wright, observed in one particular visit the wives who played bingo or cards in the reserve building club room while their men trained. The women "concentrated on the game a little too hard maybe, they laughed at each other's jokes a little too long[,] . . . and it might strike you as unusual to see a mother give her young son a quick hug for no reason at all in the middle of a bingo game."[69] In late August the company received official word. A coal-fired locomotive and six Pullman cars would pull out of Evansville for Camp Pendleton on 28 August.

Shortly before noon on the day of departure, cars and trucks began arriving at the C Company Marine Corps Reserves Headquarters on West Illinois Street, and young men in green fatigues began spilling out into a drizzling rain.[70] Carl Barnett and Charlie Gottman arrived in a pickup with Charlie's father. Charlie's mother, who had signed a release for their underage son, stayed home and, as Charlie later recalled, "took sick for a month." Raleigh McGary's wife had taken the day off from her school-teaching job in Poseyville to drive him to Evansville, and they stopped on the way to have his picture taken. "I had my marine uniform on top and my civilian clothes on the bottom," he remembered. Cpl. Ralph Hargrave of Boonville had left his car with his boss at Hester Motor Company and was driven by the head salesman, Bill Hester. Although his girlfriend would say her farewells at the train station, he had insisted that his family stay home.

Once inside headquarters, some of the men nervously checked and rechecked their gear. One anxious marine generated a little tension-relieving laughter and good-natured ribbing as the others watched him try to stuff two ham sandwiches into an already bulging bag. "Man," he said, "I expect to be gone a while. At least two weeks." For the younger reservists, who had never before shipped off to war, there was a current of excitement, though it was quickly becoming tempered with the realization that they were truly leaving home without any certainty of where they would go and when they would return. The veterans among them, most of whom had already experienced the nightmare of war, were more somber. Maj. Paul Torian, who had survived especially ferocious action in World War II, remembered being full of dread at the thought of what these young men might have to face. Guy Wright, a reporter on hand for the *Evansville Press,* asked a couple of the reservist veterans how this compared to the call-up in 1942. Cpl. Ralph Hargrave replied that "it isn't very different." However, to 1st Sgt. Walter "Sonny" Hoepner, who now had a family, the differences were crystal clear: "This time I have a company of men to look out for. Then I had only myself. The first time I was single. Now I have a wife and a three-year-old son. It's gonna be tough at the train. He won't understand what's happening."[71]

As more marines filed into headquarters, the waiting became more anxious. Buses would eventually arrive to take them to the train depot. Some of the men wandered out to the porch of the two-story Reserve Head-quarters and gazed out with unfocused eyes at the bothersome drizzle. "Outside the gate," the *Evansville Press* reported, "a few cars still waited, and occasionally a woman would roll down a window and look back at the building where her man was. In the headquarters office, Staff Sgt. H. A. Peterson sat on the floor and plinked his homemade ukelele. He sang 'Five Foot Two.' 'He'll be hot stuff in Hawaii,' someone said."[72] No one laughed at the wisecrack. At last the chartered buses rolled in to take the men to the station. Looking at the first bus that screeched to a halt in front of headquarters, the men must have felt an even greater sense of the surreal. The lead bus had just returned from Mexico City with a load of Evansville College students, and there hadn't been time to change the sign on the vehicle. The sign read "Educational Tours."[73]

Reporter Jack Pressley, musing about all those waiting at the train station for the loads of marines to arrive, wrote, "For many Korea is still a distant place—distant in space and thought. But for the hundreds of persons who stood on a rain-swept platform at the Union Station . . . Korea was all too close."[74] Wives, children, parents, and sweethearts lined the platform, waiting to say their goodbyes, some of them huddling in the rain. Maj. Paul Torian later recalled, "I will always remember that scene at the station—mothers, wives, the tears." The day reminded Torian of a vast funeral. A reporter at the gathering turned to a gray-haired woman whose shoulders were shaking. "Your son?" he asked. When she nodded, he asked if she would mind giving her name. She struggled to speak but could only stammer to the young woman next to her, "You talk to him. I can't." The young woman, Nina, said that the marine was her husband, Jess Thurman. "This is his mother, Mrs. Neala Thurman."[75] The Thurmans had been married for all of four months.

After the buses arrived, "a thin column of fatigue-clad men, carrying only overnight bags and here and there a bag of potato chips or a chocolate bar, threaded through a waiting host of friends and relatives and boarded the train." Most of the marines were smiling thinly, and some had wisecracks for whoever wanted to listen. "Standing there among all the people who had come to say goodbye to them, they must have found it hard to believe that they were off to anything more than a routine Reserve training period," the reporter observed. "But by then you noticed how quiet it was, how in all the shuffling crowd you could still hear the steady drip-drip of the rain as it ran down the sides of the Pullman cars and onto the track bed. And it came as a surprise when you saw how many of the women were holding handkerchiefs to their eyes."[76]

Finally the roll call blared over a loudspeaker. 1st Lt. Mason Wiers began assigning berths to the men and giving them their loading instructions. Dressed in green fatigues, as were the others, Wiers told the men to "go directly to your berth and stow your gear as fast as you can. That'll give you more time to be with your families." After the men had stowed their gear, they scrambled off the train and began searching the multitude of faces. Outside the train, family members stretched and bobbed their heads, trying to pick their loved ones from the sea of green fatigues. "They all look so much alike in their uniforms and there was so little time left," noted the reporter. After relatives or couples reunited, they tried to remember all the words they had planned to say. "Some were casual, teen-age girlfriends, and sisters, pride shining in their eyes."[77]

Many marines tried to reassure their trembling spouses that they would be safe. "Don't worry," Raleigh McGary whispered to his wife. "We'll be back in a few weeks. The scuttlebutt is that we will take the place of the regulars in the states so they can fight." Later he would recall that when his troopship actually sailed from California for Korea, he still thought it was some enormous mistake. To others, this scene "was like a recurring bad dream." Mrs. John Lively lamented about her husband: "This is the third time I've had to give him up. We have a daughter, 8, and a son, 6. Frankly, this time I'm scared."[78] Bill Etheridge later recalled, "That's the reason I didn't want my mother going to the station, because she had seen so many sons going off to war. There had been three. . . . I was the fourth." One Evansville family gave up three sons that day at the train station: James, Joseph, and Ralph Floyd.

Shortly before they boarded the train, eight of the Oakland City boys stood with their arms around one another's shoulders to have their picture snapped. In front of the camera, the moment to be forever suspended in time, stood Forrest Miller, Bud Fitch, Gordon Greene, Bill Marshall, Barney Barnard, Al Dickson, Don Corn, and Garold Sheetz. They did not know that one of their group would die on a barren hill in Korea, thousands of miles from the quiet, tree-shaded streets of Oakland City, where they had once been Boy Scouts and played soldier. The other seven in the photo would find upon returning home after the war that somehow their lives would never quite be the same.

The dreaded call of "All aboard!" came much too soon. "There were hurried goodbyes, last kisses, faces pressed against the windows, shouted words that couldn't be heard," as the men boarded the train at 3:00 P.M.[79] Even though some marines threw open the windows on the train for a few last shouts of goodbye, the train was moving, and they reluctantly ducked their heads back inside. Families and friends kept watching long after the train was out of sight. A reporter observed, "It was so quiet and subdued. And then the sun came out and splattered across the wet and empty tracks."[80] Almost fifty years later, Charlie Gottman said of that day, "It was the only time I ever saw my father cry."

3   *All the Boot Camp You Want*

Just before the Marine Corps reservists left their Evansville headquarters on West Illinois Street, C Company commander Paul
Torian announced that he had requested and received permission
to promote twenty of the group.[1] (See the appendix for list of
names and ranks of the Evansville reservists who left for Pendleton in August 1950.) These promotions would provide those fortunate men with a little higher pay and allotment for their families while they served. More important, the act created a needed
boost in morale among the group as a whole as the men left their
families, friends, schools, and jobs for the unknown. Few Evansville men would forget Torian's generous act. Many years later one
Evansville reservist noted, "If we had enough time and rank,
Torian gave us promotions. That was a really big help and added a
little cheer to an otherwise gloomy day."[2]

Despite Torian's promotion efforts, however, a somber mood
soon came to linger in the hot, smoky air of the six Pullman cars
as the train carrying C Company began its slow journey westward.
At first most sat quietly and stared vacantly out windows as the
late summer scenery slipped by. Outside, some of the field crops
were already showing signs of turning, and in the distance the air
hung blue and hazy in the humid August heat. At some point on
the journey word spread that a local paper had carried an article

quoting the commander of Indiana's entire 16th Marine Corps Reserve Battalion as saying, "Not a man will be in combat for at least six months."[3] Those words came across as particularly reassuring news to the World War II veterans. Six months, they reasoned, might mean the difference between occupational duty and combat. National media hinted that a quick end to the war was indeed possible. *Time* said of the week the Evansville reservists left for California that the period "was the best week for the UN forces since the war began and perhaps the turning point."[4] *U.S. News and World Report* struck an even more positive tone, suggesting that "Korea might be cleaned up by next February."[5] One veteran, however, was less than optimistic about C Company's chances of avoiding the war.

Ralph Hargrave knew of "the guys who had been in Japan being thrown into Korea" and what a terrible price the unprepared men had paid. Now, as the Evansville train traveled relentlessly westward, Hargrave grew concerned about the teenage reservists who hovered, jostling and pushing around him. "They thought it was going to be an adventure," remembered the Boonville man. Eight in Hargrave's squad were still in high school or fresh out. "They had no idea what they were getting into. They'd get off the train when it would stop and run off and get some booze. I saw an awful lot of kids, seventeen and eighteen year olds like that at Pendleton and then in Japan and Korea." The younger Evansville reservists who either read or heard of the sudden positive predictions about the war's end likely held more ambivalent feelings about the topic. Boyhood friends Gordon Greene and Bud Fitch, who had spent the summer pondering how they might stand up to combat, now faced the likelihood they would miss the fighting altogether. More important, they knew now they might well miss returning home with war stories to share with their friends and families.

After a couple of hours of travel, many of the men grew restless and became more chatty. William Marshall, who would have started his senior year at Oakland City High School a few days after the train's departure, recalled how the younger reservists soon began to roam from car to car while the older veterans started up card games or began telling "sea stories" about their experiences in World War II. Their stories soon drew the younger men like magnets. While the marines began to loosen up, the train bearing C Company picked up several cars in St. Louis and still more

Pullmans in Kansas City, where they were joined by a marine reserve company from Iowa. From there the train included almost two dozen cars stuffed with troops.

At some point in the journey an Evansville man leaned far out the back of a middle Pullman car in the caravan with a camera and snapped a picture of the back half of the train as the line slowly chugged around a long curve. "I wanted to see just how long the train was," the inquisitive marine recalled.[6] Another Evansville reservist dropped his mother a card from Amarillo, reporting that he witnessed troop trains "passing us all the time." The presence of so many men moving by rail reminded the reservist of the troop trains he had watched move through his small Indiana town during World War II and gave him a feeling of being part of a great world event.[7] In his first letter home to an aunt, William Marshall told how he "slept between St. Louis and Kansas City, somewhere in Oklahoma to somewhere in New Mexico," adding "we slept through Texas." In another letter addressed to his younger brother Jim, however, Marshall told of a much more rambunctious time. "I've seen a lot of fights since I left home," he reported. "Three on the train going out."

Perhaps the sudden shift to more rowdy behavior came about because of the increasing nervousness, as each passing mile drew these men closer to possible combat. At any rate, some of the older veterans took it upon themselves to show the younger reservists how marines were supposed to act on such a trip. The behavior ranged from pleasant to extremely combative. At some point in the trip, Bill Marshall found himself sitting in one of the Pullman cars, singing along with several other marine reservists as one of the men strummed a ukelele, plucking out such favorites as "Good Night Irene." After a while the musician announced he was tired and going to bed. A stocky staff sergeant who carried the reputation of a brawler ordered the ukelele player to continue playing, and a fight erupted. Marshall, who had gone to his sleeping berth when this fight broke out, later witnessed a long-suffering Major Torian rushing through the car to break up the altercation. Once in Pendleton, Marshall wrote a classmate, Bill Barnard, "You surely have heard Barney [Bill Barnard's older brother] speak of Sergeant Wayne Poole of Fort Branch. He was in three fist fights on the way out here."

The heat, boredom, and in some cases alcohol consumption, greatly increased tension among the men as the train progressed. "It was miserably hot and dirty—coal smoke blowing back through the open windows," remembered one marine.[8] In most cars the windows were shut to keep out the smoke, further adding to the discomfort. William Etheridge found the heat particularly difficult to deal with: "I mean it was hot. We didn't have air conditioning, and when they tried to keep the windows wide open, the smoke would roll in covering every one with soot." Dining under these conditions took away from what might have been a pleasant break from the discomfort of the trip. "They would take us into these hot Pullman cars and feed us," recalled Etheridge, "and the chow line was so long. You had to wait a long time in the heat to get your food."

To World War II veteran Bill Wright, the heat also made the trip a particularly hellish journey. "Oh, it was terribly hot. We were all packed in and in dungarees and nobody had taken a bath since we left. Everything," remembered Wright, "smelled of smoke and sweat." Teenager Charles Gottman recalled how long the trip lasted and how somber the older marines seemed to be. What few times the train stopped, the men rolled out and did calisthenics alongside the smoky train. Many took the opportunity to sneak off and get more booze. When the engine pulled to a stop at night in Needles, California, most of the C Company men decided to step out to stretch their legs. The heat that greeted them would be the most intense any of them had yet experienced. Even though the sun had set, the superheated air felt like a blast furnace. "It was the hottest place . . . I have been," wrote one reservist to his family. "Someone said it was 117 degrees."[9]

Squad leaders, such as Paul McDaniel, had been warned not to let their men get far from the train. McDaniel, however, soon found himself going with his men into town. "We went into Needles and got all the cold beer they had," he recalled. "I really wasn't a drinker myself, but the rest of the men stayed up all night before we pulled into Pendleton, playing cards and drinking beer. It got a little wild. Some of them got to vomiting, and there was a lot of yelling and some fights." Bill Etheridge also went into Needles and witnessed a number of men buying cheap, hot wine: "You talk about a bunch of sick marines. They were sick until they got to Pendleton." Just before the train pulled out of Needles, C Company reservists were ordered to line up in formation to check and make sure all were present and accounted for. One marine was missing. After about ten minutes of frantic searching by angry officers and noncoms, twenty-year-old John Elliott was discovered up front, casually talking to the train's engineer. Elliott received a quick, sharp reprimand before the train proceeded westward.

The trip was not all drinking, fighting, and card playing. William Marshall's Aunt Belle Colvin had given her nonshaving nephew a new shaving kit when he left Oakland City. Somewhere in the journey the novice seventeen year old found himself pondering nervously over the kit in a Pullman car rest room. Fortunately, a kindly older veteran, Robert Egan, noticed Marshall's puzzlement and taught the young reservist how to shave. Summing up the train trip, one Evansville reservist noted, "It wasn't a good trip. . . . All the guys were sad you know, leaving everyone."[10]

After three long, hot days of travel, the train carrying C Company finally pulled into Camp Pendleton, and the men of the unit fumbled for their seabags and quickly disembarked. One marine second lieutenant, who stood in charge of training a group of reservists at Camp Pendleton, recorded his first impression upon seeing a mob of reservists file off a train. He observed "beardless teenagers with little training, . . . pale of skin and shaggy haired. They had," he thought, "the bewildered air of raw recruits." It seemed obvious to this marine officer that none of these young men "had signed on for Reserve duty with the expectation of a shooting war."[11] The lieutenant thought that the reservist "youngsters[,] . . . despite Reserve training or because of the lack of any training[,] . . . knew little of Marine infantry and its methods."[12]

The train bearing the Evansville reservists arrived early in the morning, and once off the train, the men lined up in formation by platoons, reporting all present and accounted for. The environment that greeted the reservists seemed pleasant enough. William Marshall remembered the day as bright and sunny. Around him and his comrades lay scattered a number of two-story wooden barracks, and in the distance large, barren, sun-scorched hills shrouded in a soft haze. By midday, however, the reservists would discover the mist chased away by a pounding sun.

After reporting in, C Company shuffled off to a mess barracks for breakfast. Many of the reservists were still hung over from their drinking bouts on the train. One Evansville marine recalled how the breakfast was used by the Pendleton marine instructors to make a point: "It was just like boot camp. When we got in the chow line the mess men piled and piled the food on your tray and then came through and said 'you don't leave this chow line until you eat everything on that tray!' Of course there was a lot of them sick from drinking all that wine they bought in Needles. That's one thing I'll always remember, the smell of that chow line and all the sick people."[13] David Graham also vividly recalled the food heaping episode: "I was in line holding my tray and talking to my buddies when I turned and looked at my food. The mess man had piled at least fifteen dips of mashed potatoes on my tray. I told him 'Hey buddy, I didn't say I wanted that many potatoes.'" The mess man replied, "By God, you held the tray there." When Graham had finished and shuffled over to where the trays were returned, a gigantic marine observed that most of Graham's mashed potatoes were left uneaten. "What do you think you're doing?" the huge marine barked. Graham replied, "I'm full." The big marine began hollering at Graham, "You got that many tators, and you're gonna eat 'em all! Sit down over there and finish your meal!" Graham ate as much as he could and then hid the rest under the table. It was a portentous beginning to Graham's training at Pendleton.

That evening, and for the next two days, C Company stayed together as a unit. On 2 September 1950, the Evansville group posed for a group picture. It would be the last time the complete company assembled. The breakup came as the first of many shocks the Evansville group would experience at Pendleton. One surprised and disturbed reservist thought the company "would at least stay together for training in California."[14] C Company, however, had been luckier than most reserve groups. More often, the members of an original reserve company found themselves being separated at Pendleton upon arrival, leaving many commanding officers sadly shaking their heads in disbelief. Despite protest about the separating procedure, the disbanding of original companies was the norm, as one group of reservists from Roanoke, Virginia, discovered when they aggressively sought to stay, train, and fight together. "Can't do that," came the reply from the sergeant major in charge of placements. "I'm going strictly by the book," he told the disappointed men.[15] This practice grew out of experiences in earlier wars when regional groups stayed and fought together, sometimes causing particular communities to lose scores of their men. Such events had greatly damaged home-front morale. Conversely, the present practice of disbanding original reserve companies threw together marines who had never before interacted. One officer described his new unit at Pendleton as "filled by 215 men and 7 officers who had never served together. Half of our enlisted men were infantry trained Regulars, the other half were Reservists, most of whom were youngsters who knew little of Marine methods."[16] This situation, of course, further complicated the awesome tasks that lay before Pendleton instructors.

The day after C Company separated, homesick Bill Marshall lamented in a letter back home to Oakland City, "Today they separated us." Marshall sadly added, "The company is broke up for good." Charles Barnard, the oldest of the Oakland City boys, found himself placed in a group that was to be sent to Korea in two weeks. Marshall wrote that "Dickson, Greene, Cunningham, Fitch, and Sheetz are going to have about four weeks of training before they are sent across." The rest of the Oakland group, including Marshall, would be used at home to replace the regulars already in Korea. The latter group would also be put through boot camp. Many in the combat-ready-in-four-weeks category never endured the boot camp experience. Bud Fitch, because of his intelligence, was soon sent to San Diego to communication school, causing his worried parents back home in Oakland City to breathe a temporary sigh of relief.

Like other reserve companies pouring into Pendleton, C Company members were enduring the process that determined which men were ready for combat. This procedure loomed as the most critical portion of the call-up for marine reservists. Driving the process was the need to bring the 1st Marine Division up to strength for the secretly planned landing behind North Korean lines at Inchon. Although not evident to the casual observer, by late August the situation in Korea had shifted somewhat to the UN forces' favor. The Pusan perimeter had drawn up tight enough for embattled UN forces to shorten their supply lines and more easily place troops where needed. Conversely, North Korean lines were now greatly stretched. The North Koreans further aided the UN cause by failing to make one major thrust with a large concentrated force at weak points in the American lines.

While the American perimeter was holding, Gen. Douglas MacArthur, in charge of UN forces, convinced the Joint Chiefs of Staff that a surprise landing at Inchon on South Korea's western coast would cut off the North Koreans and bring a swift end to the war. It was an exceedingly risky and brilliantly conceived plan. More important for Marine Corps reservists, MacArthur's strategy would shape many a reservist's fate. For those marines needed for the Inchon landing but still in the states at Pendleton, the training was minimal. One marine private at Pendleton during those trying times recalled how his platoon commander summoned his men together on the first day. "Any one who doesn't want to be in a line company step forward," the lieutenant commanded. Three men did so. "Tough shit," the officer barked. The platoon never had time for night training and rifle range practice. "All their time was spent getting shots, their gear, and having their records updated if they could be found. Two days later the group was on a ship for Korea. . . . Between 7 July and 1 September, the Corps put together a division almost from scratch."[17] Experienced NCOs such as Evansville reservist Gene Koonce figured they would soon be going to Korea. Koonce remembered, "When they started interviewing us, it was apparent how desperate the marines were for manpower, especially those of us with combat experience."

The task of getting reservists prepared to carry out MacArthur's strategy of retaking the South Korean capital of Seoul after the landing at Inchon "had to be performed quickly," noted one historian, "but with a minimal degree of error; the life of the Reservist as well as those in his unit was at stake if it turned out he was untrained."[18] To enhance the process, the Corps quickly created three categories. Those labeled combat-ready reservists went through a two-week course to get them prepared to be rushed over to Korea for the upcoming Seoul campaign. This first group supposedly had two years of training in the reserves, had attended one summer camp and seventy-two drills or two summer camps and thirty-two drills, or were veterans with more than ninety days in the Marine Corps. A second group was deemed combat-ready in four weeks. This category included those who had gone to at least one summer camp and had attended a majority of the weekly sessions. A third group consisted of those with less than one year in the reserves. This latter group would be assigned to post and station billets to replace regular marines who had previously joined the division. About 65 percent found themselves placed in the first two classifications (50 percent combat-ready, 15 percent combat-ready in four weeks) and, consequently, could expect to experience some fighting in the near future.

Despite the creation of these categories, the selection process had many flaws, which was to be expected as thousands of reservists poured into Pendleton in a relatively brief period of time. A 1951 article in the *Marine Corps Gazette* noted that the time factor "did not permit the usual deliberation process of analyzing and giving practical tests." Further aggravating the problem "was the fact that while the majority of Reserve units reported with their records in excellent shape, many either became separated from their records in the hurried movement or were unable to complete them." This, coupled with the narrow time limit, "created a problem with unfortunate repercussions." Reservists unprepared for combat were more likely now to be chosen for the combat-ready-in-two-weeks category before having experienced adequate training. Further, "MOSs [military occupation specialties] were scrambled, and the payment of some personnel was delayed by as much as two months." This latter development put a further financial strain on many families of reservists and hurt morale in general.[19]

The loss of records also led to some unusual snafus. Evansville reservist Ralph Hargrave, who had been given his five shots and vaccination just before leaving Evansville, received the same set of shots when he arrived at Pendleton. When he was transferred to another company, he was given another round. "I protested, but it didn't do any good," the reservist recalled. "Two days later I was transferred to Headquarters Company, second replacement draft, and I got shots again. A few days after that, I transferred to Item Company. I got them again. That was five times I got those shots. Every time I protested and raised hell, but it didn't do any good because my records had not caught up with me."

To circumvent the problem of deciding which reservists were adequately prepared for combat after two weeks' training, each marine was supposed to be interviewed before any decision was made. The official position taken by the Corps was that "any Reservist that felt he needed more training, and so suggested, was at once removed from further consideration for immediate assignment to combat duty without prejudice."[20] In reality, this policy of selecting only those who were most ready often went ignored. William B. Hopkins, a second lieutenant at the time, told, for example, how many doctors and dentists "cooperated fully with the commandant's urgent request for more marines in Korea." (The urgency was increased about this time by President Truman's executive order exempting seventeen year olds from serving in combat.) "One World War II veteran," noted Hopkins, "had second thoughts about leaving so soon [for Korea]. . . . When he got to the dentist chair he pulled out his upper and lower plates and placed them on . . . a nearby table." The toothless marine hoped having dentures would exempt him from being sent to Korea. The ploy, however, failed: "The Navy doctor . . . gave the teeth a thorough examination. 'Now that's what I call a darn good set of teeth. Next!'"[21] The experiences of C Company members regarding this problem were often far less humorous. "There were some of the kids," recalled Bill Wright, "who told me 'I've never shot a rifle.' When I reported this to one of the officers, he just about dropped. By calling all these reserve units in, they ended up with many who simply never had any training at all."

From the administrative end, the organization and training of the men pouring into Pendleton was a logistics nightmare. Lt. Col. Ray Davis, for example, reported into Pendleton on 21 August and two hours later found himself assigned to organize and train the 1st Battalion of the 7th Marines. At that time there were no troops in his unit. All he had was a small cadre of veteran officers and NCOs. Camp Pendleton is a huge base covering several thousand acres divided into several parts. Combat-ready marines were assigned to an area designated Tent Camp Two, about ten miles away from the main headquarters area where the Evansville reservists had first arrived. (The name Tent Camp was something of a misnomer since the camp was actually made up mostly of metal Quonset huts.) About twenty miles away from Tent Camp Two lay Tent Camp One, where the combat-ready-in-four-weeks group would train. Davis, when notified of his command, got into a jeep "and drove down Rattlesnake Canyon" toward Tent

Camp Two. "Each installation along the twenty mile route—Chappo Flats, the rifle range, the artillery impact area, the infiltration course—was a reminder of the work to be done and the training that could not be done because there was no time." Davis, in dramatic fashion, declared to the officers and noncoms immediately assigned to his command, "We have a week to form a battalion. At no time in our careers will we be faced with greater responsibility—sixty percent of our men will be Reservists. . . . Many will be youngsters. . . . It is our job to get them ready for combat. If we fail they'll forfeit their lives." Davis knew time would be the great enemy. "There are only twenty-four hours in the day," he informed his group, "but we will use all of them."[22]

Evansville reservist Paul McDaniel, a veteran of World War II, vividly recalled his experiences at Tent Camp Two. "We opened it up," McDaniel remembered. "It was all Quonset huts, but the thing I remember the most was a big platform and the instructor got out on the middle of it while we sat around him. We heard a rattling sound coming from underneath." When some marines took a crowbar and raised several boards, they found "several fat rattlesnakes." When told that night to check under the Quonset huts for more rattlesnakes, McDaniel's crew found "a den of skunks instead." The lack of preparation for housing and feeding those marines being prepared to leave in two weeks quickly became evident. "There was no mess hall," one reservist recalled. "They took us on a conditioning hike. When we got back they had nothing for us to eat. That evening we found that there were no cots or mattresses for us to sleep on either. Many of the men were pretty mad at that point. Here we were going to be shipped off to fight and our own people weren't providing for us."[23]

The housing was almost always overcrowded. Bill Wright, for example, reported to his family back home that he lived in a barracks with two hundred men designed for half that many. Poor food was another common complaint from the men who found themselves in the combat-ready category. An Evansville woman, who went out to Pendleton to stay the two weeks with her husband, wrote home to say that "the men who can afford it buy their meals in the PX." Another Evansville wife, who stayed near Pendleton, told how "civilians near the base are taking advantage of the marines. Prices for cleaning and pressing or for shoe repair are terrifically high."[24] The gouging experienced by reservists and their families took many forms. One reserve officer from North Carolina, who would sail with the combat-ready-in-four-weeks group, told of returning to the apartment he shared with his wife to find "a note tacked on the door. It had been placed there by my landlord, who asked that I call at his desk." When the reservist inquired about the note, the landlord grumbled about how little money he was making on rent. The marine shot back, "Thirty five dollars a week is pretty steep." The landlord, however, began complaining loudly. "Steep! You can't get rooms any cheaper. . . . The demand is there. . . . Every day somebody comes by and wants a room I don't have." The marine finally walked away in disgust.[25]

Evansville reservist Richard Whitfield and his wife Alice had recently wed when they traveled out to California for Richard's training. Whitfield recalled how "the pay was late every month, so I'd hock four silver dollars I had until the government check came. When the money arrived, I'd go down to the pawn shop and buy back my silver dollars. The next month the process would start all over again." Whitfield, while training, also encountered animosity from regulars. On one occasion, the reservist missed a bus back from a training exercise but was able to catch a ride with a marine major and lieutenant. Unfortunately, the officers could only take Whitfield part way. "The next thing I knew," he recalled, "a state trooper pulled up to where I was thumbing for a ride and an SP [shore patrol] was riding with him. The SP was giving me a hard time, threatening to take me in for being late back to base." Hoping to calm the SP about the matter, Whitfield explained how he had already received a partial ride with two Marine Corps officers, one a major. The SP's response to Whitfield's story was "Just what we need, a couple more f——— reservists."

Paul McDaniel and the other Evansville reservists chosen for the combat-ready-in-two-weeks group endured "about ten days of extremely intense training . . . crawling under a lot of machine-gun fire and climbing up mountains." One regular, Morgan Brainard, recalled how he and the others suffered "long marches into California hills." The weary men "almost never used roads" as they struggled "up and down one big hill after another." They "marched and marched, and marched some more . . . in long files, snaking up and down the burnt . . . hills, each one larger and steeper than the one before." Few would forget the punishment they received from the pounding, relentless sun, which at times "was almost unbearable." Brainard recalled how on these long conditioning marches "we were issued a second canteen of water to wear, and we got up in long lines by the water wagon each morning to fill them before we marched out, and they would both be empty when we returned." Sometimes the marines carried light rations "and stayed out all day, returning about 5:00 P.M.," their faces "caked with dirt" and their leg muscles "tightening with pain."[26]

Many reservists, despite the intensity of the conditioning, remained concerned about the short duration of training they had received before leaving so quickly for Korea. William Ellis, an Evansville marine, complained to his wife that the two weeks of training "wasn't enough. It just gives us blisters and makes our muscles sore."[27] Worry about the lack of training also came from those in charge of preparing the reservists to fight. Misgivings, for example, turned to real concern for one lieutenant as he began to train his charges at Pendleton: "I was . . . discouraged. They seemed like kids, uncomfortable in their steel helmets, ill-fitting dungarees, some with leggings on backwards, and all milling about to find their places in the ranks." Comparing the regular marines he had trained at Camp Lejeune to the supposedly trained reservists, the lieutenant noted, "By contrast, the disheveled people before me looked like recruits in the first hours of boot camp. The DIs, the fabled drill instructors of Parris Island and San Diego, had twelve weeks to teach boys like these to march and handle a rifle. I was expected to have them combat-ready and on their way to a shooting war within only a few weeks."[28]

Some of the instructors panicked when they realized the lack of training their charges had received. One officer went to a higher up and complained about training "all Reserves. . . . I don't have a single Regular in my section." The officer then asked for "a few Regular NCOs to help break these people in." The request was promptly refused.[29] The job would have to be carried out in spite of the lack of instruction and modeling by regulars.

Some reservists would remain bitter about their uneven training experiences. The novelist William Styron, for example, would pen a searing piece about the training for Korea he endured at Camp Lejeune on the East

Coast. The story, *The Long March,* was based on two incidents there. Styron's regiment was on bivouac, when, during a field exercise, two mortar rounds fell short among a regiment camped next to Styron's group. Nine marines died. The rounds, it turned out, were defective shells from World War II. The colonel in command of Styron's regiment, for some odd reason, decided the evening of the tragedy to have Styron's group march all the way back to base camp, a distance of thirty-three miles. As Styron's biographer, James West III noted, "This would have been a demanding march even for young, well conditioned troops, men who had worked themselves into shape[,] . . . but the average reservists, many of them in their late twenties and thirties and all of them flabby from civilian life, found it a cruelly long distance." Three days after the difficult trek, Styron wrote a friend, describing the march: "We marched and marched and marched from 8:30 P.M. until 7:00 the next morning, and it was sheer hell. . . . I made it all the way with blisters on both feet the size of ping pong balls."[30] Like Styron, many reservists, because of the insufficient training time, often experienced unplanned and unfortunate treatment while in training, which they never forgot.

Reservists who found themselves classified as combat-ready in four weeks had a little more time to take in the atmosphere around them. Many in this group, however, because of the unusual needs created by the sudden call-up, would train, go to Korea, and come back to be discharged without having undergone marine boot camp. Unfortunately, within the marine culture, it was thought one could not be a true marine without this unique experience. Boot camp stands as the great test separating those who wish to be marines from those who endure and become marines. One could not wear the eagle, globe, and anchor, could not whistle the marine hymn, could not call himself a marine until the absolute final parade on the final day of boot camp. A person who had not experienced the same excruciating process yet called himself a marine was considered an imposter. Consequently, those nonboots who served in Korea, saw combat, and in some cases received decorations for valor would later find themselves frustrated by the odd circumstances in which the sudden call-up had placed them. How was it possible, they wondered, not to be marines after fighting like marines? On the other hand, there were those reservists who saw ferocious combat in Korea and then came back to the states and were required by the Corps to go through boot camp—the only time in Marine Corps history this occurred.

William Etheridge, a ready-in-four-weeks reservist, recalled his training as very tough: "They put us through a 'mini-boot.' We got up at 3:00 and got to bed at midnight. By the time we got our weapons cleaned, we'd only be left with a few hours of sleep." The lack of sleep in the barracks, however, did not affect Etheridge nearly as much as it did most of the trainees. "I could sleep any place," he remembered. "They used to tell me 'You could sleep standing up, Etheridge.'" Another advantage the young Evansville man believed he carried over other reservists was a bit of wisdom passed on to him by older brothers who had served in World War II. "Don't volunteer for anything," was their advice. Of the intense training, he remembered close-order drill, marching, rifle maintenance, and target shooting. Many of the older reservists were horribly out of shape and especially struggled with hiking up and down the steep, punishing mountains inside Camp Pendleton. "Nobody was in shape," Bob Egan remembered, "and those California hills were really high. Most of us had trouble getting half way up." In the face of this adversity, the Evansville group stuck together whenever possible. Raleigh McGary, who had not attended any of the prior summer camps or weekly training sessions, found himself being pushed and encouraged up one mountain by former Oakland City High School basketball star Albert Dickson. The younger Dickson told the out-of-breath McGary to "hang in there. The climbs," Dickson assured him, "will get easier."

All in all, the training had the most profound effect on the younger reservists, "boys [who] had just come from the shelter of home, family, and mom's cooking." Fortunately, they were also "strong and intelligent and they went to work with a purpose. They may not have been good at staying in step," one officer recalled, "but they took their weapons readily and they hardened quickly."[31] Gordon Greene, the Oakland City boy who so wished to someday tell "sea stories" to his family and friends, wrote frequently to his mother back in Indiana during his four-week training. "There is talk," he reported hopefully in his first letter from Pendleton, "that we will form into a raider battalion." Happily he also reported, "I don't have to go through boot camp." Greene, however, found the four-week regimen grinding. "We don't have time to waste," he penned his mother. "We really work hard having hikes and marches over these mountains every day." In a letter written in his second week of training, the Oakland City reservist complained, "I'll sure be glad to get this four weeks over with. Then maybe it won't be quite as tough." Greene described the base as "surrounded by mountains" where the reservists "are doing just about everything there is to do for combat training." The letter ended on a pessimistic note: "I don't know what to think about the world situation, but it looks like a long drawn out affair." Greene, as a much older adult, gave this brief account of his Pendleton experiences: "Advanced infantry training at Camp Pendleton California—September, 1950. Grueling days and grueling nights. Never got off the base—not one liberty! Went to the slop-chute a few Saturday nights to build record beer can pyramids."[32]

Greene, however, was luckier than many of the Evansville reservists, for he was able to be with two of his Oakland City friends after C Company's separation at Pendleton. "Albert [Dickson] and Bill [Cunningham] are still with me as yet," Greene related in one brief note. About half way through the training, Greene reported to his mother that he was "feeling better about the whole thing, getting adjusted to the training, and the gains we are making sure help out." The young man often reassured his mother regarding the danger he would soon likely face. "There is no reason for [worrying]," he noted in one letter. "I can take care of myself. . . . That's why we are training."

Less subdued in his description of training at Pendleton, Greene also wrote a childhood friend, William Barnard, who was still in high school, telling him, "My goodness, but these fellows are too mean for me to associate with. I think I'll give them my resignation. Yeah, that'll do it. No shit, this life could be compared to the foreign legion." Greene vividly related to his friend the tedious routines he now endured: "We'll fall in by our sacks and fall out again, then fall in. We take off our clothes and put them on,—fall out again until the gunnery sergeant is satisfied." The rugged conditioning especially shocked the nineteen year old: "We get up at 4:30 in the morning to take a long tactical march over the mountains, our captain's favorite for early morning exercise. Today we fired on the range. I got up at 4:30, and it was still dark when we got to the range." Greene's comments were also a clear indication of how little training reservists typically possessed. "I had never fired an M1 before and my darn cheek is swollen bad from the recoil," he wrote Barnard. The training experience left the young Hoosier so drained that he reported, "You know, I haven't drank a beer in weeks. I don't even have a desire for one anymore."

Typical of most reservists while in training at that time, Greene felt strongly about fighting for his country and against the perceived dangers of communism. "We could go to several places [after Korea]," he informed his mother, "such as Indo-China or Germany. Anywhere the UN needs us. It seems we are their police force in more ways than one. While we are here, we should show these Communists where they belong." Later, after living through months of grinding combat, Greene would offer a much more sober and mature view regarding fighting the North Koreans and Chinese. "Fighting," Greene wrote to his mother about six months later, "is getting mighty old."

Like so many young reservists who had to bear the complaints and snide jokes of regular marines, Greene often worried during his training at Camp Pendleton about how he would come to measure up in the eyes of regular marines on the day of final inspection. Greene recalled that tense moment in later life. "We fell out into the streets," he remembered. "Today was the first day that an officer has appeared on heaven's scene. All my muscles tensed as this tall blue-eyed lieutenant moved from man to man inspecting rifles, gear and clothing. As he inspected the man next to me, I began to concentrate on being sharp in bringing my M1 to inspections arms." When the officer came to Greene, the young Oakland City man brought his rifle "to inspection arms, pulled the bolt back and awaited the lieutenant to take the piece from me. Great! A clean take away without me holding on! Looking good!" After the ritual, the M1 was returned to Greene. "The lieutenant was ready to move on to the next man but hesitated a second and turned back to me." The officer barked at Greene:

"Who is your commander-in-chief?"
"You are, Sir!"
"Thank you for the compliment! Who is your commander-in-chief?"

"Captain Gas, Sir!"

"Who is your commander-in-chief?"

"General Smith, Sir!"

"Who is your commander-in-chief?"

"Commandant of the Marine Corps General Clifton B. Gates, Sir!"

"Who is your commander-in-chief?"

"President Harry S. Truman, Sir!"

The lieutenant gave Greene "that 'dumb so and so' look and moved on to the next man. I released the bolt on my M1 and brought it down to attention. God, I thought to myself. Why did you panic? You know this! But I wasn't ready for this sort of question."[33] Shortly before Greene experienced his first combat, he wrote his mother, "It seems like such a long time since I left home."

Bud Fitch, who left with a later group of reservists for Korea in January 1951, also grew more concerned about combat training as the time neared for his departure. In a letter addressed "Dear Folks," Fitch told how he and the other marines he trained with had recently been issued "our 782 gear—helmets, packs, rifles, canteens, etc. This is the same gear we will have when we go into combat . . . and you can sure bet I'm going to take good care of it." Fitch, who had originally been assigned to communications school in October, also passed on to his parents a bit of bad news. His mother and father had hoped that his communication training would keep him out of combat. They were now told this was not to be. "We are all infantry here," their son reported, "so I don't guess my school will do me much good." Because of Fitch's size, the husky Oakland City lad "got the B.A.R." The weapon, Fitch told his parents, "weighs about 20 lbs. and is really . . . wicked."

Conditions for later trainees quickly grew just as uncomfortable as it had been for those marines who had been sent to Korea after two- and four-week training periods. Bud Fitch noted in one letter to his mother, "We live in Quonset huts here, about 32 men sleep in a hut, so it's pretty crowded. The heads (toilets) are about a hundred yards off with no heat, and the showers are the same deal. The chow is plain and not much variety." In one bleak instance, the Hoosier reservist reported, "It has been raining all day, and we stood inspection today in the rain with our dress greens on. At least the officers had to be out in the rain with us." Fitch had more trouble in his training than some marines because the strenuous activities often caused him to accidently break his thick glasses. His parents, however, would faithfully send a new pair. In one letter to his parents he wrote, "I got the glasses and thanks a lot. They fit just right and cling to my face well." Pondering upon his bad luck in being called up with the marine reserve, Fitch later reflected, "As for the Marine Corps, I guess if you have to be in the service, you might as well be in a good outfit."

Seventeen-year-old William Marshall also faithfully wrote to his family while he trained in California. His letters clearly indicated the loneliness of the younger men who had never been away from home. "I've been homesick," he wrote. "Mostly this stuff isn't fun anymore." Playfully, however, he signed his first letter "Major Marshall." In his next letter, written three days later, the Oakland City teenager related, "I was very homesick yesterday, but I feel okay today. That doesn't mean that I wouldn't walk home if I had the chance. Some things," Marshall added, "are better than I expected, some are worse. The food has not been the best." Marshall also spoke of the unusual weather. "It gets hotter than at home [then] it gets real cold five minutes later." The young marine also complained about having to do his own laundry. "It isn't exactly fun, but I don't mind." Marshall tried to find solace in listening to his favorite music, but found it was not popular in California: "One boy has a portable radio and I hear music, but I haven't heard Ernest Tubb or Eddy Arnold yet." In another letter he complained, "I haven't heard an Eddy Arnold song since I left home. That's no kidding either. There are a few Ernest Tubb records out here but I haven't heard him on the radio." Marshall wistfully hoped that the letters his family rushed to congressional leaders might yet spare him and other high school–aged men from serving in the marines before they had graduated: "I don't know the scoop about what the senator [Capehart] said, but I believe I'd come home if I had the chance. Find out all you can about it and let me know. If it's a discharge, I'll take it and take a chance on the draft."

To ease his homesickness, Marshall, who dreamed of playing major league baseball, participated in any sporting event that happened to be available. "In one of the cards I told you about playing softball," he wrote. "I played two games, our outfit against Iowa. . . . I hit a homer and a single in each game. That made me four hits in seven times at bat. I played third base and did real well, although I threw a couple over first." In a letter dated 25 September 1950, the hopeful seventeen year old related how he believed "the war in Korea won't last but a few days longer." This belief was based on the fact that MacArthur's planned invasion of Inchon had been successfully carried out. Apparently this belief was prevalent, for Marshall told how "the teletype machine said the war should be over in a couple of days if nothing happens unexpected."

Gordon Greene also grew very homesick for the sights and sounds of his hometown. Greene wrote a friend back in Oakland City, lamenting, "I sure miss everyone, and when this affair is ended, I'll be glad to return and be recognized among the fellows again." Greene added that it seemed odd how all the Oakland City boys would soon likely be in combat together. "It sure seems funny that all of us should be going into the real thing so soon. A guy does get to wondering what is in the future for himself." Greene also demonstrated a growing maturity, telling his high school friend, who was having some difficulties, to "stay right in there and participate in every-thing that comes along. That's the only way to stay ahead, as well as to really enjoy yourself." In addition, Greene showed an increasing apprecia-tion for some of his former teachers. "You will never find a person more pleasing and considerate than Herman Cloin. He is a fine man, and the high school should be glad to have him," Greene observed.

Some of the letters written from reservists in training to friends and family back home emphasized the lighter side. Bud Fitch wrote a child-hood friend, Peg Sheetz, telling her, "I am here at San Diego going to Field Telephone School. It is a fourteen week course shortened to six and they are really throwing it at us (the course that is). Besides going to school we have the usual 'hoot and stomp' (drill), clean rifles, etc." Fitch reported that sergeant-instructors expected the reservists "to be three places at once, so we go to the place with the roughest Sergeant and get chewed out by the other two guys." Fitch added, "You get used to it after a while." The lonely Oakland City native also hoped to get his friend to send a picture of her-self. "I have been telling these guys about all the good looking women in Oakland," he wrote, "but they don't seem to believe me. How about send-ing out a couple of pictures of yourself to help me with my argument? Just sign them so they won't think it's a picture of some movie star and send them out. I need some to put up in my locker also. Anything for the boys you know." Fitch added in a more serious tone, "No kidding though, I would appreciate it."

Many of the Hoosier reservists were star struck by the Hollywood celebrities who lived nearby, and the reservists often wrote the folks back home about how close they came to these cultural gods and goddesses. "I haven't seen Tony Martin yet, but I did see Constance Moore," wrote one marine. "I don't know if you remember her, she played in the movies some.[34] Garold Sheetz wrote his sister about the exciting access the marines had to Hollywood entertainers: "I went down to San Diego to see Bud [Fitch] Friday eve and we went to L.A. and Hollywood Saturday morning. We went to the Hollywood Palladium. Frankie Carl was playing there. Later we went to the Colony Club. . . . Last Thursday night Edgar Bergen and Charlie were here to entertain us. His whole company was here with Ray Noble, the Starliters and his guest star was Jane Wyman." Reservists also often attended nearby sporting events. Bud Fitch wrote home that he and another reservist, Toledo native Bob O'Keefe, hoped to travel to Los Angeles "to see the National Pro Football League Championship." Fitch added, "They are filming a picture with John Wayne here called *Flying Leathernecks*, and we see Jap Zeros flying around smoking and all kinds of dog fights." Evansville reservist Charles Koestring was one of several marines who would be employed as extras in the film.

For the marine reservists among the former C Company group who were deemed combat-ready in two weeks, the day of departure came all too quickly. An Evansville party of about one hundred men were part of a larger group of three hundred who were suddenly ordered to be flown immediately to Japan and then to Korea. This group would just miss the Inchon landing but would be used in the campaign to recapture South Korea's capital. The night Paul McDaniel's barracks found out they would be taken to San Francisco the next morning and then flown to Korea "was pandemonium. They brought beer into our barracks and everybody drank and drank. Marines threw their empties out the windows until there was a pile three feet high. The next morning we had to get up early and fall out— everybody with a hangover."

So loud was the behavior of those who were about to go overseas that seventeen-year-old William Marshall feared those who were leaving were going "to tear the place down." The wild leaving parties also brought up once more the lingering conflict that still existed between regulars and reservists. In Marshall's barracks, for example, "an old salt" burst into the building that night after lights were out, yelling and demanding to know if anyone was awake. When no one answered the enraged man, the regular broke a Coke bottle over a stove and loudly swore until he had woke everyone who had been asleep. The angry regular "gave a long speech about how tough the Marines were and how green and embarrassing to the Corps the Reserves were. He seemed to be upset about having to fight alongside so many untrained Reservists." Finally the corporal of the guard tossed the regular out of the barracks.[35]

Some marines thought there was little to celebrate. Teenager David Graham, who found himself, as did a great number of reservists, classified as combat-ready after only two weeks of training, had grave concerns about going over so quickly: "When we were getting ready to go, I went down to see the commander to tell him we didn't have enough training—haven't even had boot camp. The commander agreed this was so, but added there was nothing he could do about the situation." The officer informed Graham, "We need people over there; we need them right now and you're the best we've got." The commander, however, promised Graham "all the boot camp you want" upon Graham's return from Korea.

William Marshall, at the time of departure of the first Evansville reservists to Korea, wrote his high school classmate William Barnard to tell him not to worry about his older brother, Charles "Barney" Barnard, who would be leaving in this first group. "I was with Barney when he got on the bus for Oceanside," he reported. "He looked good. I believe he could tame ten tigers." The homesick teenager further added, "He didn't mind leaving as bad as I minded him leaving." Of the men from the original Evansville reserve unit who served in Korea, only two officers, 2d Lt. Marion "Tex" Graham and 2d Lt. Mason Wiers, both veterans of World War II, went overseas. Both men endured ferocious combat. The other officers, such as Maj. Paul Torian, who trained marines in San Diego, were ordered to remain stateside, where they helped prepare men to fight in Korea.

Tex Graham's wife, Joan, had joined him in California. Sometime during that two-week training period, she and another woman friend, whose husband was training with Tex, had purchased some windup baby dolls that they released one evening to waddle into the next room where their husbands were resting after a long day of conditioning. The mechanized dolls had a message taped on them for the men to see. "This is our aim." Apparently the plan worked, for a few weeks after her husband left for Korea, Joan Graham discovered that they had conceived their first child in California. The exciting news, however, was dampened by the chance that the baby might never see her father alive.

Most of the Evansville reservists still at Camp Pendleton would soon find themselves aboard troop ships sailing west. The night before one of these groups of reservists shipped out, Joseph Owen, a regular officer, recalled how he listened to his wife lament about the unfairness of the reservists' plight. "It isn't fair," she said. "Sending men like that into combat, . . . untrained I mean." Owen, however, offered his wife a more positive assessment of the situation: "We're working on the men. They're coming along. . . . Our officers are good—and we have some of the best NCOs I've seen and that includes our Reservists." Owen added, "Don't worry. We'll fight like Marines when we get there."[36] Almost all of the Evansville men flying or shipping west to Asia were destined to be together again soon at a place called Chosin.

4   *Just the Night Before, We Were Laughing*

In the beginning, many of the Marine Corps reservists who found themselves so abruptly called to duty in July and August of 1950 hoped to be used in noncombat roles, relieving the regulars to do the fighting. Indeed, the first group of marines to arrive in Korea, in late July, the 1st Marine Provisional Brigade, were able to leave their previous assignments so quickly because the first rush of reservists had slipped in to fill those regulars' positions. The Provisional Brigade played a pivotal role in maintaining the ever-shrinking Pusan perimeter, buying time for UN forces to come up with a plan to turn around the fortunes of war. MacArthur later revealed how he had envisioned just such a scheme in the dark early portion of the conflict. Visiting the battlefield just a few days after the shocking invasion, MacArthur had "watched the smoke from the artillery and mortar bombardment pockmark the horizon." While observing "the great columns of terror-stricken refugees pouring south . . . he conceived the notion of a great amphibious landing behind the enemy flank" at Inchon.[1]

In pulling off his vision, MacArthur had specific plans for the Marine Corps. In July he had declared to Gen. Lemuel Shepherd, fleet marine commander, "If I had the 1st Marine Division, I would make a landing at Inchon and reverse the war."[2] The brilliance of MacArthur's design can be seen if one imagines Korea as the state of Florida. Down at the very southeast corner would lie the vulnerable Pusan perimeter. Just below the belt line of the state, on the west side, would lie the capital, and a few miles west of that, a seaport. MacArthur's plan called for a surprise landing at the seaport with troops swiftly moving toward the capital. Once secured, the troops would then move south and east to cut enemy supply lines.

The scheme was potentially even more dramatic because the great tides that surged at Inchon, the second highest in the world, precluded any major landing for all but a few days each month. Many of the top military leaders had opposed the shaky mission, seeing it as "a quixotic project, destined to disaster."[3] Yet MacArthur's dramatic presentation of the idea to the Joint Chiefs of Staff swept away all criticism, and the risky landing, dubbed Operation Chromite, took place on the morning of 15 September 1950. The endeavor turned out to be successful beyond anyone's wildest dream. Looking back, one military historian noted, "In a world in which nursery justice decided military affairs, Operation Chromite would have won the war for the United States."[4] As this assessment suggests, the apparent final victory was a heartbreaking illusion.

The Pendleton marines who found themselves boarding planes in California in late September 1950 would be arriving too late for the Inchon landing and would be used instead to help in the quick thrust to secure Seoul. Later, some would criticize MacArthur's shortsightedness in not going southward to attack the North Korean flank, thereby missing the opportunity to destroy the enemy. As it turned out, the North Korean army, once it realized its precarious situation, fled so rapidly northward that the UN forces in the Pusan area were unable to engage and destroy them, and many did indeed evade the trap. At the time, however, most believed the enemy force, or what was left of it, could be taken care of later. As a dramatic gesture, the publicity-conscious MacArthur wanted to hand back the capital to President Syngman Rhee as soon as possible.

The first group of Evansville reservists now flying westward from California carried little if any opinion regarding the handling of the war beyond wanting actions taken that would shorten the conflict. Gene Koonce, however, still worried about the reservists' lack of training. "We ran the obstacle course one time at Pendleton before we boarded planes for Korea," he recalled. The planes Koonce spoke of were Pan Americans chartered by the Marine Corps to rush over a group of about three hundred men. The one Koonce climbed aboard "was a strata cruiser with a double deck." Evansville native Jim Stearsman recalled that the men flew on six planes with Stearsman traveling on the last one. The flight itself would take thirty-six long, uncomfortable hours, with stops in Hawaii and Wake Island. Barney Barnard wrote reassuringly to his parents back in Oakland City, "There are many clouds below us, but everything is swell up here." For many reservists, the trip was their first on a plane. Wrote the observant Oakland City native, "The boy next to me had never been in a plane before, and he was jittery for a long time while we were warming up and getting into the air. Several of the people on this flight had never been on a large plane. However no one has been sick as yet." Young Barnard tried to put on his best face for his worrying parents, telling them how some of the marines on his flight were "vets of the South Pacific, a lot of sergeants and corporals that have several years service."

Some of the Evansville group especially remembered their short time on Wake Island. "It was 115 [degrees] down there," recalled Paul McDaniel, "and when we stepped off the plane, it was like a blast of hot air. They had great big portable fans going in the dining room, so we ate in there." The men were told they had about two hours to kill before leaving, so several wandered around the tiny island that had so recently been the scene of World War II struggles with the Japanese. In his brief excursion around the island, Charlie Deffendall recalled seeing "a large number of rusting Japanese tanks and other equipment scattered along the peaceful beach." The eerily quiet scene served as a grim reminder to the Evansville men of the horrors of war.

The landing at Tokyo International Airport was a difficult one for some of the planes. "The strata cruiser did just fine, but two planes hit an air pocket and just dropped several hundred feet," remembered Gene Koonce. Buses were brought in and the men rode to Yokohama Naval Base, where they stayed about four days, receiving some liberty time to see the sights. Eventually the marines trekked to Otsu for a little more training before being sent to Korea to help in the liberation of Seoul. The conditioning they received in Japan tended to leave the travel-weary men even more fatigued, as evidenced by a letter one reservist wrote to his mother: "Boy am I tired. The unit just came in from an eight mile hike." Fatigue, however, was not the only problem the man reported. "The smell is worse than anything else," he wrote. "The Japanese farmers carry the 'night soil' [human waste] in wooden buckets on their shoulders. When they are upwind it is really rough." The reservist also commented on the food, which he noted was "better than Pendleton," although the milk, he observed, had "a funny taste—like something has been put in it." Also, the marine complained, "the people don't fry the bacon long enough. It seems too raw and greasy."[5] Obviously the cooks at Otsu did not prepare food as well as this reservist's mother.

After a short time in Japan, the group received orders to load their sea-bags onto trucks for the ride back to the planes that would fly them into Korea. Gene Koonce and Paul McDaniel noticed one of the Evansville men, Henry Maley, standing around without his gear. Maley sheepishly came up to his friends and said, "I guess I'll see you guys back in Evansville." Koonce demanded to know why he was not going with them. "I've got double vision. They gave me a waiver," Maley meekly replied. Both McDaniel and Koonce lit into their friend. "You coward! You've got the nerve. Here we are going to Korea while you stay here. What in the hell are you going to do in Japan anyway?" Maley answered that he had offered to train the younger reservists who were not ready for combat. "You couldn't train anything," McDaniel snorted. Maley, who possessed an unusually high-pitched voice, began to plead with his two friends not to think so badly of him. "You shouldn't feel that way," he said. "I'm sorry—please don't be angry." McDaniel howled, "Get out of here. We don't want to see you anymore!" As the truck rolled out, the distraught Maley ran a long distance after his friends, still pleading for their understanding. If McDaniel and Koonce had not been so angry, the scene might have been humorous. As it turned out, the men were all destined to meet again at the Chosin Reservoir.

Kimpo Airfield, the primary air base for nearby Seoul, was still not completely secure when the planes carrying the Evansville reservists and other marines circled to land late in the afternoon of 27 September. Paul McDaniel was told that the North Koreans "were still firing at the planes as

they came in, so we stayed up high enough to get away from the gunfire."
One of the reservists who rode on Jim Stearsman's plane lit up a cigarette
just as the aircraft started to land. "The guy was probably nervous," Stearsman recalled. "We all were. Anyway, Lieutenant Wiers stomped over and
knocked the cigarette out of the guy's mouth." The officer told the stunned
marine "smoking lamps are not lit in a combat zone." When the planes
finally descended and the men scurried off, the sight of another plane
belching forth black clouds of smoke at the edge of the runway greeted
them. An Evansville reservist wrote his father that the marines had landed
"right in the middle of the whole works. . . . In the distance we could see
Seoul burning and the shells bursting in the town."[6] Paul McDaniel heard
someone shout, "'You better run up here and get your ammunition right
now!' We went by some little houses that were built on the air base where
I grabbed two bandoliers of ammo."

Other marines also grabbed up weapons and supplies. "Everyone is
loaded for bear," observed one Evansville man in a letter. "I am carrying an
M1 rifle and 10 clips of ammo. Some of the boys have automatic pistols
and carbines with 100 rounds of ammunition."[7] Despite being heavily
armed, many of the men, most of whom were novices to war, grew
extremely nervous. At this juncture, McDaniel recalled, "We hadn't been
assigned to units yet, so they told us to bunk down in a nearby building
that was part of a university. We were told we would spend the night there,
and then tomorrow we would fall out to join a unit that was going to secure
Seoul."

Some of the new arrivals feared the possibility that an enemy soldier
might sneak up and hurl a grenade into the building that they were to
sleep in, so many sought other accommodations. John Elliott and Paul
McDaniel threw up their shelter-halves together and made a tent. Nearby,
Charles Deffendall wandered around the perimeter of the airfield looking
for a safe place to sleep. Deffendall, who harbored a rather negative attitude toward authority, had been unnerved by the sights and sounds he witnessed upon landing at Kimpo. "I told myself, Charlie, you'd better listen
for a change to what they tell you or you may not get back." Shaken, the
young man sought a secure place where he might pass the night. "I saw
some concrete bunkers and figured they'd be safe," he recalled. Sticking

his head inside one of the structures, Deffendall discovered two rotting human corpses—North Korean soldiers—"one faceless, and the other with its brains oozed out." Needless to say, Deffendall spent a long, restless night trying to sleep outside one of the bunkers, contemplating what he had just viewed.

McDaniel, a veteran of World War II, and the younger John Elliott spent most of the night quietly talking about their plans for when they returned home. Nearby a schoolhouse with big, screened windows had been turned into a temporary prison for the growing number of captured North Koreans. "They had put all these Korean prisoners in the school and a lot of them were just walking around looking out," McDaniel remembered. "It was so creepy that I couldn't sleep. I'd look up and they'd be looking back at me through the screened windows." Completely worn out by their flight, Barney Barnard and some others stayed in a graveyard, which the Oakland City native described as "just mounds of earth, no markers or anything." The night was as uncomfortable for Barnard as it was for the rest of the nervous arrivals. "It was very cool," he wrote his father that evening, "and I don't think it helped my cold very much." The young man also complained that he wore "the same clothes I had in Japan. My socks are something to see—blackened. The dust here is very bad so there isn't much use in changing clothes or shaving or anything else for that matter." On a more positive note, Barnard told of "the first good meal that has been passed out for a week—hot dogs, potatoes, peas, and pineapple—also hot chocolate."

On their second day in Korea, the new arrivals were split up and sent in a number of different directions. Charles Deffendall recalled the new arrivals boarding amphibious vehicles and crossing the Han River. When Deffendall and another Evansville native, Donald Inkenbrandt, reported to their assignment, a gruff gunny sergeant demanded to know why they were so late. Without thinking, the rambunctious Deffendall responded, "'Why are you so early?' Then I realized just how big that gunny really was. Luckily, he just gave me a hard look and walked away." Richard Eberle, an MP in World War II, received one of the more prestigious assignments—a bodyguard to the top marine in Korea, Gen. O. P. Smith. Barnard and three others from the Evansville group "were transferred to the 1st Engineering Battalion."[8] Joining Barnard was Jim Stearsman, who soon found himself assigned to help "place a pontoon bridge across the Han River to help the marines take Seoul." Tex Graham, one of only two officers who came with the Evansville group to Korea, was assigned to Headquarters Company, where he was given the important responsibility of carrying map overlays and messages from Command Headquarters to Regimental Headquarters.

Paul McDaniel recalled a group falling out the next morning on a soccer field while off in the distance "there was a lot of firing going on, so we were all kind of jumpy." The selection process seemed haphazard and driven by expedience: "All these different guys were called to different infantry units until it got down to where there were only two of us left out there on the field." Finally the two, McDaniel and another NCO, went to a nearby house to find out what was going on. "The captain inside placed the other guy in machine guns, then he turned to me and asked if I'd ever fired a 3.5 Bazooka. I told him I'd only fired the 2.5s from World War II. The captain said, 'no different, just bigger.'" Many of the Evansville reservists, including McDaniel, now came as replacements into the 3d Battalion, 5th Marines, commanded by a tough thirty-two-year-old lieutenant colonel named Robert Taplett. A hard-fighting tactician who cared deeply about his troops, Taplett always earned accolades from his men.

McDaniel, who ended up in Headquarters Company, was told his group would be used in mopping up around Seoul. "When we got up to the fighting," he remembered, "our group came in contact with Item Company and suddenly here were all these Evansville guys yelling and jumping around, happy to see me—David Graham, Chester Krueger, Billy Groves, just a whole bunch of them. Believe me, it was good to see their faces again." McDaniel would not have been so excited if he had known the fate that awaited Item Company at the Chosin Reservoir. "We came to call Item 'Jinx Company,'" noted one of McDaniel's friends, Gene Koonce. "They were just thrown together so quickly, and that caused a lot of problems. And then they just had some downright bad luck." The new arrivals were soon down to business. McDaniel's group spent the next night "on a mountain with tin cans strung all around for security. I had a hand grenade lying right beside my cheek, but it didn't have the pin pulled out."

Sometime during the night, McDaniel woke up to a loud commotion. "I heard the tin cans rattling. Suddenly, everyone woke up yelling 'who is that?' It turned out it was one of our guys relieving himself."

Soon after arriving in Korea, Evansville reservist Gene Koonce found himself leading a patrol along an unpaved road. The patrol's task was to guard the convoys of trucks now streaming by on the way to Seoul. Koonce was walking point when his group started taking fire. Ordered to form a skirmish line, the marines advanced smartly across a rice paddy. "I was running up on a dike, running hard, about a fourth of the way across when something exploded and knocked me down face forward," Koonce recalled. "When I looked around I saw three men down; they looked like they were in pretty bad shape." Koonce had tripped a land mine but had been running fast enough that he missed the brunt of the blast. "Nearby I saw what looked like a croquet stake and realized it was a land mine tripping device. I hollered, 'Minefield! back up!'" Koonce "got shrapnel and a concussion" in the explosion, suffering the first of several wounds he would receive in Korea. Koonce was more worried, however, about the dangers of the unmarked minefield than his injuries. "Battalion Headquarters was told about the incident, and the paddy was supposed to be marked off." Headquarters' lack of response, however, would soon prove costly.

Item Company, which had a number of Evansville men, came along shortly after Koonce's misstep had triggered an explosion. For some unknown reason, the dangerous minefield had not been posted. The marines of Item, including David Graham and the popular John Elliott, with whom Koonce had attended Evansville College back in Indiana, traveled in trucks. When the vehicles came under small-arms fire, the officer in charge had Graham and the rest pile off the trucks and go across the rice paddy to set up a blocking position at the base of a nearby mountain. "Several trucks were going to be traveling through shortly, and the officer didn't want the North Koreans coming down the mountain attacking the convoy," Graham recalled. "Soon several of us Evansville guys were headed across the paddy toward the mountain. Chet Krueger probably stepped on a land mine. The shrapnel went right by me and hit John Elliott, who was walking behind. Someone shouted mortars, but I knew it was a land mine." Several marines gently picked up the injured Elliott and carried him back to the road. "The Corpsman told us John wasn't injured too badly, and he would be alright. We got back on the trucks greatly relieved. We thought Elliott was going to be our leader; he had corporal rank and had attended a military academy. A little bit later, someone came back and said that Elliott had died from shock."

When the dismal news of John Elliott's death begin to circulate among the scattered Evansville reservists, it rocked the group to its core. Paul McDaniel remembered how the news "broke me up—just the night before we were laughing in the tent we shared that first night at Kimpo." Another member of the old Evansville Company, Barney Barnard, wrote home that "one of the boys who came over from Evansville stepped on a mine the first day he was on line. The boy's name was Elliott." Although the Evansville group had been promised at least six months of training before seeing combat, Elliott died just over a month after leaving Evansville. "They didn't give those people enough training to protect themselves on the line," Barney Barnard wrote his father. Gordon Greene, who now trained in Japan, wrote a friend back in Oakland City, telling him, "I have just heard tonight that one of the young guys from the Reserve unit was killed. Man, I don't know how to explain what a feeling it is to hear that someone you know got it. It sure doesn't help out your morale."

As the war continued, the Evansville marines had little time to deal with the first death of one of their own. Most of the group experienced some combat in and around Seoul as the capital was secured. One letter home from a Hoosier marine reservist gave some indication of the savage fighting that took place during this time: "You have read about the things the North Koreans did to our army people—well they buried three Marines alive, so our division didn't take any prisoners for three weeks. It wasn't very nice, but nobody is going to do that to our men the way they did." The marine went on to point out that "the South Koreans were even worse to the ones they captured, but that's all in war I guess." The marine had seen enough to write his mother and tell her he hoped his younger brother, who was a high school senior, didn't "want to join the Marines. My experiences have been bad enough on me. Only a fool would want to get into the service," he declared.[9] Reservist Gordon Greene, a friend of the Barnard family, cautioned a younger Barnard brother, William, to "stay shy of this outfit. It sounds like a grand and glorious life, but we have a wonderful reputation to live up to, and you are expected to keep it so." The letter added, "Speaking of college, that is where you belong. You can stay clear of all this and have some fun too." Despite these admonitions, the teenager would eventually join the Corps and retire with officer rank.

Besides the fighting, living conditions were also difficult. Barney Barnard wrote from Kimpo to some of his boyhood friends back at Oakland City, telling them, "I haven't shaved or washed for five days and I'm beginning to feel kind of crummy. The water situation here is poor. Enough to drink and cook and that's about all." Barnard also complained about the weather: "The nights are very cold now. I have a hard time every night since we have been here. . . . The wind blows the red soil into every hut and into all of our food." Still, the young man couldn't help but share some of the excitement of battle with his friends back home. "The front," he reported, "lies about three miles due north. Last night I could see the big guns shelling Seoul, but they were so far away I could only hear the dull thuds." In the same letter the marine engineer told how "General Mac came past yesterday going to Seoul. He was going to give back city hall to the South Koreans, after the Marines took it, of course."

The caravan that Barnard saw was an impressive one. *Time* magazine reported, "'It's just like old times,' said Douglas MacArthur to the assembled big wheels at Kimpo Airfield. The Supreme Commander's silvery new constellation SCAP had just flown in from Tokyo for another historic ceremony of liberation." MacArthur traveled from Kimpo to Seoul "in a five-starred Chevrolet Sedan trailed by four other staff cars, and forty jeep loads of newsmen and lesser brass." On the occasion in Seoul, MacArthur gave a short speech then turned to President Rhee and announced, "Mr. President, my officers and I will resume our military duties and leave you and your government to the discharge of civic responsibilities." Rhee was overwhelmed with tearful gratitude.[10] Paul McDaniel remembered how his marine unit was relieved by the 1st Cavalry for the occasion of MacArthur's official returning of the capital back to the South Korean president: "We were pulled off of the side of the road and were told the 1st Cavalry was going to take our place in Seoul for the ceremony. We just sat there in our dust-covered clothes as truck after truck of army personnel roared by. They all had on those yellow scarves, and here we were all scroungy looking." MacArthur wanted the Seoul ceremony to be mostly an army affair. Only four marines out of several scores of army and diplomatic dignitaries were allowed to attend the services. Marine colonel Chesty Puller was especially angry at not hearing the Marine Corps singled out for their major role in the capturing of Seoul. "They never said a damn thing about the Marine Corps. Can you imagine that? Who the hell do they think carried this whole fight?" Puller fumed.[11]

As the Inchon/Seoul phase of the war drew to a close, the members of the Evansville group could breathe a sigh of relief. Although the sudden death of the highly regarded John Elliott had been tragic, it now seemed likely that the rest of the men would soon be going back home or, at the very worst, face some kind of occupation duty. MacArthur's Inchon strategy had indeed caused the North Koreans to cut and run. Only in Seoul did they make a determined stand, and, as Chesty Puller noted, the marines had taken care of that problem. Now United Nations troops hotly pursued the remnant of the once-proud North Korean army. For a brief moment in October, UN forces paused at the thirty-eighth parallel while leaders pondered whether to cross that line. The pondering did not last long. Secretary of State Dean Acheson argued that the UN could not be expected "to march up to a surveyor's line and stop," and Gen. Douglas MacArthur stood in full agreement.[12] National Security Council paper number 81, produced on 1 September, recommended the United States "persuade the United Nations to pass a resolution authorizing [American] forces to cross the 38th parallel to destroy the North Korean . . . army and to provide for the unification of Korea by free election." For political reasons, however, the final UN authorization remained highly ambiguous on the reunification effort, the UN recommending that "all appropriate steps be taken to ensure conditions of stability throughout Korea."[13] By mid-October, as U.S. troops moved up the peninsula, all that seemed to remain was the mopping up of the fragmented North Korean army.

The crossing of the thirty-eighth parallel by UN forces did not go unnoticed by North Korea's neighbors. At the time of the invasion of Korea, and throughout the war, the United States believed the initial invasion had been jointly planned by North Korea, China, and the Soviet Union. More recent information suggests, however, that although the Russians were aware of the possibility of North Korea's intended invasion and had given their blessing to the endeavor, neither they nor the Chinese were ever directly involved in planning the war.[14] However, by early August 1950 the Chinese were forced to consider the necessity of intervening in the war. One Chinese military leader, though, described the unprepared Chinese army as "a fat man in urgent need of a diet."[15] General Peng gave the final opinion from the military point of view to a group of that country's military leaders: "China will become involved in hostilities in Korea only if the integrity of the Democratic People's Republic [North Korea] is directly threatened." Peng noted hopefully that there seemed "no likelihood of such a disaster."[16]

Politically, the Chinese were just as adamant about North Korea's survival as a nation. The Chinese premier, Chou-En-lai, declared as early as September that his country would "absolutely not tolerate foreign aggression [in Korea] nor will they . . . tolerate seeing their neighbors being savagely invaded by imperialists."[17] The United States, however, seemed in no mood to take the Chinese seriously on the matter. General MacArthur all but guaranteed that neither Russia nor China would come into the war now that North Korea was obviously defeated. MacArthur's pronouncements, because of his legion of past successes, now carried the weight of a god's. *Time* magazine declared that one of the primary reasons for the "final victory" in Korea lay in "Douglas MacArthur's vast superiority over the enemy generals in strategic planning."[18]

Most cultures have maxims and proverbs that warn of the dangers of pride, but the possible ending of the Korean conflict on such a surprisingly positive note overcame any concern of possible turnarounds on the part of American news media. By early October, folks back home in places like Evansville heard wonderful news from the press about the war's glorious finish. *U.S. News and World Report* bragged in a sudden burst of hubris that the United States, by "winning" in Korea, "was again top dog in the world."[19] *Newsweek* observed happily, "Everybody loves a winner" and gloated that "North Korean's great ally, the Chinese Communists[,] . . . made not a move to save them." President Truman and the Democratic

Party seemed to be big winners also, as the off-year election soon to take place would now likely go their way. "The President's advisors," *Newsweek* reported, "were telling him that a Korean peace by congressional election time was now possible."[20] One national magazine carried a number of triumphant photos, one showing happy, waving GIs giving the old World War II "V" for victory salute. Another photo, this on the front of the magazine's cover, showed a marine with a captured North Korean. The caption read "U.S. Fighting Marine: Winner And Still Champ."[21]

The change was indeed breathtaking. American forces in the early portion of the war had known only retreat as four understrength and "peacetime-soft divisions occupying Japan" had found themselves facing a tough, brutal, well-trained, and well-equipped army.[22] At the very worst moment of this phase of the war UN forces found themselves desperately holding only a small bit of land seventy-five by forty miles. Now, miraculously, only four months later, the war looked to be only a matter of cleaning up. By late October *Newsweek* declared that the conflict in Korea had wound down enough for the magazine to begin reporting less about the war and more about national affairs: "And so with this issue *Newsweek* meets changing news values with a change in its format of the past several war weeks."[23] The Korean War, boasted another article in the same magazine, is "the first war in which America's kids have had a chance to show their [World War II] big brothers they've got the stuff too."[24] Column writer and retired air force general Carl Spaatz bragged shamelessly that "the air plane beat the coolie in Korea."[25] In an eerily prophetic vein, however, *Newsweek* noted the surprise shift in fortune "seemed almost too good to be true."[26]

The day before the first Evansville men had landed at Kimpo, near Seoul, Gordon Greene, who still trained at Pendleton with the combat-ready-in-four-weeks group, wrote his mother back in Indiana that his unit would "move out Saturday. The chances are that our destination will be Japan," he told her. The young Oakland City man confided to his mother in another note that he actually looked forward to the ocean trip "for the reason that we will get a little more spare time." Greene added a reassuring line, telling his worried mother that the situation in Korea was "looking a lot better now." The troop ship, the USS *General Walker,* loaded up in late September, and two sets of Oakland City, Indiana, parents, the

Cunninghams and the Dicksons, hurriedly drove almost two thousand miles to see their sons depart. Unfortunately, they arrived just as the troop ship left port. "We couldn't talk to them," Greene noted, "because they were too far away for us to hear them. I suppose they were disappointed, traveling so far and not getting to talk to us." The situation, however, was not quite as bleak as Greene believed. Many years later William Cunningham recalled how as he gazed at the huge throng on the dock, trying to pick out his mother, "a very attractive young woman in a tight sweater materialized among the crowd. Suddenly marines all over the *General Walker* began to wave and whistle frantically at the young girl. I was taking a good look too, until I realized my mother was standing right beside her. If it hadn't been for that young girl, my mother and I probably never would have made eye contact. As it was, at least we got to wave at one another."

Despite Gordon Greene's hope that the ocean journey would provide relief from the marines' difficult regimen at Pendleton, the trip was an uncomfortable one. For World War II veteran William Wright, the journey was the second time he had traveled on a troop ship. Wright, who had left a young bride back in Evansville, found the sleeping conditions almost intolerable. "There were four or five bunks stacked one on top of the other with very little head room," he recalled. Most of all, however, Wright fretted and worried constantly about his wife, Evelyn, who had little experience driving a car and now found herself without any nearby family members from whom to pull support. "I was worrying about her all that time. She was just on my mind for the entire trip." Bill Etheridge had a stroke of good fortune regarding his assignment aboard the ship: "One of the sergeants on board had served earlier with my brother in the Corps. When we got aboard he told me to get some of my buddies and sign up for his detail. We had the task of chipping paint, so we were top side most of the time." Etheridge's assignment turned out to be one of the best of the voyage. "We chipped and painted all the way over and never pulled any KP," he remembered. "We'd see those other poor guys coming up from below; they'd just be worn out while we were walking about for hours a day out there in the sunshine." Few men on the troop ships bound for Korea were as lucky as Etheridge and his friends. On a later voyage, Evansville reservist Charles Gottman, who spent most of his time down below "with the hatches battened down," remembered how the ship's screws "would come out of the water and the whole ship would shake and you'd think the thing was going to break apart. You'd have to fight for a place to stand on top-side." The rolling seas made most of the men sick to one degree or another, and many of the marines down below soon discovered it was an advantage to have a top bunk.

Young Gordon Greene found the voyage something of a mixed bag. "Golly, there are a lot of guys who are sea sick," he wrote his mother. "The first five days were the roughest. . . . I darn near felt like turning my guts wrong side out at times." Once Greene adjusted to the roll of the ship, however, he reported, "The food is excellent, and we have a lot of spare time. We're almost north of Midway, about half way to Japan." As a sign of things to come, Greene told how the weather had begun to change. "It is a lot colder out here now. . . . We were issued two pairs of winter underwear and a field jacket."

After a two-week voyage, the USS *General Walker* pulled into Japan. Now these marines faced two more weeks of training to get them ready for Korea. At Camp Otsu, the men marched and took long conditioning hikes. Veteran Raleigh McGary, who had left a wife back in Poseyville, Indiana, set up his shelter-half with another marine out on an airfield about the time a heavy downpour began. As the water rose at his feet it suddenly dawned upon the Hoosier native that "things were not going to turn around where we would soon be going home." McGary got severely sick to his stomach at this point.

Although McGary and many of the older men found the new environment uncomfortable, younger reservists, who came from small towns and rural communities and had never traveled much before, found their time in Japan exciting. Greene reported to his mother from Japan, "This place is really a better one than any I have been to yet. It is very interesting because I see something different every day." In another letter Greene told how he "and Albert Dickson are going into Kyoto today to shop." Greene, however, found some conditions in Japan disturbing. To Bill Barnard, Greene wrote, "The Japanese have no means of transportation except bicycles and street-cars, also some old charcoal burning buses. Their houses are crowded together more than our slum districts, and living conditions are extremely bad. Their clothing has been patched and repatched. Most of it is army clothing, especially those fatigue pants. The don't have toilets as they just squat anywhere at anytime. So when we are marching down through these little villages, we often smell some very foul odors."

Toward the end of their stay in Japan, the reservists grew restless, no doubt due in part to the changing weather. Gordon Greene told how "it's really getting cold here, and snow is expected soon. I am wearing heavy underwear too and I really appreciate them." The call-up experience had already had a shaping effect on the once-eager-for-adventure Greene, who now told his mother, "I don't know when this will end, but I plan on going back to school. I know one thing, I don't want to have to go through this again." Occasionally, the easing of tensions for the marines while at Otsu took odd twists. William Wright and the three other men who made up his fire team found a dilapidated rickshaw. "We were scheduled to leave for Korea in two days and decided we would have some fun," he recalled. The four marines purchased two cases of beer and spent their last day or so in Japan taking turns pulling each other around the base. "We'd run for a while and then stop and drink two or three beers, then we'd run some more." Knowing the men would soon be sent to Korea, the authorities took little notice of this peculiar activity. "On the last night in Japan we put the rickshaw on top of a mess hall roof," Wright remembered. "When we got out to sea, however, we sure paid for our fun. All that beer drinking and then running just tore up the linings of our stomachs." Still, such episodes helped relieve the stress of some of the marines while they trained, but mostly waited, in Japan.

While the combat-ready-in-four-weeks group fretted in Japan, back in Korea, marines, including the first group of Evansville reservists, continued to mop up after the Seoul campaign. Barney Barnard told his father, "The weather here is turning," the nights "getting colder and colder." Like his reservist counterparts in Japan, Barnard soon found the routines of war tedious. "I have seen the dawn for three days in a row. First I had guard, then a work party, then guard again last night. The only thing we guard," the marine went on to complain, "is the water and the food, keeping other companies from stealing the stuff." Barnard found some time to relax by keeping up with sporting news. "We got to hear three innings," he wrote, "of the third World Series game. I have read about the other games in *Stars and Stripes*. It's a good paper, except all the credit goes to the army for capturing every airfield and town." On a more serious note, the young marine told his father that the whole division was preparing to move out: "I know where we are going, but I can't really say. If we are real lucky, this landing won't have to take place." The conditions that mandated the date of the Inchon landing also dictated when Barnard and the division could depart. "We might leave by the 15th," he wrote. "The tide goes back down so low [after then] that the ships can't come in."

Paul McDaniel's unit was called back to Inchon about this time, and on the first night stayed in an abandoned factory. "We saw a bunch of woven mats in there," he recalled, "and thought they'd be good to sleep on, certainly an improvement after sleeping in our bags on the ground. I stacked three or four of them and laid down but then I started scratching. The mats were just covered with fleas. So we went back outside, back to the sleeping bags." The next day McDaniel remembered his group going out on the Inchon mud-flats. When the tide came in McDaniel heard the marines' destination. "We're going to Wonsan," an officer told him. "Everybody said, 'Well, where's Wonsan?'"

General MacArthur had been told by the Joint Chiefs of Staff in late September that his military objective was now to "conduct military operations . . . north of the 38th parallel in Korea." The directive, however, had limiting factors. "Under no circumstances . . . will your force cross the Manchurian or U.S.S.R. border of Korea," MacArthur was ordered. Initially only Korean ground forces were supposed to be used in the northeast part of the country, where Korea touched Soviet territory.[27] This latter strategy would soon be discarded in the rush northward. The supreme commander now developed one of the most questionable strategies of the war: he split his forces. Lt. Gen. Walton Walker, who had up to this time directly commanded the troops in Korea while MacArthur directed the UN forces from his headquarters in Tokyo, grew particularly "disgusted by MacArthur's determination to maintain a divided command." To the long-suffering Walker, the decision suggested MacArthur had given in to one of his "notorious weaknesses for favorites—granting his own chief-of-staff, Gen. Ned Almond, one of the two command positions." On the other hand, some doubted Walker's ability to carry out the final offensive unassisted.[28]

The final push to end the war required that Walker lead the 8th Army up the west side of North Korea and capture the capitol of Pyongyang. Ned Almond would now command X Corps, which included the marines. Initially, X Corps was to make landings at the eastern ports of Wonsan and Iwon and then march across the peninsula to help Walker's 8th take Pyongyang.[29] However, the capital fell so quickly that X Corps would quickly receive a new directive: move north and east to secure that part of North Korea. Also, in the changed plan, Almond's troops would be available to wheel and protect the 8th Army's flank if that maneuver became necessary.

Almond would now have the veteran marine shock troops Walker had initially used so frequently at the Pusan perimeter, plus the rest of the marines who came later. Of course Walker was still upset by the fact that he had originally been given the mission of coordinating support for all forces in Korea. Now Walker commanded only in the western theater. As one historian noted, the plan just "didn't make sense."[30] Another critic of the MacArthur strategy called the split of the UN forces "a misguided masterstroke." It made more military sense, some experts have argued, for MacArthur to have let X Corps, with the marines, continue to chase the fleeing North Korean army instead of abruptly pulling it up and moving it overseas to the east side, "but MacArthur was so obsessed with 'strategic masterstrokes' that he permitted his fantasies . . . to overshadow the realities on the battlefield of Korea. He bungled a chance to win the war in October." Some military leaders have been more generous regarding MacArthur's supposed blunders. Gen. J. Lawton Collins pointed out, regarding MacArthur's plan, "how it is easy to Monday morning quarterback an operation long after its completion."[31] At the time the whole matter looked to be a mopping-up task anyway.

X Corps' voyage to the east side of Korea developed into one of the most dismal sea trips marines had ever endured. Paul McDaniel recalled, "I never wanted to join the navy after that. My stomach just churned and churned. It was really a hellish trip. We slept in hammocks down below, three decks down, ladder after ladder." Dining under these circumstances seemed almost impossible. "We ate from metal tables which were fastened to the floor. You'd try to eat while the tables just pitched and rolled. We were out twenty days, and I could only eat eleven of those days." To add to X Corps' problems, the North Koreans had planted three thousand mines around Wonsan, so that the troopships full of marines had to buy time going up and down the coast, plowing through choppy waters while the mines were removed. The miserable voyage became known unofficially as "Operation Yo-Yo." One second lieutenant remembered, "We had come aboard combat-loaded. . . . There was little fresh water . . . and less soap after the first week of Operation Yo-Yo." Soon "the holds stank with unwashed bodies and sweaty clothes." Food also ran low. Many came down "with a low grade flu and the corpsmen had nothing to give the men but . . . aspirin. After a week, the toilets in the tiny heads were inadequate for the men afflicted with 'the runs.' The stench below decks made the air unbreathable."[32]

Barney Barnard told of the difficult conditions in a letter to his mother: "We are still out in the Sea of Japan. This makes the tenth day." The marine reservist apparently did not know about the minefields. "I guess the generals are trying to decide what to do with us," he reported. "We are running out of food. . . . Something has got to happen. We have been going up and down the coast for better than a week." In spite of the harsh conditions, there was one ray of hope. Rumors soon began floating around among the marines regarding a possible quick end to the war. Some of the Evansville reservists demanded of one of their former squad leaders, Paul McDaniel, to know when the reservists would be going home. McDaniel went to where the officers loitered and told one lieutenant, "Sir, the men are driving me crazy. They want to know when we are going home." The officer replied, "Tell them we're going to be home by Christmas."

One of the sea-bound marine reservists wrote his family in late autumn, relating a less cheery but still optimistic view of what was likely to happen: "The news over here seems to be looking good. The Division may get to go to Japan for Christmas. That would be better than staying in Korea or on board ship."[33] The combat-ready-in-four-weeks marines who sailed over from Japan suffered no less than their comrades who had left earlier from Inchon. They too had to endure the misery of Yo-Yo. One

Evansville reservist told how the group "boarded ships at Kobe, Japan, and quickly got into high seas. You stood up to eat on the old liberty ships and the food trays would slide back and forth, and when you'd go to the head all that stuff would be sloshing around on the floor—it was a stinking mess."[34]

By the time the marines began to land at Wonsan in late October, plans for deploying X Corps had already changed. Instead of wheeling westward to join the 8th Army in its fight for Pyongyang, which had already fallen, the two groups would now have distinct and separate missions. The new orders "established parallel zones of action" for both sets of troops, with the rugged Taebaek Mountains serving as a dividing line. The 8th Army under Walker would move up the west side of North Korea while X Corps would clean up resistance in the northeast, moving all the way up to the Yalu River and the Manchurian border.[35] The two armies would now be completely separated. However, this potentially dangerous situation did not seem to matter much now. On 20 October, one of MacArthur's primary intelligence officers, Gen. Charles Willoughby, suggested that the end of the war had finally arrived: "Organized resistance on any large scale has ceased to be an enemy capability. Indications are that the North Korean military and political headquarters may have fled to Manchuria."[36]

Much to the surprise and later disgust of the marines, Wonsan had already been secured by the time the regulars and reservists landed. One reservist complained in a letter that "the army over here is working quite a play upon us [about] landing without opposition. You would think we could get a break sometime without getting razzed by the army."[37] In the otherwise heroic annals of Marine Corps lore, the landing became "as anti-climatical as the Marines ever made."[38] Reservist Jim Stearsman remembered the Wonsan beach as "beautiful. There was white sand for over two miles and tall pine trees." Once ashore, the marines quickly discovered they had to adjust to the extreme weather conditions. North Korea, reported one surprised reservist, has "a kind of biting cold. . . . I am O.K. as long as I stay out of the wind. It would be very rough to spend the winter in the dugout which I have built. One end is partially opened and it is so cold even now, at night with a fire." A week later the same marine told his family how a major had ordered that "no fires be started from 7 A.M. to 7

P.M. It is supposed to save firewood."[39] He also noted that "the Army gets to sleep in buildings."[40] Much worse weather conditions were yet to come.

Despite deteriorating weather, the situation at least seemed preferable to having to stand up and fight a resistant human foe. The marines figured that they would only face some fighting from broken North Korean units fleeing toward Manchuria, or from small determined bands who, having escaped to the rugged mountainside country, now waged guerrilla warfare. Raleigh McGary wrote to his wife about this time, telling her hopefully, "What we're going to do is a matter of much speculation, but I'm not going into that. I hope we are leaving Korea." Teenager William Etheridge spent his first night on the line at this juncture: "I had three veterans, thank goodness, in my fire team. . . . We were dug in up on a ridge, and man, it was cold. I don't think I slept much at all that evening." Gordon Greene wrote his mother about this time that "there isn't anything to worry about because we are only mopping up around Wonsan." A few days later he wrote, "We are on a mountain on the outskirts of Wonsan. There is scarcely any fighting at all. . . . The gooks have taken to the hills and there will be guerrilla warfare for a while yet." Sadly, the "mopping up" operation required the lives of some marines. Marine engineer Barney Barnard, for example, told his father of "laying out a new graveyard" at Wonsan. "They have about fifty people to put in it, . . . all from the Marines," he reported. In the same letter the young man told his father about a communion service he had attended that morning. "It was the second since I arrived in Korea." Barnard also wrote his younger brother, naïvely telling him in early November, "I may get to see a little action yet. Not that I want to be shot at, but I am tired of just sitting around loading and unloading boxes for the officers." Barnard would soon get his wish and then some.

Gordon Greene, who twenty years after Korea wrote an unpublished autobiographical novel, called "Boondockers," about his experiences there, landed at Wonsan in late October. A comparison of Greene's letters home with episodes in the novel indicate that his story precisely follows the young reservist's experiences in Korea. In one portion of "Boondockers," the main character, Ramig, gives a vivid first impression of the regulars and reservists who came to Wonsan: "There was no set uniform—

mongolian piss-cutters, gung-ho caps, helmets, filthy dungarees, scroungy field jackets or tanker jackets, beards, mustaches, and bare-faced kids."[41] Perhaps because of the easing of tensions, the old animosity between regulars and reservists reappeared about the time of the Wonsan landing. Reservist Gene Koonce had a feisty answer to any regular's verbal jab: "I told them when a regular can't hack it, they send in the reserves." Koonce also recalled how his group "got our first big boost of reservists while we were at the railhead [Chinhung-ni]. I remember Ross Compton, a veteran of fighting on Iwo Jima, who was over thirty and therefore older than almost anyone else in our unit, was treated unkindly at first by the regulars. But once they realized that Ross knew more about combat than anyone else, they thought he'd hung the moon." Oddly, reservist Gordon Greene discovered he liked being with the regulars, perhaps because he felt more secure there. "I'm in a platoon who are all Regular Marines and they are easier to get along with than the Reserves," he observed. Greene proudly wrote his mother that his unit, Able Company, "is supposed to be the best in the 1st Marines." Some reservists, such as Glendal "Jeep" Ellis, who also served in Able Company, never came to feel completely comfortable with the regulars, who he felt constantly "looked down upon us, even in Korea."

The marines' specific task, after landing at Wonsan, would now be to move from the coast northward to Hungnam and Hamhung and then on into the rugged interior of North Korea, toward the Chosin Reservoir. Almond expected marine general O. P. Smith to push his men quickly in the direction of the Chosin Plateau and on toward the Manchurian border. Smith, however, following the more conservative marine practice of establishing strong supply bases as advances are made, moved too cautiously for the impatient Almond. Certainly Smith had cause for worry. Only one slender thread of unpaved mountain road wound up through the peaks to the Chosin Plateau. From Hungnam on the coast to Yudam-ni, the farthest penetration of any marine units, lay a distance of seventy-eight rugged miles. At Chinhung-ni, about forty-three miles north from the coast, the unpaved road was two-lane and the terrain comparatively level. From there, however, the route became especially treacherous: "The road takes its abrupt climb into a tumbled region of mile high peaks. Funchilin Pass, comprising eight . . . miles, represents an ascent of 2500 feet. . . . The road is merely a twisting one-way path, with a cliff on one side and a chasm on the other." The trail-like road passed through Koto-ri, more than fifty miles from the coast. The tiny village rested on a rugged plateau. Hagaru was located eleven miles farther north of Koto-ri at the south end of the sprawling Chosin Reservoir. Higher still sat Yudam-ni, on the west side of the reservoir. Remote Yudam-ni could only be reached by traversing the four-thousand-foot Toktong Pass.[42]

To Almond, X Corps' assignment looked easy enough, and he desperately wanted to reach the Yalu River before General Walker's 8th Army on the west side. One of Almond's chief aides remembered "all units were racing to see who could cover the most mileage everyday. The Yalu River became the objective."[43] General Smith, however, did not buy into the hurried and haphazard plan. Too quick a thrust would leave his marines widely scattered from Wonsan to Yudam-ni along a single and very vulnerable road. Smith protested vigorously to Almond, but the army general dismissed the marine leader as being too conservative.[44] Despite the pressure placed upon Smith by his commander to move rapidly northward, the general now set upon the task of establishing fortified supply bases along the perilous route. These bases soon took shape as the columns of marines marched north up the winding mountain track: first at Chinhung-ni, then at Koto-ri, which stood at the halfway mark to the reservoir, and finally at Hagaru at the southern tip of the Chosin. Each base contained an airstrip and a fortified perimeter. The primitive road linking the operations would soon become famous as the Main Supply Route, or, simply, MSR. Smith's slow process frustrated Almond, but Smith stuck to his guns. Unfortunately, Almond maintained more control over elements of the army's 7th Division, which settled on the east side of the Chosin in late November. This group of about three thousand GIs would lack the supply bases and close support the marines typically established, leaving the soldiers as "scattered elements . . . [un]connected physically or otherwise."[45] It would be a recipe for disaster. Then, in the middle of November, while Smith plodded and carried out his slow but cautious plan and Almond fussed and fumed about delays, a new enemy made itself known.

Had the Chinese not come into the war, it is likely that members of X

Corps would still have long remembered the terrible winter conditions of that campaign. Although the Korean Peninsula sits at about the same latitude as Indiana, winters at the high elevation of the Chosin Plateau are controlled by bitterly cold Siberian air masses. Night temperatures can bring numbing cold. Winter struck northeast Korea with an especially savage fury in November 1950. On the tenth the temperature dropped to minus ten degrees without warning. More extreme temperatures soon followed. "The cold was so intense men became dazed and incoherent, some went numb, others cried in pain," noted Edward Murphy.[46] By late November temperatures were well below zero, not factoring in wind chill. Inactive GIs and marines often froze to death in their foxholes. Truck drivers now found themselves struggling to carry out their jobs in the most difficult of circumstances, for the roads in the Chosin campaign "were among the poorest and most precarious of any used in war by American forces. No American armies," noted the military historian Roy Appleman, "before or since have fought in as harsh or hostile an environment."[47] The cold often paralyzed trucks and drained batteries while troops riding in the back of three-quarter-ton trucks sometimes froze. One survivor of the 7th Army group recalled how a "¾ ton truck started to honk. I stopped my jeep and ran to investigate. Two of the men had passed out from the cold and the other men huddled up against them, trying to revive them with their own body heat."[48]

The marines who moved toward Koto-ri on 10 November took an extremely hard jolt from a duo blast of wind and cold. "A lot of men went into shock. Others cried. Some became upset, agitated, very nervous." The suffering marines were quickly placed in warming tents, "large tents with camp stoves that burned fuel oil." These tents would soon become "a way of life until the division returned to a warmer climate."[49] Farther north, at the main supply base and headquarters at Hagaru, the temperature fell to several degrees below zero. In early November, "accompanied by winds of thirty to forty miles per hour the wind chill fell to minus 60 degrees."[50] One marine officer wrote home about the fierce cold, telling how "it was the worst I'd ever seen. . . . Night before last and yesterday it was terribly cold. . . . There's about five inches of ice on the stream and the only way I can keep my canteen from freezing is to keep it empty."[51]

Neither the eighth or the tenth, however, would be the coldest nights the marines would endure. Barney Barnard wrote his father about this time, "If it weren't for our sleeping bags and our parkas, we would freeze to death during the night." Fortunately for the marines, said Barnard, they had been issued "heavy winter clothing. The shoes are ten inch leather with rubber soles. They also gave us very heavy socks, parkas, and heavy pants which are supposed to be wind proof." Gordon Greene also spoke of the dreadful cold in a letter to his mother. "Boy it sure is getting cold here," he reported. "The ground is freezing and the wind really blows down from Siberia." Although Greene told of how difficult it was being out in the weather during patrols, he also told his mother that "I stay warm though. We dig our foxholes pretty big and cover the bottom to keep the dampness out." Greene also complained in a more earthy description to a friend how "the weather is getting worse than the gooks. First it gets colder than hell, then the Siberian wind blows down and freezes our balls off." Greene added, "I haven't had a bath in eighteen days." Greene gave yet another account of the desperate weather conditions in "Boondockers": "Fire wood became a problem in record time. Captain Hayward had to put a stop to Marines hacking on power line posts after one squad of Marines chopped one in half, leaving it dangling. One abandoned house disappeared completely after the first day."[52]

Raleigh McGary, the Posey County native who originally thought the call-up was just a mistake that would soon be rectified, now endured, along with Gordon Greene, incredibly cold and harsh living conditions at Chinhung-ni. He wrote his wife of what he suffered, telling her, "I'm sitting in our nice warm tent wrapped around our oil stove freezing to death. The weather around here isn't like anyplace I've ever seen; it gets almost warm when the wind isn't blowing, but when it does it comes from the north pole." In another letter he told his wife, "It sure would be nice to take a bath and change clothes. I'm still wearing what I left Japan in and instead of changing, I just add more. All I change is my socks and not very often on those. I've managed to wash 3 times and shave once. My teeth are in a pretty filthy condition." As McGary observed, the cold greatly affected hygiene. In another letter, written on 19 November, McGary lamented, "I sure would like to get someplace where I could clean up. I've been pretty dirty before, but I never went filthy for a month before. My hands and face are dry and cracked from the wind and cold. I'm just generally in a miserable state."

The desperate cold could also be a great equalizer. McGary, for example, reported to his wife about the colorful chaplain who served his unit: "You would probably be interested in our chaplain. I haven't been to church since that time in California, but I must look like a good clean church going Marine because he always stops and talks to me." The reservist reported that the chaplain "is as dirty as I am (and him a major) and wears a .45 pistol and a jungle knife. It isn't obvious that he is a chaplain and I suppose the gooks would kill him the same as me. He is always going around asking if everything is alright. He must be about 40 but is pretty healthy (as all Marines are)."

The 1st Marine Division in northeast Korea faced other grim difficulties, along with the abominable weather conditions and the lack of basic necessities. At Inchon only 15 percent of the marines were reservists. Toward the end of the Seoul campaign the number of reservists who had served as replacements had risen to nearly a third of the fighting force. Now, in what everyone hoped to be the final phase of the war, reservist numbers had exploded to where they made up at least half of the marines' manpower total. The great majority of the reserve replacements were untested teenagers and young men in their early twenties, such as Gordon Greene, Barney Barnard, and William Etheridge. Marine leadership could only hope that no major fighting would erupt. Luckily, a sprinkling of World War II veterans, the so-called two-time losers who had experienced some combat, were in the mix. Many, such as Paul McDaniel, Ross Compton, and Gene Koonce, served as noncoms.

The reservists from Evansville who were now in northeast Korea as a part of X Corps soon found themselves scattered all over the X Corps area of responsibility. At the beginning Barney Barnard stayed close to the coast with a group of engineers, but in late November he found himself traveling to the more dangerous village of Hagaru, just south of the Chosin Reservoir, to help construct an airstrip. He described his journey as one over "a one-way trail with many hairpin turns." Gordon Greene, Jeep Ellis, William Etheridge, and Raleigh McGary, among other Evansville men, came to be assigned to the Chinhung-ni railhead, about forty-three miles north of the coast and at the edge of where rugged ridges of mountains stood like great forbidding walls. Ralph Hargrave, Paul McDaniel, Gene Koonce, David Graham, Robert Egan, Tex Graham, Ross Compton, and several other former members of the old C Company reserve unit went all the way north to Yudam-ni, while William Wright served as a lineman at Hagaru.

Paul McDaniel received a particularly interesting surprise just before his group left the railhead at Chinhung-ni and moved north toward the reservoir: "We're up on this mountain waiting for orders when I hear this high-pitched voice down below on the road. 'Does anyone know where McDaniel is?' Man. I thought there's only one voice like that, so I hollered down, 'Maley, is that you?'" Henry Maley had heard over in Japan that the marines would be home by Christmas. "I signed my waiver so I could come over here," Maley informed the amused McDaniel, "but I'm not getting in your unit." Maley went on to announce proudly, "My unit is up ahead of yours." When the Chinese hit the marines three days later, McDaniel recalled that "Maley's unit was right on the point." The group was all but wiped out, but Maley miraculously survived.

Even by mid- and late November the Evansville men and the other marines of X Corps believed the war would soon be over. On 12 November, Barnard wrote, "There isn't much resistance right now. . . . There are several thousand army troops back at Wonsan. It is rumored that they are going to relieve us: I hope so. This weather is out of my line—my feet are cold all the time up here." Barnard's boyhood friend Gordon Greene was just as hopeful. On 17 November he wrote, "We are somewhere near Hamhung. So far we aren't receiving any contact with the gooks. I don't hear any news, but it seems to be about over. We hear all kinds of rumors about going home now."

While the marines dreamed of going home, the Chinese had busied themselves that October and early November sneaking thousands of troops into North Korea. The Chinese leader, Mao Tse-tung, had earlier told his military generals that "when a neighbor is in mortal danger, it is hard just to stand by and watch." When it seemed certain the UN force would push clear to Manchuria, the die was cast. Recent scholarship suggests China "reluctantly entered the Korean conflict, not to further world communism but to protect itself from invasion by a powerful enemy threatening to use the atomic bomb." Mao and his supporters, however, were convinced they could keep the war "limited and non-nuclear."[53] The ironic thing was that the United States had already won the war. Had UN forces not approached the Chinese frontier, the Chinese would have most likely stayed out of the conflict.[54] Stranger still stood the story of how so many thousands of Chinese soldiers slipped into North Korea without being seen.

Three hundred thousand to as many as five hundred thousand Chinese soldiers came into the mountainous north undetected. In hindsight the primary reason for the lack of detection seemed to be poor intelligence work and overconfidence on the part of the Americans. Eighth Army leadership followed the line coming out of Supreme Headquarters in Tokyo and the main intelligence officer there, Maj. Courtney Whitney. Amazingly, Whitney saw nothing that indicated Chinese intervention. Meanwhile, Chinese soldiers moved stealthily through the trackless mountains, staying out of sight of patrolling UN forces. Still, there were signs. On 25 October 1950, South Korean forces reported capturing a Chinese prisoner. The prisoner admitted that he was part of a Chinese force of unknown strength that "had lately crossed the Yalu."[55] From this point on, the number of Chinese prisoners mounted. Intense interrogation of captured soldiers suggested that elements of at least six enemy Chinese field divisions were present in North Korea, with a total of 180,000 men.[56] Oddly, up to the moment that the Chinese trap was sprung, experts saw "no indications of open intervention on the part of Chinese communist forces in Korea."[57] MacArthur argued that neither the Chinese nor Russians would be foolish enough to come into the war now, and Whitney's information from the field, though apparently flawed because the Chinese were coming into North Korea in small groups and at night avoid detection, supported MacArthur's contention.

On 15 November, Chinese military leaders fretted over a giant relief model of North Korea at the Chinese arsenal in Shenyang. The Chinese officers "quickly noted that the model had changed drastically over the past few weeks. . . . There were additional Chinese airfields in Manchuria, newly developed hill tracks through the wilds of North Korea—and, south of the Yalu River, a fresh forest of red-starred wooden markers revealed the growth of Chinese strength in North Korea." The most impressive array of markers massed around the Chosin Reservoir, where a new force of more than a hundred thousand troops were gathering to wipe out the marines. This field army was led by Lt. Gen. Song Shilun, who, now forty-three, had already participated in the famous Long March of the 1930s. Two of the three armies under Shilun, the 20th and the 26th, had previously been scheduled for an invasion of Taiwan. Another field army, the 27th, along with one division of the 30th, made up General Shilun's command.[58]

Several problems confounded Shilun and the other officers who pondered the coming campaign against the marines. Maj. Gen. Liu Fei, who commanded the 20th group, noted the deteriorating weather. "It's snowing thicker than cowshit on the Reservoir," he commented. General Peng, overall commander of Chinese forces, observed how the prior attacks on UN forces in early November had not caused the enemy to withdraw from North Korea. "This is unfortunate, because China now has no alternative but to teach the imperialists a lesson. . . . The Ninth group," said Peng, "will encircle and exterminate the U.S. Marines around the Chosin Reservoir. This should be possible, bearing in mind the enemy's scattered dispositions across difficult country."[59]

Chinese confidence might have seemed overblown on first glance. They had hardly any tanks and very little field artillery. Typically they attacked using only mortars, light machine guns, and hand grenades. Further, without motor or even animal transport, the Chinese faced major supply problems. The brutal cold that so harassed American troops was even more cruel to the Chinese, who "wore [only] a two-piece reversible . . . uniform of quilted cotton and a heavy cap with fur lined flaps. [Their] shoes were canvas . . . with crepe rubber soles. . . . Few troops wore gloves." Many thousands were destined to freeze to death. Crossing the Yalu, "they were given a four day food supply . . . of rice, millet, or soy beans carried in a pack." Later food had to be "donated" by the North Korean population.[60] On the other hand, Chinese troops likely stood as well trained as their North Korean counterparts and skillfully employed night attacks to unhinge their enemies. "Using large quantities of hand grenades, light machine guns, and mortar fire," they liked to take the fighting "to close range." Further, the Chinese "usually approached from the rear, after drawing enemy fire by sniping and bugle or pipe music." They feinted, probed, or withdrew "in order to test enemy reactions or to confuse and intimidate them."[61]

The average Chinese soldier was also well versed in why he was fighting in North Korea. Down to the lowest private, each Chinese soldier understood the overall strategy to be used against the Americans, and why that strategy must be carried out. Indeed, American interrogators often distrusted the first reports of captured Chinese because they seemed to know too much about what the Chinese leadership planned to do on the battlefield. One captured Chinese soldier who had fought for the Nationalists told the Americans he had switched sides because the Communists "feed me." General Shilun announced to his men just before they marched into Korea that the Americans planned to invade China and that "they were being sent . . . to save the homeland" from invasion.[62] The final advantage the Chinese possessed involved sheer numbers and the element of surprise. Tens of thousands of hidden Chinese now lay secure in the mountains as the marines of X Corps snaked slowly toward the Chosin.

In late October and early November, Chinese forces, hoping to warn the Americans from going deeper into North Korea, gave the 8th Army a bloody nose in several intense and shocking engagements. Marines on the east side also engaged in several bitter struggles but were able to hold their own. MacArthur became somewhat unraveled at this time, asserting that the Chinese's coming into the war stood as "one of the most offensive acts of international lawlessness of historic record."[63] *Time* magazine dismally noted that top leaders were unsure why "the Chinese had sent troops into North Korea so late in the game."[64] *Newsweek* declared that "at the very moment when final complete victory seemed within grasp, the forces of Communist China suddenly intervened, reversed the tide of triumph, and struck dangerous blows deep into UN lines."[65] *U.S. News and World Report* warned that "China's Mao, by sending in his troops to fight United Nations forces, is willing to chance a big war. . . . The turn this time seems bad, really bad."[66] Then, as quickly as the Chinese had appeared and delivered a heavy blow, their soldiers melted away. "Suddenly, mysteriously, inexplicably, the Chinese had gone to ground."[67] Just as mysteriously, American leadership took no notice of the possible meaning of the Chinese attacks. It was as if the attacks had not occurred.

Some military analysts suggested at the time that the Chinese had carried out the attacks simply to save face and, having done so, had withdrawn. At any rate, the UN supreme commander, with the Chinese attackers apparently gone, now led a force of 100,000 men and believed he had the enemy trapped in the jaws of a great pincer. Chinese withdrawal, however, only served to lure the UN forces deeper into the Chinese noose. In the northeast, a force of more than 120,000 battle-tested soldiers moved secretly to surround the 14,000 marines in the Chosin area, while in the west, 180,000 Chinese marched to cut off the 8th Army. The Chinese planned to do more than just bloody the marines. When they launched their attack on the east side, Radio Peking interrupted their regular broadcast many times to announce that "the annihilation of the United States First Marine Division is only a matter of time."[68] Chinese pride was apparently no less than America's. A report made by Chinese intelligence after China's initial contact with American troops stated "their infantry men are weak, afraid to die and haven't the courage to attack or defend. . . . They are afraid when their rear is cut off."[69] While this might have been a fair assessment after some of the fighting with the 8th Army, the Chinese would soon get an unwanted surprise in their dealings with the marines on the west side of the Chosin. Meanwhile, marine reservists, many of them still teenagers, were about to get a dramatic taste of combat and face a predicament of almost impossible proportions.

On the eve of the planned final push to the Manchurian border, Gordon Greene wrote his mother. By this time the usually optimistic Oakland City teen understood that the cleanup of North Korean troops loomed as a much more difficult task than previously thought. "We had hopes for awhile of getting home for Christmas," Greene told his mother, "but it looks like we will spend the winter here. Any thing might happen you know, this world is so unpredictable." The letter was signed, "As ever, Gordon."

5   *Home by Christmas*

Despite the reassuring communiqués pouring forth from Tokyo Headquarters in mid-November, the marines who toiled on the east side of the Taebaek Mountains had ample warning signs that all was not well. After landing at Wonsan, Hoosier reservist Raleigh McGary was stationed near the railhead at Chinhung-ni. During the initial Chinese attacks and withdrawal in early November, McGary stood guard with a number of other marines on the perimeter of this important supply base. Occasionally his group went out on patrols, where they encountered sniper fire and blew up enemy ammo dumps. "I remember the first time I came under enemy fire," McGary recounted. "I had stopped to light a cigarette when a machine gun opened up, kicking up dirt all around me. On instinct I jumped into a ditch and then heard a voice command us to move out. Bullets were flying around everywhere but we moved out anyway. I sure didn't want to be left there by myself." Although it soon became apparent that Chinhung-ni had unwelcome visitors in the area, the well-fortified and well-defended perimeter could likely withstand any assault. On the other hand, if the marines were to leave the safety of the perimeters of any of the bases that had been recently established, there hung the question of their survival. Most despairing was the potential situation further north, along the single, threadlike supply road that wound to the cold waters of the Chosin.

Higher up the MSR, at Hagaru, which lay at the southern end of the reservoir, marine units had split, with one group, RCT-7, traveling to the west side of the Chosin Reservoir and another group, RCT-5, tracking to the east side. Colonel Taplett's 3d Battalion, 5th Marines, in which so many Evansville reservists served, made up part of the latter set. Thanksgiving fell on 23 November that year, and the military leadership wanted their fighting forces to receive special treatment for a change. Hot meals were trucked in all along the MSR for the occasion. Somewhere on guard near Chinhung-ni, Gordon Greene ate "turkey, potatoes, green beans, tuna dressing, mince pie, fruit cake, nuts, candy, and fruit."[1] Paul McDaniel, with Taplett's 3/5, wolfed down his Thanksgiving meal within sight of the cold gray waters of the Chosin. "I came down off a mountain with two other fellows, and we sat in a snow bank to eat our meal," he recalled. By the time most of the marines who hunkered down at the front got their meal and found a warm place to eat, the food had frozen. Some used a little C-4 plastic explosive to warm their grub. "But what this did," recalled one marine, "was to make the outside warm and leave the inside frozen, so we'd stick a knife in the middle and eat it like a popsicle."[2]

About this time McDaniel recalled receiving shoe-pacs to protect his feet from the cold, and "these big heavy parkas. They were warm, but very bulky and difficult to move around in." The parkas were indeed heavy. They were knee length, pile lined, with a hood. By itself, the coat weighed more than marines' warm weather uniforms. The marines were also issued at this time "winter weather snow trousers, also heavy to wear, plus a new set of regular weight dungarees. . . . In addition there were flannel shirts, new long johns, and heavy socks. The leather and canvas mittens" the marines now received "had trigger fingers with thin woolen gloves to wear inside." The shoe-pacs, which most marines came to curse, were "big and cumbersome" and twice the weight of the regular marine footgear. It turned out that this improved shoe was "clumsy for climbing and slippery on ice."[3] Gordon Greene wrote home, telling a friend, "I have so much clothing on, I couldn't run if I had to." But Greene and the other marines who now huddled uneasily in North Korea were glad to get the extra clothing and new shoes even if they made moving about difficult. As Paul McDaniel noted, "It just kept getting colder and colder." The cold that McDaniel spoke of, along with the geographic remoteness of the marines' position, greatly added to a growing feeling of uneasiness that quietly spread throughout the units.

Some Evansville reservists carried an extra burden of concern in the anxious times the marines now faced. Among the Evansville area men who found themselves near the Chosin Reservoir were two brothers—James and Donald Crouse. Pairs of brothers in this theater were typically unable to keep track of their kin, but fortunately, Jim Crouse served in an engineering company where he often went out on reconnaissance patrols. Not knowing what lay ahead, Crouse was comforted in knowing that this duty would enable him to keep in relatively close contact with his brother, even if fighting began.

Ralph Hargrave, one of the older reservists, who was also a World War II veteran, also felt a heavy cloak of concern descend about this time. Hargrave had been tortured by a premonition since leaving Japan that something terrible was going to happen. "I didn't want to go. Somehow I knew what I was going to get into." The Boonville, Indiana, man had wisely set his sights on becoming a telephone switchboard maintenance man. "I got the switchboard MOS and then went into an artillery company," he recalled. "I thought I had it made." Hargrave, however, soon discovered he was going north to the Chosin. "I found out I wasn't going to Regimental Headquarters after all. Too many guys had pulled the same stunt I had and had also received an MOS as a switchboard repairman. They sent most of us to the field." Hargrave had Thanksgiving on the east side of the Chosin, along with some of his former C Company comrades from Evansville. "The meal was good but it froze before it could be eaten," he remembered. Another thing that bothered Hargrave was the home-by-Christmas rumor that flashed through Hargrave's group like wild fire: "I knew that was a darn lie. There was no way they could have got us home even if nothing had been going on. Anyway the rumor had all those poor boys hollering, 'We're going home—we're going home by Christmas!'"

Not every marine near the Chosin Reservoir got to eat a Thanksgiving meal on the twenty-third. The night before, on the east side with Taplett's group, Sgt. Gene Koonce had been assigned to hold a ridge above the main camp. Because of the extreme cold weather, Koonce had his men make fires to warm themselves. "We still hadn't seen any sign of the Chinese, and I was afraid some of the men would literally freeze to death without fires." A lieutenant down below thought differently about the matter: "Lt. Charles Mize called up and told us to 'put out those damn fires!' I argued with him but finally relented." The next morning, as punishment, Koonce was sent out "as an observer" on a patrol with a larger group of marines. "This is when we ran into the first Chinese," Koonce recalled. "I don't know how far we'd gone north, but we engaged them in a firefight. Ross Compton's handling of a machine-gun section saved the day, and we brought back a prisoner."

Koonce and Compton had been a part of a platoon-sized reconnaissance patrol that killed five Chinese soldiers and took one prisoner. Finding no sign of large-scale enemy activity, the patrol turned back just short of the northern tip of the Chosin. This was likely the farthest north any marine unit penetrated. The Chinese Koonce and company had run into were apparently an advance scouting party of the enemy's 80th Division of the 27th Army. So disturbing was the encounter to leaders back at the 3/5 command post that Colonel Taplett made a hurried trip north by helicopter to check the situation out. At the time, however, it remained unknown as to the number of Chinese in the area or their intentions.[4] Koonce recalled one positive outcome of Taplett's visit: "Colonel Taplett ordered the disciplining officer to make sure we got our Thanksgiving meal when we returned."

The officer in charge of the marine forces on the east side, Lt. Col. Raymond Murray, had sent Taplett's 3d Battalion four miles beyond the village of Sinhung-ni. It was here that Taplett's men had dug in. Except for the action Koonce's patrol stirred up, all else stood quiet and peaceful on the east side.[5] This calm would not last. On about 25 November, Murray's group was issued new orders to move down around the southern tip of the reservoir and join the marines on the west side to help in the move to Yudam-ni and beyond. First, however, the 5th Marines were to wait for a force of about three thousand army personnel, the 31st and 32d Regiments of the 7th Army Division, to replace them. The army task force was led by Lt. Col. Allan MacLean, with Lt. Col. Donald Faith as second in command. Faith had family from Washington, Indiana, near the city of Evansville, where the C Company reservists had trained. Another man in the 32d group, Sgt. Charles Garrigus Jr., grew up near Oakland City and was an in-law of sorts to Tex Graham of the Evansville reservists. Garrigus's sister, Delores, had married Graham's brother, Tex. Graham now served as a map runner for Taplett's command post.

Marine officers encouraged MacLean and Faith to use the well-fortified perimeter they had discovered, which offered a full view of all approaches. The army, however, chose to dig in elsewhere. Gene Koonce recalled, "The army came in to replace us a couple of days after Thanksgiving. We'd found some concrete bunkers and were staying there. Our commander, Colonel Taplett, suggested the army use our positions, but they ignored the suggestion. I saw so many ROKs [Republic of Korea, i.e., the South Korean army] mixed in with them, I thought they'd be in trouble if they were attacked." In a letter to a family member, reservist Barney Barnard noted the difference between the GIs he now observed coming through Hagaru on their way to the east side of the Chosin and his fellow marines: "There seems to be quite a few army people around here now. . . . I am really glad that I am in the marines, not that I like it over here, but there is more spirit in one company of marines than in a whole army division. Over here every marine helps every other marine whenever he can." Bar-nard added, "Naturally, we steal anything we can from the army. They always have more gear than we do." Only about 10 percent of the army task force on the east side of the Chosin survived the coming Chinese on-slaught.[6]

While the 5th Marines rushed on 25 and 26 November to join their comrades on the west side of the reservoir, Barney Barnard labored at Hagaru. In a letter he assured his father that "everything is going all right up here." Barnard, an engineer, soon bent himself to the work of helping to construct an airstrip. He proudly told his father, who also had an engi-neering background, how one sergeant "didn't remember how to figure the cuts and fills, so I had to show him how it was done. These people did-n't think I knew anything at all about field work. You would get a kick out of the stakes we were using," Barnard added. "Some of them are 2x4s cut into three foot lengths. We just have to use what we can find around here." The airstrip Barnard now labored on proved to be an important life-saving force in the later struggle to escape the Chinese trap.

Evansville reservist William Wright also served at Hagaru as a communications man. The first view of Hagaru reminded Wright and the other marines "of old photographs of a gold-rush mining camp in the Klondike. Tents, huts, and supply dumps were scattered in a . . . haphazard fashion about a frozen plain crossed by a frozen river and bordered on three sides by low hills."[7] On one side rose a large landmass called East Hill. Wright remembered the village as "being in the bottom of a bowl surrounded by mountains." On the way up to Hagaru Wright had seen "little villages where kids came out, their skin blue with cold. We'd throw them chewing gum and candy as we rode by on trucks." Farther north on the way to Hagaru, however, Wright saw his first dead marine: "Except for the cold, it was a pretty day. The air's so clear in a higher altitude. Suddenly our truck stopped and someone said, 'there's a dead marine over there.' We all jumped out and saw the body in the bottom of a pit. And that right there made it all matter. It just changed our attitude right there."

Another marine who came into Hagaru on 16 November remembered struggling against a temperature of twenty-one below. "It was so bad," he noted, "that each guy watched someone else's face to check for white spots on their skin."[8] James Murray, an eighteen-year-old marine who served in the 7th Regiment and traveled through Hagaru on his way north to Yudam-ni, remembered, "You'd be talking to someone, and you would actually see the blisters pop out on a guy's ear. November of 1950 was the worst month I ever spent in my life." The village of Hagaru, however, had several heated houses in which some of the luckier marines were able to sleep on wooden floors. Soon tents dotted the area around the village and the smoke from fires and warming stoves climbed into the cold air. Barney Barnard wrote that he was "living in a building and our room has two stoves. There is snow almost every night." Barnard noted the ever-increasing activity around the village: "Work hasn't been slowed down at all by the snow. There are machines all over the place. I think the job [building an airstrip] has to be done in 17 days. With all the changes in plans . . . we are kept on the run all day long." Soon giant floodlights were brought out so the work on the airstrip could proceed around the clock.

The marines of X Corps who had gone further north to Yudam-ni endured what were perhaps the most formidable conditions. The tiny village nestled in the center of a broad valley "surrounded by five great ridges. . . . Each of these ridges extend several thousand yards and include many peaks, spurs, and draws."[9] The area offered scores of places from which to launch surprise attacks. To make things more difficult, the marines who came to Yudam-ni had to negotiate the four-thousand-foot Toktong Pass. On the morning of 26 November, the weather was bitterly cold: "The ground was so hard you couldn't dent it with a pick. . . . You could tell at a glance that if the Chinese controlled the hills around the valley, then life at the bottom would be miserable."[10] The next day, the twenty-seventh, the marines at Yudam-ni were to begin attacking west, groping toward the 8th Army. Altogether, ten thousand marines waited at Yudam-ni to carry out their orders. The group consisted of ten rifle companies thinly scattered over five ridges. The supply dumps nearby had only three days' supply of food, three of fuel, and two of small arms ammunition.[11] Thus the stage was set for MacArthur's final push in northeast Korea.

Despite the sudden and ferocious attacks in early November by the Chinese, MacArthur had soon regained his typical confidence. On 24 November 1950, the supreme commander flew to Sinanju Airfield in the far northwestern corner of North Korea to be present for the 8th Army's part of the final offensive. The general seemed cheerful enough as he toured the area for several hours in a jeep. Afterward, MacArthur issued a confident message: "The United Nations massive compression envelopment in North Korea against the new Red armies operating there is now approaching its decisive effort. . . . If successful, this should for all practical purposes end the war [and] restore peace and unity to Korea. . . . It is that for which we fight."[12] Much later, however, MacArthur wrote that the tour of the 8th Army brought him great worry: the 8th's entire line looked to MacArthur "to be deplorably weak in numbers."[13]

It was at this time that MacArthur made one of his most memorable and regrettable utterances. Some would later claim the statement was made in a flippant manner. Other reports, such as in *Time* magazine, related the comment as a possibility MacArthur genuinely hoped would come to pass. While at Gen. John Church's division command post on the twenty-fourth, MacArthur told Church, "I have already promised wives and mothers that the boys will be back by Christmas."[14] A wire service piece reported that MacArthur said to Church, "Tell the boys when they reach the Yalu they are going home. I want to make good on my statement that they are going to eat Christmas dinner at home."[15] *Newsweek* observed that MacArthur had remarked, "I hope to keep my promise to the GIs and have them home by Christmas."[16] Flippant or not, MacArthur's words gave the "final" push in North Korea a new and darkly ironic name—the Home-by-Christmas Offensive.

Back at the railhead at Chinhung-ni, Raleigh McGary found himself stationed on one of the higher points around the well-fortified perimeter with three other marine members of a fire team. Getting to and from the remote observation post to headquarters for meals had been such an ordeal of climbing that McGary and the others had decided they preferred "the c-rations to the weary hike." Thus the four marines lounged in their rocky outpost on the opening day of the final offensive and idly watched as a marine company left the base. Before the last man left the area, however, the four witnessed the company pinned down by heavy enemy fire. "That's when we knew we were surrounded," McGary recalled. Later that evening a lieutenant came to the outpost and told McGary's fire team, "'Headquarters has just received word that ten thousand Chinese on horseback were coming this way.' I was always kind of a smart aleck, so I told the lieutenant, 'Hell, lieutenant, don't tell us—call Roy Rogers.' The officer did not think that was very funny." The horsemen did not show up. Regardless, it was evident that the marines at Chinhung-ni would encounter major problems from an unknown number of Chinese if they left the relative safety of the perimeter.

On the day the Home-by-Christmas Offensive began, Raleigh McGary wrote his wife from Chinhung-ni, "I don't know if I should tell you the gossip—but I will. It seems we are supposed to stay here until we go home. That will be by the 8th of Dec. (we leave Korea at least). Every time I have told you any such news we have moved farther north. I'm taking another chance." Two days later, before McGary realized how perilous the

1st Division's situation was, the reservist reported, "My pen is frozen up and doesn't write so well. I didn't have time to mail the first part of this letter as we have been pretty busy and losing sleep every night. It seems impossible to get a good night's sleep in a combat area. . . . We had about an inch of snow late last night. I was standing watch so I nearly looked like a snowman when it was over." McGary closed the letter optimistically, "I'll have to get this in the mail, so I'll close with barrels of love. See you Christmas—I hear MacArthur said."

Up at Yudam-ni, the push north, then west, to link up with the 8th Army would quickly grind to a halt. While the perimeter there had seen no action on the night of 26 November, the cold that night had been all but unbearable. On the morning of the twenty-seventh, the 2d Battalion, 5th Marines, in numbing cold, lunged out of Yudam-ni and launched the primary attack along the valley road. Meanwhile Taplett's 3d Battalion, 5th Marines, began to tackle some of the more strategic heights above the valley floor.[17] The movements of all marine groups, however, quickly broke down. By nightfall the 5th Marines had made only modest gains of about fifteen hundred yards. As it turned out, the lack of progress would be a blessing in disguise, for it meant the marines would have a smaller area to defend when the real Chinese attack fell. The Chinese assault would be the blow the Chinese hoped would start the annihilation of the 1st Marine Division.[18]

The group to which many of the Evansville reservists belonged, Taplett's 3d Battalion, 5th Marines, had arrived from the east side of the Chosin at about noon on the twenty-seventh, while the initial marine push out of Yudam-ni was "in full progress."[19] Taplett placed his men in an area at the base of a huge land mass that included Hill 1384 and nearby Hill 1282. The latter was a particularly important hill, for it stood "as the strategic point leading to Yudam-ni."[20] Taplett's men were to take the point the next day from the 2d Battalion. The total number of marines on the night of the twenty-seventh at Yudam-ni included "ten under strength rifle companies of both regiments [5th and 7th] on the high ground around Yudam-ni, two battalions of the 5th [the 2d and 3d] in the valley near the village, and two rifle companies, Charlie and Fox, of the 7th in isolated positions along the . . . route to Hagaru."[21]

Despite the thinly scattered positioning of the marines in the difficult terrain, the Yudam-ni perimeter itself "encompassed an impressive array of Marine supporting arms."[22] However, the marines would face an almost impossible task if they tried to move out of the valley. The hills around Yudam-ni swarmed with tens of thousands of Chinese, and the fourteen-mile route back to the larger headquarters at Hagaru, where an air base was hastily being constructed, lay along a narrow, vulnerable track. On the night of 27 November, the marines who tried to sleep in the hellish cold at Yudam-ni hung on a very precarious limb.

Once the sun set, the temperature quickly began dropping toward its official bottom of twenty-five below. (Many accounts claimed temperatures much lower than even this.) Marines soon grew numb as they lay on the frozen ground. Almost as disturbing was the effect of the cold on carbines and BARs. "The weapons froze to such a degree that they became unreliable, or, in some cases, completely unserviceable."[23] While marines struggled with the cold and strained to see through the pitch-black darkness, thousands of Chinese began to stir in the hills around the marines. They included assault battalions of the 74th and 89th Chinese army divisions. This group had been sent to northeast Korea with the specific assignment of destroying the 1st Marine Division. The "knockout blow" would hammer at the northwest arc of the Yudam-ni perimeter near where Taplett's men shivered in the cold. Another Chinese division, the 59th, had already completed "a wide envelopment to the south . . . to cut the MSR between Hagaru and Yudam-ni."[24] The battle amounted to three massive Chinese divisions against two understrength regiments of marines. In addition to sheer numbers, the Chinese possessed the very important elements of mobility and surprise. Chinese general Shilun ended his final message to his troops before the battle for Yudam-ni by saying, "Soon we will meet the American Marines in battle. We will destroy them. . . . Kill these Marines as you would snakes in your home."[25]

Surreal bugle calls pierced the darkness when the first Chinese attacks came at Yudam-ni. Screaming, the Chinese hurled grenades as their machine guns opened up. Mortar shells also began to rain down on the marines, who soon learned that their enemy attacked "ceaselessly and without regard to losses."[26] Sometime during the shocking attack that evening the Chinese were able to seize the strategic Hill 1403. A platoon of about forty men from Item Company became surrounded there, and only twelve eventually came off the hill alive. One Evansville reservist who survived, Floyd Riggs, recalled how the Chinese "turned machine guns loose at us. I could see fire coming out of the barrels right at me, but they must have been bad shots." Riggs was not hit but had to lay down "and play dead the rest of the night. . . . It was forty below." The survivors soon had company as Chinese soldiers came to plunder the dead. "I could feel the sweat in my socks freezing on my feet, but I was afraid to move them. I spent most of the night praying," Riggs reported.[27]

Hill 1282 also became the scene of extraordinary fighting. The Chinese kept up a continuing attack, sending formation after formation so that the "northwestern slope of Hill 1282 [soon] lay buried under a mat of human wreckage."[28] Unknown to Taplett and his command, the 3d Battalion's headquarters tent had quickly fallen into "a no man's land." Enemy bullets began ripping through the tents while the fearless Taplett studied his maps, regimental reports, and issued instructions.[29] Taplett was unaware of how dangerous his situation was until two marines slid down a hillside and told the lieutenant colonel a large force of Chinese had attacked them on Hill 1384. Suddenly grenades ripped away part of the command post tent. Everywhere Taplett looked there were Chinese. Chaos reigned until George Company, led by Lt. Charles Mize, came to the rescue. His men quickly cleared the area of Chinese.[30] In the melee, however, executive officer Maj. John J. Canney was killed.

Evansville native Lt. Tex Graham had just left the main headquarters and was treading his way through the dark to Taplett's command post when the attack fell. "I had gone a few yards down the road when all hell broke loose—flares popped up, grenades, machine guns, mortars—it was just chaotic," Graham recalled. He rolled over into a ditch as bullets flew everywhere. "I had no responsibilities other than to get the map overlays to another place, and I carried no arms, so I figured I would just lay there for a while and try to figure out what to do next."

While Graham lay stuck in a ditch, Paul McDaniel, another Evansville reservist, experienced his own hair-raising escape near Taplett's command post: "It had just come my time to go to the warm up tent. All at once bullets started ripping through the canvas. Me and another guy just took off. We didn't even try to find a flap. The Chinese were coming down the hills blowing bugles, and screaming." McDaniel and some other marines quickly tried to find a low place in which to lie, in order to escape the barrage of bullets. "Then the Chinese began shooting mortar shells all over the place. It seemed like each time I moved, where I'd been a few minutes before, a mortar shell would explode." Finally, McDaniel's group found a place to stay by some marine mortars that were firing up into the hills where the Chinese were. "Our mortar fired from about eight P.M. that night until four A.M. the next morning," McDaniel recalled.

Robert Egan lay on the frozen ground somewhere on the valley floor when the fighting began: "The first night I was with a marine who had been shot in the head. It was a terrible wound. The man, a reservist, had a wife and children back home, and as he lay there dying he kept moaning, 'Who's going to take care of my family?'" Sgt. Gene Koonce's platoon fanned out "on a frozen stream right below a spur of Hill 1384" when the first assaults came. "I saw a lot of marines coming down the mountain in a panic. A guy next to me saw I was shaking and asked me if I was scared. I told him yes, but that wasn't why I was shaking. It was just so unbelievably cold on that ice." Three companies went up the mountain that night to try to knock off the Chinese.

The number of wounded marines mounted quickly. "The seriously wounded filled the few [aid station] tents initially available, and the others were protected from freezing by being placed outdoors, side by side, and covered with tarpaulins while lying on straw. Everything was frozen," remembered one officer. "Plasma froze and the bottles broke. We couldn't use plasma because it wouldn't go into solution. . . . We couldn't cut a man's clothes off to get at a wound because . . . he would freeze to death." The officer further noted, "A man was better off if we left him alone. Did you ever try to stuff a wounded man into a sleeping bag?"[31] Gene Koonce remembered stumbling into an aid station about this time: "A corpsman cleaned and packed my wound, but it was so difficult to sleep on the cold ground that I just went back to my squad."

The situation looked bleak when the sun came up the next day. Robert Egan knew something was wrong when he saw a group of ROKs fleeing down a hill: "Our sergeant, an old salt, tried to get them to go back up, but they'd been spooked by what they saw. I could tell the sergeant thought it was a bad sign. All of a sudden there were Chinese everywhere." Later that morning Egan heard another old master sergeant say darkly, "We're going to have to learn how to surrender." The will to survive, however, quickly renewed the marines' spirits, and men could soon be heard talking confidently about fighting their way out. The Americans knew they would not be alone in their struggle. The perimeters at Yudam-ni, Hagaru, Koto-ri, and Chinhung-ni had plenty of artillery firepower, and during the day planes swarmed above the mountains and valleys below, dropped deadly napalm, and bombed and strafed the Chinese. However, several difficult tasks had to be accomplished before the marines could escape the trap at Yudam-ni. Hill 1282, for example, had to be controlled by the marines.

On the morning of the twenty-eighth, Robert Egan and another marine stumbled up strategic Hill 1282 as replacements. As they slipped and climbed up the steep mountain, bullets kept kicking up around them. Egan and his companion thought fellow marines had mistaken them for Chinese. "We kept yelling 'It's us! It's us!' but the bullets kept popping up all around." To his sudden horror, Egan realized the shooting came from the Chinese: "The marines just laughed when we got up on the hill. A marine machine-gunner told me, 'If I had been shooting, you wouldn't be up here.'" Another problem soon presented itself. The young marine who came up with Egan kept standing up, offering his profile to snipers. Egan told the boy to get down, but the marine paid no attention. "Then I heard a thud," Egan remembered. "A bullet hit the kid right in the head. It was so cold the steam rose up from the wound. A corpsman came and got him, and on their way back down a mortar shell got the corpsman too."

The fight for Hill 1282 took place in an unbelievably hostile environment. Gene Koonce recalled "at least a foot of snow along with twenty to thirty below zero temperatures in the evenings." The Chinese were determined to take the hill, believing the large mountain mass held the key to destroying the marines at Yudam-ni. Koonce and a group of about forty-five other marines went up 1282 on the third day. Their group was the sixth platoon to be sent up to fight the Chinese. Koonce recalled how once the small band of marines got there, "about five hundred Chinese made a determined attack" on Koonce's undermanned group. "We got in some old marine foxholes and used frozen Chinese to stack in front of our positions. The sound of bullets hitting frozen bodies made a sound I'll always remember."

The intensity of the battle took a quick toll on the leadership. Koonce recalled, "About three days before, we'd just got a new platoon leader and a staff sergeant, so I went back to platoon guide. They both got killed in a short time, as well as two of the three squad leaders—the third was wounded." Then while Koonce's platoon and squad leaders were going down at a frightening rate, another crisis loomed: "I saw a machine-gun section from weapons located in the wrong place. They were pinned down so I went down there to help them. A mortar round came in and I got hit— a piece of shrapnel fractured my wrist, and two other pieces of hot metal lodged in my back." While Koonce was helping another wounded marine, he received a gunshot wound to the shoulder. The rugged Evansville native continued in spite of his injuries: "I moved the machine-gun section down about twenty-five to thirty yards where there was cover and a better range of fire. Snipers were everywhere. We had a young corpsman who had never seen combat, and he got wounded. On top of that, there were all of these head wounds from snipers."

Incredibly, Koonce's difficult day was just beginning. "After I moved the machine-gun section, I went back up to platoon CP [command post] and was told the lieutenant and staff sergeant lay wounded down on the side of the hill," Koonce recalled. He went to see if the two marines were still alive and received another gunshot through the fleshy part of his lower torso. Still the marine reservist plowed on: "I could see when I got to the lieutenant and sergeant that they both had head wounds and were probably dead." At that point the plucky World War II veteran took command of the platoon. Once in charge, the wounded Koonce faced yet another crisis: "Another attack came from the left. Me and two runners and a wire man grabbed a couple of cases of grenades. We started throwing grenades down on the Chinese, and they hurled concussion grenades back at us." The two runners backed off, but Koonce continued to pitch grenades as the Chinese drew closer. One of the Chinese grenades exploded close by, knocking Koonce down and causing the reservist to begin bleeding from the mouth and ears from concussion. Koonce, however, was able to get back up. When the Chinese attack slackened, Koonce sent a runner back to the platoon CP to find if his group could get a corpsman from another platoon.

About this time Koonce trekked part way down the hill with another man to bring back wounded marines. Returning from this chore, Koonce threw his binoculars back to the marine who was with him. "See if you can find those damn snipers," he ordered. The two men found a foxhole and took cover. The other marine peered through the binoculars for sometime, then reported he couldn't see any signs of snipers. As the two men were standing there, Koonce remembered, "the lights went out." A sniper had fired at the marine with the field glasses, and the bullet had hit both him and Koonce. When Koonce came to, he heard the other man groaning. "I felt around his head and couldn't find anything at first. Then I saw his left ear was gone. He started to go into shock. I shook him and told him, 'You're not that bad; you've lost your ear but you saved my life.'"

The bullet had torn off the marine's ear and had continued over the brim of Koonce's head gear, leaving a deep crease in the metal. The first hit had deflected the bullet just enough to cause it to slightly change its trajectory and in the process likely save Koonce's life. The impact on Koonce's helmet, however, had knocked the Evansville reservist out cold. As soon as his head cleared, he went back to the fighting: "I pulled the wounded marine up by his parka and pushed him up the slope." By the time Koonce got to the top of the hill, the platoon had a new corpsman. The platoon had also received a new commander, and when the lieutenant saw Koonce's condition, he ordered the sergeant "to get his ass to the aids station down below." Somewhere between the grenade attack and the sniper incident, Koonce had been shot through the two cheeks of his mouth, as he had been barking orders. Luckily, the bullet had not hit the jaw bone or any teeth as it passed through Koonce's open mouth.

The bitter struggle for Hill 1282 was also remembered by the Chinese. Chen Chung-Hsien, a Chinese squad leader, recalled during one brief period of quiet, how "snow fell in great flakes, fluffy as down. . . . Soon the blackened shell holes were blanketed in white. . . . Looking about me I saw the battlefield littered with the bodies of American soldiers shrouded in snow." Chen's commander had told his fellow Chinese that as long as

1282 stayed in Chinese hands, "the enemy will be pinned down where they'll be annihilated by our brother units." Like Koonce, Chen would receive several severe wounds. The worst came on the first night of attacks. Chen had fired a heavy machine gun to cover the charging Chinese. "I immediately removed the cotton-padded quilt from the gun and opened up," Chen recalled. "But after one round of shooting the water in the radiator was frozen. . . . I was greatly vexed and tried to unscrew the muzzle. But the moment I gripped the . . . metal my hands stuck fast to it and the skin was ripped clean off." Somehow the tough Chinese soldier succeeded in changing the barrel and continued firing to cover the advance of his fellow troops. By the end of the night, only he and another man survived in his area of the fighting.[32]

While marines and Chinese fought savage battles up at Yudam-ni, another group of marines, Fox Company 2/7, under Capt. William Barber, found themselves cut off and surrounded on a hill that sat just off the main supply route near the Toktong Pass. Barber's group had been given the assignment of guarding the MSR at this strategic point, and the officer had chosen "an isolated hill just north of the MSR for his company's perimeter."[33] The Chinese desperately wanted the hill Fox Company now occupied because it guarded the escape route from Yudam-ni to Hagaru. The enemy now spared no men for their assaults. By the morning of 28 November, almost five hundred dead Chinese littered the area around Barber's perimeter.[34] Throughout the days of the Yudam-ni withdrawal, the Chinese continued to hurl attacks against the marines of Fox Company, slowly whittling down the defenders' numbers. Fox Company, however, grimly hung on while relief columns from Yudam-ni and Hagaru tried but were unable to break through to them.[35] Yudam-ni and Fox Hill, as it would come to be named, were not the only places marines struggled to survive during those last days of November. Farther south, at the southern tip of the Chosin Reservoir, the main headquarters and perimeter for the marine operation located at Hagaru was about to face its own life-or-death struggle.

The significance of Hagaru lay in its location. Once the Chinese had cut the MSR in several places, Hagaru, "with its supply dumps, hospital facilities, and partly finished C-47 airstrip was the one base offering the 1st

Marine Division a reasonable hope of uniting separated elements."[36] While it was obvious this essential base had to be held at all costs, the resources available to carry out the task were sorely limited. Only one rifle company and a third of a weapons company, along with two batteries of artillery, were present for defensive purposes. To make matters worse, marine leadership realized that the relatively small number of men available to defend Hagaru would have to be scattered along a four-mile perimeter, which meant that the commanding officer had to make "the choice between being weak everywhere or strong in a few sectors to the neglect of others."[37] In short, any decision regarding the posting of men around Hagaru was a crap shoot.

East Hill loomed over the village and was considered one of the likely points of attack. Because of the shortage of men, however, few marines could be used on this strategic location. Fortunately, ample artillery firepower was available to help if any major problems occurred from that direction. This firepower, however, was about the only positive element the marines at Hagaru had going for them. Adding to the confusion in the perimeter were hundreds of North Korean refugees who had poured into Hagaru. Mostly women and children, William Wright recalled, "they lay on the frozen ground covered only with thin blankets. It was almost beyond bearing to hear the children scream and cry during fighting or when our artillery would open up. We just had to push them away or step around them to do our jobs. It was heartrending not to be able to comfort those terrified children."

Wright, one of the Evansville reservists, served as a telephone lineman and was one of the first on the morning of the twenty-seventh to see Chinese forces: "A tank had knocked down a telephone line to a machine-gun pit. I was up on the pole, maybe thirty feet or so, and replacing the line. My hands were so cold I put them under my armpits to warm them up. This gave me time to look around at what was going on in the camp. It was about ten o'clock, a beautiful morning. The sky was so clear and blue. Away off some high tension lines ran up the side of a hill and I suddenly noticed movement in the cleared area that ran alongside these power lines." To Wright, the marching men in white coats looked like a parade. "I just couldn't believe it," he recalled. "I hollered down to the pit below, 'what's that up there?' A marine using binoculars quickly identified the moving men: 'Hell, they're Chinese!'" When machine-gun fire erupted, Wright clambered down the pole and hurried back to his unit to grab his rifle and receive his assignment.

The firing of machine guns scattered the first Chinese Wright had spied. "The occasional crackle of small arms fire," however, would continue on into the night.[38] The busiest group that day were marines of the 1st Engineer Battalion, which included Oakland City native Barney Barnard. The airstrip was only about one-quarter completed on the twenty-seventh. Working on the strip turned into a herculean task. "So difficult did it prove [for graders] to get a bite of the frozen earth that steel teeth were welded to the blades. Where the pans were filled, however, the earth froze to the cutting edge until it could only be removed by means of a jack hammer."[39] Barnard and his fellow engineers were told that they would work through the night under the recently installed floodlights. Barnard described to his brother in a detailed letter how difficult the work grew because of the cold. He also spoke of the determination of the marine engineers to finish this important job: "The scrapers are having trouble with clay freezing to the pans. They run about four trips, then shut down while we chip the frozen clay off. It takes time, but this strip will be completed. We may have to get out there with shovels, but it will be finished."

About 10:30 that evening the air was still and quiet except for "the muffling clank of the dozers."[40] Suddenly three red flares shot into the night sky to the southwest, followed by three blasts on whistles. In the beginning the marines experienced only the probing of small patrols, then white phosphorous mortar shells fell on the marine lines. The main attack came shortly after the mortars. The enemy hurled forward despite horrible losses. This particular attack was a showpiece of Chinese fighting strategy. White-clad troops came pouring down the slope and into the marine lines so suddenly that they "seemed to emerge from the very earth."[41] Shortly after midnight, the enemy broke into the perimeter and surrounded a command post tent and a portable mess galley. William Wright noted that once in the marine perimeter, "the Chinese seemed disoriented. They milled around the mess hall." Several houses in the village were set afire by the marines. "The flames helped silhouette the Chinese for us to shoot," Wright recalled.

The next morning the marines reorganized and killed or ran the Chinese out. Wright and the others placed their bayonets on their rifles "and went charging after them." The Chinese "screamed and ran." Several Chinese had moved that night on the vital airstrip that Barney Barnard and other marine engineers desperately labored to finish. The marine workers continued at their posts even as bullets whizzed around them. Finally, a marine engineer, 2d Lt. Robert McFarland, frantically organized a number of heavy equipment operators and swept through the area, driving off the Chinese. Several engineers were injured in this fighting, but the essential airstrip was finally cleared.[42]

The first encounter of the Hagaru marines with the Chinese had been a close call. "If the enemy had decided to effect a major breakthrough at this time, he would have experienced no trouble," asserted one marine officer who was there.[43] Luckily, the perimeter held. The next day Wright and some of his fellow marines were ordered into shifts—four hours on, four hours off. When "on" they often trekked up into the surrounding hills. "When we were 'off' we'd sit down in the valley and watch the show on the hillsides," Wright recalled. Once the Evansville reservist witnessed a group of marines encountering a group of Chinese high up on a mountain: "You could tell they couldn't see each other until the last minute. It was very dramatic." In another instance Wright watched a courageous display of defiance: "A long column of Chinese were coming up the valley, and several of our planes roared in to napalm and strafe them. But one Chinese soldier just stood there shaking his fist. I couldn't believe it. It took about three runs before our planes got him." Wright had several narrow escapes but found his time up on the mountains around the Hagaru perimeter to be most intense.

One night, Wright, five other marines, and an officer climbed two-thirds of the way up a mountain to set up a defensive line to keep the Chinese from coming down on the perimeter. "We laid on the frozen ground the whole night," Wright remembered. "Our rifles would freeze up and we'd have to slowly click them. . . . The M1 rifles would freeze up so easily."

It was hoped that Wright's small band would fool the Chinese into believing that many more marines were in position on the mountainside: "The Chinese would come down, and we could see them. They would only be a few feet away. We'd look up at them, but we did not fire. . . . If we fired, they'd know how many of us there really were. If they knew there were only seven of us up there, they could easily overrun us and come down into the camp." The night turned surreal: "The Chinese would come down and look at us and then run back up the mountain. Then they'd come back down again and hide behind the trees and look at us some more. It was a long, eerie night, but the bluff worked."

Wright was the only reservist in the group who had endured the long night of bluffing the Chinese. "One marine, a regular, laid right beside me and cried the whole time. I kept him covered up with a poncho. He ended up getting the Bronze Star. In fact, they all got Bronze Stars, but me." The next morning, on the way back down the mountain, Wright's group was halted by a marine officer who sent them to another place where the Chinese were supposed to be coming back up from the perimeter after a night's attack. "We were ordered to set up an ambush. There was a big machine-gun pit; I don't know whose it was, but we were in that pit waiting for them. We were scared to death because there were only seven of us, and we were told to expect hundreds of Chinese." Wright recalled that the men in his group were soon "all praying. We were all saying whatever scripture we could remember because we knew we were going to die." Miraculously, however, the Chinese turned to go back up the mountain another way.

The situation at both Yudam-ni and Hagaru continued to worsen. Hagaru was completely surrounded, and its undermanned defenders fought bravely as the perimeter continued to shrink. A force of men from Koto-ri to the south had been fighting northward toward O. P. Smith's headquarters to reinforce the beleaguered Hagaru. On the night of 29 November, however, Smith received word that this group, dubbed Task Force Drysdale, faced heavy attacks and requested permission to turn back. Few of the men from this convoy broke through, and many bodies were left, along with equipment, by the sides of the narrow MSR. Task Force Drysdale, however, was not the only group who endured a near massacre.[44]

Elements of the 7th Army on the east side of the Chosin Reservoir also faced a life-or-death situation. Completely surrounded and without winter gear, the three thousand or so soldiers faced the real possibility of annihilation. On 30 November, Lt. Col. Donald Faith, who came to command the force on the east side after the disappearance of Allan MacLean, decided the only chance his men had of surviving was to break through the Chinese lines and escape to the marine perimeter at Hagaru. The night before the army's attempted breakout was a brutal one. Shortly after midnight the Chinese attack built up to greater intensity than all the other previous attacks. "All through the night," recalled one survivor, "we heard the cries from our friendly wounded within the perimeter who were suffering from the cold."[45] "Five times before dawn" the Chinese "penetrated the American lines." Each time a breach occurred, Faith organized a handful of men to throw the Chinese out of the perimeter. So desperate was Faith for men "that he grabbed walking wounded from the aid station and led them to the front line to plug holes." By morning some men were so fatigued "they actually fell asleep in the middle of the battle."[46]

Because desperately needed medical supplies for Faith's men were completely exhausted by the morning of the breakout attempt, their condition was especially poor. A surviving officer described the hellish scene: "By dawn on December 1 members of the task force had been under attack for eighty hours in subzero weather. None had slept much. None had washed or shaved, none had eaten more than a bare minimum." To add to the deteriorating situation, most of the men were wounded or crippled in some way by the bitter cold. "Everyone seemed to be wounded in one fashion or another. . . . Frozen feet and hands were common. The wounded who were unable to move about froze to death. Trucks and jeeps and trailers were ransacked for ammunition and any kind of fabric that would serve for bandage or clothing." Just as discouraging on that bleak dawn, a rapidly declining weather situation loomed: "Everyone could see that the weather was growing worse, which meant the loss of air support and aerial resupply; that relief from Hagaru in force less than regimental size could never reach us; that another night of determined attack would surely overrun the position."[47]

Colonel Faith was eventually killed, as was the courageous Gibson

County, Indiana, truck driver, Charles Garrigus Jr., who bravely refused to leave the wounded and drove the lead vehicle of the convoy. Faith would receive the Congressional Medal of Honor for his heroism, and Garrigus was awarded the Distinguished Service Cross "for his valorous conduct."[48] None of the bodies of the 7th Army GIs who perished on the east side of the Chosin were ever brought back to this country. Of the original group of three thousand, only about three hundred would stumble or crawl into the marine perimeter.[49] The day before the army debacle, at a hurried conference at Hagaru on 30 November, Almond reluctantly ordered Smith to evacuate X Corps to the coast. Smith, however, announced his intention of bringing out the dead and wounded and all of his equipment. The evacuation from Yudam-ni would begin on 1 December.

On the day after the first Chinese attack at Yudam-ni, Ralph Hargrave, the Boonville, Indiana, reservist who had hoped to become a switchboard maintenance man, found himself being rushed, along with thirty-six other marines and a lieutenant, over to where Dog Company, 5th Marines, had encountered heavy losses. "After climbing over hills and mountains all night," the replacements "stayed in the area two or three days. Nothing much was going on then," Hargrave reported. "When we got back to the main base we were ordered to burn everything we couldn't carry." The inferno made an awesome sight. As the marines later stumbled and fought toward Hagaru, an officer had turned to look back "at the tall columns of smoke billowing skyward. . . . There was a lot of stuff burning—tents, fuel, ammo, everything we didn't need."[50]

Shortly before the marines left Yudam-ni, Hargrave's group was sent out once again, this time "to set up on a line in a valley. Forty of us were strung out over a half a mile, lying prone during the night on the frozen ground." The Chinese pounded Hargrave's squad the entire night. At about daylight, Hargrave and the other marines witnessed a chilling scene: "Three or four hundred Chinese were coming straight at us down the valley to finish us off. We knew we had had it. As the Chinese advanced across the valley, the dawn began to break and suddenly our planes came roaring in at tree-top level. They used napalm and rockets and just busted up those Chinese." Hargrave felt he had been miraculously spared.

In the withdrawal south to Hagaru, Taplett's group, one of two battalions fighting to the north of Yudam-ni, would face the ticklish assignment of disengagement, a maneuver "equivalent to letting go of a tiger's tail."[51] George Company, where Gene Koonce served, encountered the greatest problem in 3/5's move. The company still hung onto Hill 1282 and consequently were in the closest contact with the Chinese. So tight was the brutal no-holds-barred struggle, that grenades, as Sergeant Koonce had discovered, had become the preferred weapon of choice.[52] The maneuver to disengage, however, was eventually accomplished and the weary marines of George stumbled off 1282. As they came down, Koonce encountered an old acquaintance from the Evansville reserve group, a handsome blond teenager named Billy Grove. Grove, who now served in Item Company, was upset because he had fallen asleep while on guard duty back down at the railhead before the Chinese had thrown themselves into the war. A sergeant had found Grove asleep and told the man he faced a court-martial for his neglect of duty. The frightened marine now poured his heart out to the older veteran. Koonce reassured the teenager by telling him, "You'd be in the stockade now if that sergeant had really meant it." Koonce believed the threat was made to keep the young marine from ever going to sleep again while on guard duty. Feeling somewhat relieved, Grove quickly stepped off to join his comrades from Item.

As George Company withdrew from 1282, ammunition left behind was destroyed just as rockets, bombs, and napalm from American planes hit the Chinese. Artillery and mortar shells rained down on 1282 as well, and the mountain mass "seemed to erupt in one tremendous explosion."[53] Taplett's group would now have the essential mission of leading the point and clearing the MSR so the marines at Yudam-ni could proceed southward, and 3/5 would be arrayed appropriately for their important endeavor: "All hands were ordered to secure their sleeping bags to their belts or across their shoulders. Cans of fruit cocktail and dry rations were stuffed into large cargo pockets of their parkas. . . . Ammunition was crammed into pockets and web belts."[54]

Ralph Hargrave learned that his group would act as a rear guard for the withdrawal. During this action, Hargrave did not sleep. He remembered temperatures falling to twenty-five below, not counting wind chill. At some point in the operation, the rear guard unit began drawing small arms and mortar fire from the angry Chinese. Hargrave and the other marines "hit the deck just seconds before a shell exploded about twenty feet away." The powerful blast blew the handle off Hargrave's entrenching tool and pulverized his canteen and the back of his parka and pack. Although several pieces of hot shrapnel were now embedded in the Hoosier marine's back, by Hargrave's count, he had experienced his second miraculous escape at Yudam-ni.

On the day that Hargrave had learned of his group's assignment, Taplett's battalion had come to the base of a strategic mountain, Hill 1520, along the escape route. The land mass loomed as a great obstacle to the marines' retreat and had to be cleared of entrenched Chinese if the thousands of cold and weary Americans behind Taplett's men were to press southward. Item Company was handed the difficult and crucial assignment of going up the mountain. To beef up the Item unit, reinforcements from Headquarters Company and artillery were used as well.[55] Capt. Harold O. Schrier, one of the marine participants in the original flag raising on Iwo Jima, was the leader of the Item group. Reservist Paul McDaniel also found himself suddenly assigned to Item as the unit started up. "We hadn't gotten very far down the road before the Chinese started firing down on our trucks," McDaniel recalled. "Taplett came running up and told us that we were not going to get out of here unless we went up that mountain and cleared off the Chinese. I went running down along the road with the Item boys, and the Chinese were shooting down on us like crazy. I couldn't figure how we were ever going to get up that mountain with all those cliffs overhead."

Across the road McDaniel and some of the others spied a shallow ditch. The marines ran and slid across the icy road as bullets splattered all around them. Once on the other side they hastily fell into the ditch. The older McDaniel, who stood over six feet and weighed close to 250 pounds, soon became a focal point of leadership. "I saw a gully, so I took off and started up there and soon everybody else was swarming up the same ditch, heading up the mountain as the firing continued. It was horrible climbing. You'd go up about twenty feet and slide back ten. And it was like that all day." As McDaniel scrambled up the steep mountainside, he took some comfort in the dozen or so letters from his mother he carried tucked away inside his coat. One ended with these two words heavily circled, "Be careful!" Luckily for the men scaling the mountain, fellow marines on the valley floor kept firing upward to keep the Chinese from completely stopping Item's progress. McDaniel particularly recalled how relieved he was when he looked down from the treacherous hill and saw the trucks carrying the wounded starting to lunge forward.

When dusk approached, McDaniel's group was not yet to the top of the mountain. Item Company now faced a very dangerous situation if they could not reach the summit and knock off the Chinese by nightfall. McDaniel remembered at this point how "it was just starting to get dark and we were getting close to the top. I was getting where I could climb a little bit better, even as heavy as I was, and all at once I heard a 'pop pop pop.' Some marines were just in front of me about a hundred feet up and I heard them holler 'hand grenades!' Suddenly Item company faced an avalanche of Chinese concussion grenades rolling down the mountain into their midst. McDaniel was "trying to climb up the slippery slope when all of a sudden here comes a thundering herd of marines sliding down on top of us. When the hand grenades started exploding, the marines up ahead had turned and were running back down the mountain." Several marines were killed or wounded on this occasion.

When darkness came, the marines on 1520 were still scrambling to regroup after the grenade attack. Then the Chinese sent up a flare and the desperate word went out among the marines "to hit the deck so they won't see us."[56] A short, informal meeting of company leaders led to the decision to go a little farther up, to where a small valley seemed to offer some shelter for a defensive perimeter. Back down in the valley, Bob Taplett could hear the firing and actually see some of the fighting but had no means of communication with Item Company. "The wounded who trickled, then poured down the heights" got some of the terrible story across to Colonel Taplett. They told how Item had been caught in a draw and cut apart "by cross fire from the high ground on either side." The position, as it turned out, was impossible to defend, and the Chinese closed in.[57]

Paul McDaniel and the other marines on 1520 now fought a desperate and mostly losing fight for survival. "It was slippery and it was dark and everybody had a hand on each other's shoulders as we moved down there to that low place where Schrier had ordered us. We quickly made a perimeter facing out every which way because we didn't know where the Chinese would be coming from." McDaniel remembered that the perimeter "was like a small church full of people. There were about 150 of us, and we were in this tight circle. So we all plopped down and another flare went off and then it got deadly quiet. We were trying to figure out where the flares were coming from. Then the Chinese started firing down, and we started zeroing in on where their firing originated." The marines seemed to be getting the better of the struggle when all of a sudden a large number of Chinese "came running in amongst us. I was already lying down crawling and there were guys all around me. Americans and Chinese were fighting, rolling, and grunting in hand to hand combat."

McDaniel now witnessed a macabre dance of death as Chinese soldiers and American marines actually embraced in fighting. McDaniel wisely decided that he "wasn't about to stand up and get hit. I was running out of ammunition too. I had gotten down to where I only had four rounds left. At this point the battle had turned into utter chaos. There were no clear battle lines, and there was a lot of crying going on and moaning and groaning. I heard dying marines calling for their mothers. It was the most terrible night I ever endured." As the Evansville reservist lay in the midst of the carnage, he began to pray. He promised God that if he ever got out of there he would "be the best guy you've ever seen." About that time McDaniel "felt something like a bee sting" at his ankle.

The "bee sting" was actually a bullet. McDaniel had been shot through his left ankle joint and the bullet had continued into his other ankle. As the wounded marine lay there, the night turned completely quiet "except for some continued moaning and groaning. I think some of our guys who survived had slipped off while the fighting was going on and headed down to the road." As time went on, Colonel Taplett became more aware of what had happened to Item. Late that evening Captain Schrier had radioed Taplett telling him that his men would have to "attack across the plateau to another spur ahead of me." Taplett now feared the worst. Item and another company sent up 1520 were too far apart in his estimation. About midnight, communication from Item caused Taplett to realize his fears had become reality. Schrier reported, "I'm running into a buzz saw up here.

It's going to be a disaster."[58] Veterans of World War II who survived that night thought the engagement on 1520 "worse than Iwo Jima."[59] Item Company would disappear that night as a unit.

The place where Paul McDaniel lay wounded was about "four city blocks up the mountain." When the dawn came, McDaniel saw that he was surrounded by scores of dead Chinese soldiers and American marines. The surviving marine, shot through both ankles, faced a bleak predicament. He thought it was unlikely that anyone would rescue him: "It was just starting to get a little bit light, and I looked around and there were bodies laying all over the place. I decided if I didn't get out of there at that moment, I would never get out. So I cradled my left ankle and got my carbine and started sliding." McDaniel had not gone over twenty feet when he came upon a Chinese soldier sitting on a rock "right in front of me. I grabbed a pine tree branch to stop my motion and sat there watching him. I thought, if he makes one move, I am going to blast him off of that rock." Finally McDaniel slid right by the sitting soldier and through "another bunch of Chinese that were laying all over the place. I kept on going down that hill until I saw someone stepping out on a path." The man McDaniel had come upon was a marine out looking for survivors from Item. McDaniel told the fellow marine that he thought he was the only one left alive when he started down the hill. The marine told the Evansville reservist "to sit back and I'll drag you down. He got hold of my coat and he drug me a good ways down the mountain." The marine placed McDaniel in a shallow ditch while he and other marines went up to look for more survivors. McDaniel had encouraged the rescuers to make sure and look. "I wouldn't leave," McDaniel told them, "until someone goes up there and checks it out."

While McDaniel lay in the ditch near the bottom of the mountain, another Evansville reservist, Robert Egan, had gone up Hill 1520 the morning after the attack to help look for wounded marines. Very few men had volunteered for this dangerous work, and a chaplain had come along the MSR begging marines to leave the movement south and go up on the mountain to look for survivors. "I wasn't thinking about why no one else wanted to go until I got up there," Egan recalled. Meanwhile, Paul McDaniel still lay a little ways up 1520 where he had been left in the freezing snow. McDaniel had begun to think that he was going to be left behind, for he could see the last few vehicles moving out on the road below. "About that time along comes old Bob Egan," he recalled. "He and another marine got me over to a truck." Egan had saved his friend's life.

Lt. Col. Ray Murray, commander of the 5th Marines, came to Taplett's forward command post the morning after Item Company's night of anguish. He found Taplett's battalion drastically drained by its efforts. Taplett told his superior "to look around. We've been cleaned out." Nearby, Captain Schrier, who had been severely wounded in the neck at the Item perimeter, struggled to wolf down some food being spooned to him by another marine.[60] Item's efforts had not been in vain. Hill 1520 had been abandoned by the Chinese, and the marine caravan could continue to lurch toward Hagaru. Less than twenty able-bodied Item Company marines, however, were fit to fight the next day. The Chinese had paid an even higher price, as about four hundred of their dead were counted around the area where Item had made its desperate stand.[61] Billy Grove, the worried reservist from Evansville, did not come down from 1520. The young man's body had to be left on the lonely mountain.

Once past Hill 1520, the march to Hagaru became more chaotic. David Graham, one of the few remaining members of Item Company, remembered, "Every time we'd go around a corner, I'd want to just drop. We'd been so long without sleep or much food and the cold had really sapped us. But every time we came around a bend someone would holler, 'hurry up, they're just behind us!' That would give us another breath and we'd keep on going." Graham, who had been somewhat heavy in high school "and could never run," found himself "running anyway." Trucks in the long strung-out convoy would pass Graham; then minutes later the same trucks, most of which carried wounded, would bunch up "and we'd run past them."

Charlie Mize, who led George Company, "had never seen troops look so hopeless or care so little." They had hardly eaten for days "and were now too tired to stomach the frozen . . . rations." Mize offered his worried men encouragement. "We are in a hell of a mess. But you and I together have gone through many battles. We've always done the job, and we can do it again."[62] Reservist Ross Compton, also of George Company, was thirty-one and because of his age was called "Pappy" by the younger marines.

Compton kept running into marines, especially teenagers, who had sat down by the road and seemed to be resigned to dying. "I'd holler at them to get up and if they didn't, I'd kick them real hard to get them mad. I had to do this several times to a few of the fellows who kept falling back and sitting down. They were just so tired and cold and stressed out that they didn't think they could go on." Mize's and Compton's encouragements caused the marines of George Company to dig down deeper into their souls and continue the numbing journey southward.

The last three or four miles to Hagaru, Tex Graham had jumped up on the side of a truck and almost wished he had not: "The driver whipped the truck around like a mad man, trying to get the vehicle to Hagaru. I thought I would fall off and be run over." A wounded Ralph Hargrave was initially placed on a truck for the three-day ordeal from Yudam-ni to Hagaru. Hargrave watched in horror as many of the men riding on the truck were wounded again and again by Chinese fire raking the vehicle. "I got so weak from the cold and not having anything to eat that I couldn't stay on the truck. Also, I didn't want to get shot, so I got off the truck and limped along the side away from the fire for protection. Still, I was having trouble keeping up and was falling further and further behind. I didn't want to be left, so I got a rope and made a loop. The truck ahead had tent pegs in the rear. When the truck got to going too fast, I'd throw the loop over the peg. I wore the toes out of my shoes being drug, but I got to Hagaru."

Paul McDaniel had been thrown into a truck at the foot of Hill 1520 and remembered the incredibly difficult journey to the safety of the perimeter at Hagaru. "We were lying in the trucks, and they'd move about a half of a block down the road, and then bullets would start splattering off of the side boards. Naturally I wanted to see, and so I'd peek between the slats. There were Chinese running along the top of the mountains shooting down, and our guys were down on the road firing back up at them." Often the Chinese would set up roadblocks that had to be cleared out before the convoy could move again. McDaniel remembered "one of the NCOs coming up to our truck and telling us that we were hung up again. He asked for volunteers among the wounded who could walk to go up and fight. Many marines reluctantly went forward. I felt sorry for them. I was lying there on that truck, and they would take off, and boy, you'd hear a fire fight like you'd never heard before up ahead. A few minutes later, they'd drag the newly wounded marines back. They'd throw the wounded up on the trucks along with the ones who had gotten killed." Somewhere on the journey to Hagaru the convoy halted and the exhausted McDaniel fell asleep just as a heavy snow began to fall. When he woke up, "everything was all white. I raked the snow off. I had my parka pulled up close to me and it was all covered with snow. It must have been about six inches deep."

The journey was not completely without its humorous moments. Ralph Hargrave watched as two marines stole a load of tent pegs from a jeep trailer in order to make a fire: "We had a good fire going and all of a sudden here comes a colonel walking down the line. It turned out it was his jeep, his trailer, and his pegs. He saw the fire and ran over to take names. One of the marines, a reservist from Indianapolis, spoke up and admitted he was the one who had thrown the pegs into the fire." The colonel raged. "Besides destroying government property," he shouted, "those were my god-damn tent pegs!" Many years later, whenever Hargrave would travel through Indianapolis, he would telephone the former reservist who had stolen the colonel's property. The first thing Hargrave would say, even before he identified himself, was "Those were my goddamn tent pegs!"

As the caravan of ragged, exhausted marines moved slowly south from Yudam-ni, marine leadership decided that Fox Company would be sent help to pull them from their desperate situation. Fate's tricks are sometimes playful. In the fall of 1973 retired marine lieutenant colonel James A. Murray came to Oakland City, Indiana, to become president of Oakland City College. The town was the former home of several C Company men, and the college would be the alma mater of William Marshall, Gordon Greene, and Albert Dickson. On the night of 1 December 1950, however, Murray was a nineteen-year-old marine private preparing to follow Lt. Col. Ray Davis across several uncharted ridges in an attempt to rescue Fox Company. "The snow-covered peaks all looked alike and the guide stars were lost to sight when the column descended into valleys," Murray noted.[63] He remembered how the marines would come to crevices "of which the span and depth were impossible to judge. Colonel Davis would jump first and we would follow." So dangerous and intense was the journey that two of the men in Davis's party went completely berserk and had to be restrained. Unfortunately, both died before they could be evacuated.[64] Despite the difficult conditions encountered by the marines as they climbed over the mountains, the rescue attempt was successful. Murray, however, the lowly private who would one day become president of an Indiana college, was severely wounded just as the marines arrived back at the MSR. The teenager was quickly stacked alongside several dead marines. A small helicopter was about to take off and corpsmen were trying to decide if any of the marines who lay in the nearby pile were perhaps still alive. Murray had apparently gone into morphine shock and lay on the frozen ground, completely paralyzed, as a marine came by one last time to check. "I'm sure they thought I was dead because I couldn't move. But I could cry. I willed tears to flow down my face. One of the Corpsmen shouted, 'Hey! Murray's still alive.' So I was one they strapped on the helicopter." Luckily also for Fox Company, Murray and his companions had been able to somehow navigate over impossible terrain to come to the aid of their beleaguered comrades. Lieutenant Colonel Davis would be awarded the Congressional Medal of Honor for leading this heroic effort.

The marines from Yudam-ni started coming into the Hagaru perimeter about noon on 3 December. Gen. O. P. Smith had supported the end of the march by sending out a relief column made up of tank-mounted marines and English Royal Marine Commandos. The ragged marines of Yudam-ni were especially impressed by their British counterparts. David Graham of Item had been unable to keep the strict water discipline demanded by the Marine Corps and carried an empty canteen. "I knew better than to ask a fellow marine. We were expected to keep good water discipline. I had run out of water and I was eating snow when some Royal Marines came by. One of them asked, 'Why are you eating that snow laddy buck?' I told him I'd run out of water so he held his canteen out and gave me a long drink of his."

Hagaru quickly became the sight of a "tearful, stirring reunion. . . . Bear hugs from strangers and hands pump[ing] in admiration and thanksgiving."[65] Many of the marines who marched, rode, or staggered in needed immediate medical attention. "The first thing I did," recalled Gene Koonce, "[was go] to a hospital where a corpsman pulled off my shoe pac and then my socks. When the socks came off so did my frozen skin." The shocked corpsman told Koonce that his feet looked extremely bad and that he had severe frostbite. The Evansville reservist had new socks put back on, and because of his severe frostbite and multiple gunshot and shrapnel wounds, was tabbed to be flown out. Luckily for Koonce and other marines, the airstrip marine engineers such as Barney Barnard had struggled so hard to complete now allowed planes to enter and leave Hagaru. Ironically, while Koonce stood in line to board one of the planes, he was almost killed in a strange incident: "Several marines and I were standing there talking when I saw a guy next to me pull a pin on a grenade and drop it. I yelled 'Fire in the hole!' as I picked up the grenade and ran over to where I could throw it out of harm's way." When Koonce stepped back, the crazed marine pulled another pin and dropped another grenade. This time the grenade exploded before anyone could react. The second blast injured several men, though Koonce was mostly unscratched.

Before Koonce stepped on a plane, he faced a second incident. "I had a Russian pistol I'd taken off a dead officer at Seoul," he recalled. "When I started to board the plane, a corpsman stopped me and said that I couldn't take the pistol on the plane. I told him I wasn't giving it up. The corpsman kept bugging me about it. Between the guy dropping the grenades and the fellow trying to get the Russian pistol, I decided I'd be better off joining my company." Koonce ended up walking out. "I knew I could still help my buddies, and we still had a long way to go."

Robert Egan spent his first night in Hagaru sitting in the field by some other men: "It was almost dark when I sank to the ground. I talked to the guy next to me for sometime before I realized he and everyone else there was dead. The fellow who had been staring out at me had died with his eyes open." Egan quickly moved away to find the living. Shortly afterward, he witnessed another heartrending scene: "I saw a wounded Chinese prisoner, a very old fellow who was shot in the stomach. He was in great pain and kept pointing to his head for someone to shoot him. He knew he was going to die anyway. The officers, however, would not let us touch him."

Paul McDaniel was still on a truck when he came into Hagaru. "They unloaded us and took us into a schoolhouse," he remembered. "The doctors were so busy going from one to the other. They were doing surgery, and all kinds of stuff was going on when a doctor came over to me and said, 'Let's get this boot off.' So the doctor had an assistant to take a knife and cut my boot off, and that's when they saw that the other boot was full of blood. So they cut that boot off too." McDaniel was quickly chosen as one of two marines to be flown out in a little two-seater plane. "The Chinese were shooting out at us as the plane took off, but I was so thankful to be leaving I didn't care. I knew I was going to make it."

McDaniel and the other severely wounded marines were flown all the way to Tokyo International Airport. "They carried us out into the center of a big open area and then they started bringing in other stretchers from other planes," he recalled. "There must have been about thirty-five or forty of us laying in there on the floor. Suddenly a group of American men and women came over to where we lay. The women especially just went crazy. One of them went and got me a cup of hot chocolate. I had a pretty good beard and was covered with dirt and grime. I hadn't had a bath in about three months. On top of that, in that cold, your eyes get filled up with a kind of white mucous. I must have looked terrible, but she brought me that cocoa, and her and the rest of the Americans there just started making all over us."

Ralph Hargrave stumbled into Hagaru having not had anything to eat for three days: "We got frozen cans of pork and beans which we busted open with our rifle butts. We'd beat the beans into small enough chunks to eat." Hargrave had had his mess kit blown off of his pack while defending Yudam-ni, so when he saw hotcakes being served the next day at Hagaru, he tore a flap off of a cardboard box to use as a plate and grabbed an empty bean can for a cup for his coffee. "Those were the best hotcakes and coffee I ever had in my life," he recalled. Once in the safety of the perimeter at Hagaru, Hargrave was placed in a tent and told he would be evacuated. The next day the marine walked down to the airfield and waited for the plane that would take him from the frozen hell he had correctly anticipated he would experience in Korea: "I waited all day to be flown out. The last plane that came in before dark was loaded with replacements. The crew chief said they would take out only thirty people. I quickly counted and saw that I was number thirty in line and thought, thank God. I could just feel the warmth of that hospital in Japan. When I stepped up to get on the plane the chief stopped me and said he was sorry but now they were only going to take twenty-nine marines. It liked to broke my heart." Things were so bad now that Hargrave, although weak from shock from his wounds, was ordered back to his unit. Hargrave, however, was unable to find his sergeant so that he could report in and consequently was listed as missing in action to his family back home.

Once the marines from Yudam-ni flocked into Hagaru, morale soared: "The Hagaru perimeter presented a scene of bustling activity. . . . Trucks and jeeps bound along bumpy roads[,] . . . twin-engined planes roared in and out."[66] A total of 4,312 casualties were evacuated by air as those marines who could walk prepared for the next leg of the breakout—the trek to the perimeter at Koto-ri. The evacuation greatly aided the next phase because now the convoy would not have to worry about and care for so many severely wounded marines. In addition, 537 replacements were flown in. Reporters came as well. Marguerite Higgins of the *New York Herald-Tribune,* for example, interviewed many of the weary marines. Higgins observed that the marines who stumbled in from Yudam-ni had "the dazed air of men who have accepted death and then found themselves alive after all."[67]

Gen. O. P. Smith, realizing that the Yudam-ni troops needed extra time to recover in order to be ready for the next difficult portion of the fight, even though this also meant the Chinese would have time to prepare and could still cut off and destroy the bulk of the 1st Marine Division, gave his men needed rest. Indeed, the Chinese had been "assembling troops and supplies both at Hagaru and along the MSR to Koto-ri." Up to seven Chinese divisions were so stationed.[68]

The journey to Koto-ri was as difficult and hair-raising as the evacuation from Yudam-ni as cold weather and stress turned the journey into a nightmarish marathon. Many marines now shuffled along like wooden zombies. Reservist William Wright, who had helped defend the perimeter at Hagaru, noticed on the second day out the body of a dead Chinese soldier. The body lay next to a big wooden case, and the curious Wright walked over to check things out. Wright's water had frozen in his canteen so he was sucking on a piece of ice to slake his thirst. "I kicked the body over with my foot," he recalled, "and a booby trap went off." The dead body took the force of the blast, hurling blood and human gore all over Wright and the piece of ice he held. "I just wiped the ice off on my coat and kept on licking it. I was that tired and that thirsty."

Near the place where Wright had seen his first dead marine on the way up to Hagaru, his group stopped for a short while. Seeing the dead now had much less impact on Wright and the other marines: "We went into this power station to get out of the wind and the cold and were able to go to sleep for two hours or so because the convoy had backed up. There were all of these frozen Chinese in there, and I was so tired I laid on one for a pillow. It was four o'clock in the morning and so cold, and we were surrounded by dead Chinese bodies and we just slept anyway." The Chinese kept up relentless harassment from the mountains, having zeroed in their mortars on the marines down below. When one attack came, Wright got behind a truck "by the rear wheels. I was laying down and shrapnel blew the tires out. I could hear the spew right above me."

The march seemed to be growing more chaotic to Tex Graham, and he held grave doubts about whether he would be fortunate enough to see his unborn child: "The hills were so big, and it was so cold that I had resigned myself to the possibility [that] I and the rest of us might not get out. It just seemed too bleak to me at the time." Seeing American planes fly over and pound the Chinese was a big boost to morale. "They'd drop food and ammunition to us, and strafe and bomb the Chinese. On the days it snowed, however, the planes couldn't fly and we'd begin to worry again. I really believe if we'd had three days during which the planes could not have flown, it might have gone the other way." In one instance on the march out, Graham recalled being near the front of one group of men when Chinese machine guns suddenly pinned the column down. "Colonel Taplett came forward to see what the hold up was. I told him about the Chinese machine guns and he said, 'We can't let that stop us, let's go,' and he led us forward. Taplett was simply fearless, a true leader." The Chinese could be just as fearless. Graham also remembered looking out across the fields in front of American machine-gun positions and seeing stacks of dead Chinese who had charged into the jaws of death. "The fields would be filled with dead bodies," he recalled.

Some of the strangest episodes in the move south involved the way hundreds of Chinese soldiers came into the American lines trying to surrender. "Every time we were attacked, some of the Chinese would come in with their arms up," recalled Bill Wright. "Then when we were attacked some more we'd make those who had given up leave, but they'd come back and wander around where we were trying to fight. It was a very strange scene." Robert Egan encountered "scores of Chinese surrendering when we moved to Koto-ri and beyond." The kind-hearted Egan fed some of the Chinese Lifesavers, which the marines had been given for extra energy in the cold. "They'd smile up at me when I handed them one. The funny thing was there seemed to be more of them in our lines than there were us." About this time, Egan saw a young marine lying on the ground crying. "I went over and asked him what was wrong. 'I'm hit,' he said, and showed me a small hole in his stomach. The wound didn't look too bad so I told him to hang on until the corpsmen arrived. He sat there and died in just a few minutes."

The marines' problems were far from over, even as the main group moved out of Koto-ri and marched toward the coast. On 4 December, a crucial single-lane bridge that spanned a deep gorge had been blown by the Chinese about three miles south of Koto-ri. Between the cliff and the sheer drop off, there was no way to go around. Treadway bridges were hurriedly flown in, and after much tense work, a temporary span was put in place. Correspondent Maggie Higgins had traveled down from the blown bridge and watched as the marines begin to file pass. Robert Egan, who sat on the front of an army truck, had his feet wrapped in burlap sacks. "How come you have sacks on your feet?" she asked Egan. Egan recalled that Higgins "was a very attractive woman, and after all we'd been through, it was great to talk to her. I just told her the sacks were to keep my feet warm." Later a photograph of Egan with his burlap sack feet would appear in a number of national news media sources.

On 2 December, a marine reconnaissance patrol had gone to the Funchilin Pass, which lay just south of the blown bridge. Encountering large numbers of Chinese, the patrol pulled back, but not before establishing Hill 1081 as a key terrain feature. Intelligence reports offered grim news to the three marine companies who would soon be moving north to seize this important location. Hill 1081 was defended by elements of the Chinese 60th Division and newly arrived elements of 76th and 77th Divisions of the 26th Army. More disturbing, the 60th group was considered to be one of the best in the Chinese army.[69] Like Hills 1282 and 1520, 1081 was about to enter the annals of marine lore.

On 8 December, marine units began moving south out of Koto-ri. At the same time, the 1st Marine Battalion of the 1st Regiment moved up from Chinhung-ni about ten miles away to secure Hill 1081. A swirling snowstorm hit as the 1st Battalion, which consisted of Able, Baker, and Charlie Companies, began its journey, and it continued most of the day. The plan to secure 1081 called for Charlie Company to take the "south-western nose of Hill 1081 and to hold it while the other two companies pass through."[70] Able Company faced the hardest task. They were ordered to attack through Charlie Company and fight to the crest of the hill. Baker would attack along the left flank of Able Company.[71]

Several Evansville reservists trudged north from Chinhung-ni as a part of the 1st. Glendel "Jeep" Ellis and Gordon Greene served in Able, Raleigh McGary belonged to Baker, and Bill Etheridge, Albert Dickson, and Evansville native Robert Whitehouse marched with Charlie Company that fateful morning. On the way up to 1081, Whitehouse, a mortar man, lugged "six rounds of mortar ammo through three feet of snow." Whitehouse recalled, "You could hear bullets hitting all around us, but there was no place to hide." Just as dangerous was the frigid cold. "When you took a leak, it would freeze before it hit the ground." Whitehouse and the other marines also found themselves "pissing on our rifle bolts to free them up."

Raleigh McGary too recalled "getting fired upon all the way up there. We took off about three in the morning and at first the weather wasn't too bad." By midmorning, however, the snow was falling from the sky in buckets. Somewhere en route to 1081, McGary's group "started drawing fire from a large spur, so the lieutenant comes over and orders my fire team to go up the hill and secure the area where the firing came from." McGary left his pack down on the road and went up. "We were ordered to stay there while Baker went through." Unfortunately, McGary and his squad were unable to see when the company had passed through and another company came along. "Finally one of the fire team members said, 'We better get down there, it's been long enough.' The other three left, but I waited a few minutes more. Finally I went down to the road to get my stuff and it was gone—my sleeping bag, my pack, pictures of my family, letters from home—all gone."

It took McGary quite some time to catch up with his group: "Meanwhile I was hungry. I hadn't had any food to speak of for two days. Finally I came up to a few marines who stood around a fire. They saw how miserable I looked and offered me some of their food—a can of chicken and vegetables—the worst rations we had." McGary forced the food down. "That night I didn't have a sleeping bag until later when I got the bag of one of our dead," he recalled. "But it was impossible to sleep. If it hadn't snowed so much that night and created some insulation, I'm sure that I would've frozen to death. The next morning when I woke, I had to dig my way out of the snow." McGary had one especially close call on 1081. When a Chinese machine gun opened up on him, McGary "jumped into a ditch nine inches deep. Somehow I got myself completely hidden down there. Fear can do that. The fellow next to me got hit in the helmet, the bullet went round and round inside and just scalped him. Blood streamed down his face. I saw him the next morning all bandaged up, but at the time I figured he was dead for sure."

Gordon Greene and Jeep Ellis of Able edged up 1081, but somehow, during the climb, Greene lost sight of his reservist friend "going up in the hills." Ellis was an assistant BAR man but remembered carrying the heavy weapon since coming ashore at Wonsan because "my BAR man was lazy." Ellis experienced some intense fighting the first evening on 1081. "When it got dark, the Chinese came at us. They'd throw concussion grenades and if they'd had good metal, I wouldn't be here today. I don't know how many times I was thrown up into the air by the blasts. We were scurrying around all night like animals shooting at the muzzle flashes." In a letter to his parents, Ellis wrote of the initial charge up 1081: "We came around some rocks, and they opened up on us with machine guns. The bullets were so close I felt them go by. Several marines were hit in the first attack, and the lieutenant said we'd have to charge the pill boxes." Ellis's group soon discovered that two of their automatic rifles were frozen and they had but three hand grenades left. "I had one, and that killed two guys in one pill box. Then my M1 rifle froze up—every time I fired, I had to pull the bolt four or five times." The next morning Ellis and the other marines discovered that almost everyone had "frozen feet." When the Evansville man came off the hill, his feet were so frostbitten "they thought they might have to amputate."

Bill Etheridge, the former Evansville Bosse High School football player, arrived at the foot of 1081 with Charlie Company. Etheridge especially recalled the cold and the effect the brutal weather had on the Chinese: "When some Chinese soldiers surrendered to us, their cotton uniforms were just frozen solid on them." The time the three companies spent on Hill 1081 would be the coldest that group would see in Korea. One marine captain remembered how one of his men "began swearing and yelling so loudly from the cold that I thought he had gone berserk." A captured Chinese report revealed that more than 90 percent of its soldiers had suffered some form of frostbite.[72]

Etheridge's company held the road at the base of the hill while Able and Baker climbed up. During one portion of the battle, Etheridge's group was ordered "to go up the hill and help bring down casualties. . . . We brought twelve or so people down and that was the roughest part of it because I saw a couple of guys I knew who'd been alive when they'd gone up the night before. We had gone through all of our training together." Even a minor wound could be deadly, Etheridge noted. "It was so cold and there was no way they could give a guy plasma. I heard a corpsman say that half of the guys would have made it if it had been warm."

One marine in Able vividly recalled having to endure wading through at least two feet of snow and visibility that "dropped to seventy-five yards." Passing through Charlie Company, where Etheridge and Albert Dickson stood trying to stay warm, the Able marine described the Charlie Company men as looking "like frozen mummies, huddled together in drifts as we went by. They said they didn't envy us because it was probably colder on top of the hill."[73] Albert Dickson, who as a Boy Scout leader in Oakland City, Indiana, had experienced many nights of camping out of doors, found the environment near Hill 1081 to be almost beyond endurance. "It was the coldest winter there in a hundred years, and we were sleeping outside," the young reservist remembered.

The initial climb for Able up 1081 was difficult. One marine reported, "Most everyone slipped and fell several times, and as we drew near the crest we were pretty well soaked through. The snow was in our boots, down our shirts and pants, and it covered our faces and weapons and felt awfully icy. Strangely, I found I was enormously thirsty, but my fingers were so numb that I gave up trying to get at my canteens, and I wondered how I would do if I had to reload my weapons."[74] Gordon Greene, who had so innocently dreamed of combat that summer back at Oakland City, Indiana, endured plenty of real action as he inched up the mountain along with his Able Company comrades. Greene recorded a version of his experiences in "Boondockers." In one episode on Hill 1081, the main character, Ramig, and his squad had just come under a grenade attack, and the marines quickly responded by hurling grenades of their own up at the Chinese:

> Ramig tossed a grenade to Andrews and noticed that Hamm was scrambling up the ridge line in the direction from where the enemy grenades had come. Ramig followed him and found upon reaching him that his BAR was jammed. Hamm was kneeling in the snow and trying various magazines but to no avail. Even the magazines that Ramig offered didn't work. During the frenzy, Ramig happened to glance up and felt all his strength leave his body. He was staring directly into the muzzle of a Chinese heavy machine gun. Trying not to panic, he turned his head back to view Hamm's frantic efforts to get his BAR to work, knowing that at any second his body and that of Hamm's would be ripped apart.[75]

The final assault on the crest of 1081 came on the morning of 9 December. Capt. Robert Barrow led Able, but not before he had his men test-fire their weapons. This was a wise move, for many of the rifles had frozen in the previous night's cold. After a deadly struggle through the morning and afternoon, Able claimed the prize, but not without paying an awful price. Roughly 100 marines were left to fight of the original 223 who had marched out of Chinhung-ni. The price, however, had to be paid. The marines now held the key height between Koto-ri and the railhead.[76] During a portion of the final battle for the crest, Gordon Greene experienced the "fog of war": "I was standing with the first platoon in the middle of a blizzard on a narrow hogback ridge not knowing where in the hell the Chinese were."[77] The next day, around four o'clock in the afternoon, as Able stood triumphant on top of 1081, Greene's squad was told "to check all the bunkers for Chinese. Drag them out and shoot any who blink." The marines paired up and tossed bodies "one-two-three down the slope watching them ricochet from tree to tree as they rolled down the hill."[78]

Ironically for Greene, his closest brush with death on 1081 occurred after the Chinese had been thrown off. While he and some other marines lay resting around a fire, an American plane accidentally strafed the group. "All hell broke loose. . . . I must have flinched and ducked simultaneously. The guy who was on my left fell into me knocking me backwards. . . . There was a flurry of action, and I heard voices around me. Someone grabbed me and asked me where I was hit. I was too stunned to reply. I think I told them to look at the guy who had fallen on me. . . . Later I realized why the corpsman asked me where I was hit." The man who had been sitting beside Greene now had his brains splattered all over the area. "I had bits of flesh and blood," remembered Greene, "all over the side of my face and the hood as well as the upper portion of my entire parka. All of this came from the guy who had been sitting beside me. That plane that had made the strafing run must have been firing .50 caliber stuff at us."[79] Greene's childhood friend, Albert Dickson, also remembered "being strafed by our own planes. They hit so close that the spent cartridges rained down upon us."

Raleigh McGary recalled watching the marines who now moved south as they paraded by Hill 1081, the hill he and his other comrades had helped secure. The night before the first marines had started trickling by McGary's position, the Poseyville, Indiana, man had slept beneath the shelter of a large rock that stood along one side of the road. The next morning, when McGary came out from under the large boulder, he found frozen icicles of blood, the blood of Chinese soldiers, hanging down from the rock. McGary's prominent position over the MSR also offered a ringside seat to the unforgettable sight of thousands of marines marching by: "I'd yell and ask some of them where they were from, and they'd answer back as they moved past. My group was about the last out. I saw so many wounded just strapped to the trucks passing down below. Those trucks also had the dead piled up on them like cord wood. The trucks were just shot up to pieces."

After the many narrow escapes the marines had experienced in the move to Chinhung-ni, the final leg to Hungnam and the ships that took the marines back south seemed anticlimactic. Barney Barnard reported to his father that it was on this portion of the evacuation that "I had my little accident. I was riding on the fender of one of our trucks, and another truck met us at a narrow place in the road." A sharp piece of metal sticking out from the passing vehicle caught Barnard "just where I sit down. For a minute I thought something had been broken." At sick bay, however, Barnard was given good news. He was "only bruised and would go back to duty soon." William Wright's actions, once the marines stopped and waited to be loaded up at Hungnam, were likely typical: "We were told to stay awake if we could, that we'd be eating in two or three hours. My group went into this building and laid down on the floor on our sleeping bags and slept for twenty-four hours."

By 14 December, X Corps had gathered on the coast to begin the evacuation. All beaches were clear by 24 December. Roughly twenty thousand marines of the 1st Division had escaped the Chinese trap. The marines suffered a total of 4,418 battle casualties, including 604 killed in action and 192 missing. Enemy losses were estimated by the Americans at 37,500, including 25,000 killed.[80] One set of military historians noted that the marines' retreat from the Chosin Reservoir "was an epic of courage, endurance, and loyalty to comrades." Conversely, the Chinese army, which opposed the marines, "could not reappear in the field until March, 1951."[81]

It is important to remember that the men of the 1st Marine Division "were almost evenly divided between Regulars and Reserves, the Reserves coming from a hundred and twenty-four selected cites in the nation," including C Company, 16th Infantry Battalion, Evansville, Indiana.[82] Not surprisingly, the gulf between regular and reservist would greatly diminish during the heat of the Chosin campaign. Col. Robert Taplett, in an interview for this book, remarked that "the majority of our replacements came from the reserve. They distinguished themselves in battle, both at the Chosin and at the ensuing breakout, particularly the reserves found in Item Company. This company was the primary unit involved in our breakout from the Chinese encirclement at Yudam-ni." Taplett further noted that when Item attacked Hill 1520 "a company of over two hundred men was reduced to twenty. But their actions were the key to our escape . . . to Hagaru." Taplett especially remembered many of the members of the Evansville reserve group, including "Tex Graham, Paul McDaniel, who was wounded on Hill 1520, and Sergeant [Gene] Koonce." From Taplett's point of view, there were no distinctions to be made "between a regular marine and a reserve marine."[83]

Marine reservists in North Korea soon came to understand how close they had come to death or to capture. Henry Maley, the reservist who had almost stayed in Japan, wrote to his wife telling her, "I can't describe to you how terrible everything was. I'm lucky, very lucky." Gordon Greene wrote his mother as soon as he could and told her, "One thing's for sure, I owe my life to God and to yours and everybody's prayers back home." Greene was just as solemn about his escape when he wrote a teenage friend, Bill Barnard. Usually Greene's letters to Barnard contained humorous stories and occasional macho posturing. Now, however, Greene wrote, "My luck has brought me through, I shouldn't say my luck for it is really my trust in God and I know this to be true, believe me. I haven't reached the Harvey Alpine stage, but I will go to church when I return." Barney Barnard penned his father in the middle of December, telling him, "Our trip back [from the reservoir] cost us more than the public will ever know. A lot of our men didn't make it, and a lot of trucks, jeeps, and tanks, were pushed over the mountain side." Barnard was most proud of his work on the airstrip at Hagaru because "it saved several hundred lives by getting the wounded back for treatment. I consider it quite an honor to have worked on that strip. It was worth all the cold hands and feet I got there."

A Chinese colonel, who came to the Chosin area in late December 1950, became greatly absorbed by the many humped up human-shaped mounds of snow he observed as a driver took him along the former X Corps MSR. The mounds looked like the snowmen the colonel had made as a child in Manchuria. It was only when the car stopped and the colonel approached some of the strange snowmen that he realized he "was ringed by . . . snow-coated Chinese corpses." His driver told him there were thousands of these in the area. All told, the Chinese estimated that they lost forty thousand men to the cold, the combat, and the Americans' artillery and plane attacks. Later that evening the Chinese colonel, who had earlier discovered the nature of the frozen mounds of snow, stood in a command post at Chinhung-ni and watched a Chinese general softly tap on a wall map. "They're gone," he told the colonel. "We could not stop them."[84]

6   *It Looks as if I Were Mad at Something*

About the time X Corps was fighting its way to Hungnam and
evacuation, Gen. Walton Walker's beleaguered 8th Army abandoned northwest Korea and quickly scrambled south. Because of
the speed of their retreat, the Chinese were unable to pursue or
attack Walker's fleeing men, enabling the 8th Army to establish a
new line of defense at about the thirty-eighth parallel. There
Walker waited anxiously to see what the Chinese would do next.
Ironically, the situation of October 1950 was now reversed. Now it
was China's turn to decide if they would seek to drive across the
thirty-eighth parallel. Meanwhile, American morale sank once
more. Nevertheless, the situation offered more security than
when UN forces had been split apart and scattered far from main
supply bases. More important, the UN supply lines back to the seaport of Pusan had been substantially shortened. Now units could
more easily replace lost weapons and vehicles, as well as stock up
on other necessities of war. The proximity of the Chinese and
their spectacular success, however, placed every American soldier
under great mental strain. Hundreds of thousands of enemy soldiers were believed to be close by, "within one day's march," and
Walker's new defensive line looked vulnerable to an all-out Chinese attack.[1]

While the 8th Army held its collective breath along the thirty-eighth parallel, the 1st Marine Division began a well-earned rest. The ships that carried the division from Hungnam transported the marines to the safety of the Pusan area, to the town of Masan, dubbed the "Bean Patch" back when it had been used by the 1st Provisional Marine Brigade in those difficult days of July and August earlier that year. The Bean Patch was a large cultivated area with room to spare for all three marine infantry regiments. The division was soon placed in reserve in order to "build up the physical condition of men who had lost weight during the Chosin Reservoir operations." The commander of naval forces in the Far East quickly responded to the food needs by sending fifty thousand rations of turkey, causing General Smith to declare that his marines "had turkey coming out of their ears."[2] The environment was certainly an improvement over what the marines had endured up north. One marine reservist from Indiana wrote home, telling his family, "Our tents are set up in neat rows with small sidewalks that we have made of rocks running between them. They gave us cots last night, and it's quite a relief to get off the ground." The private added, "The officers have electric lights but the wiremen have not reached the peons yet."[3] Another Hoosier reservist wrote his father that the rest had turned him "into a bum. I never want to get up in the morning or go to bed at night."[4]

Christmas was a time of great healing for the weary marines. Gordon Greene joyfully wrote his mother about all the packages from home that had finally arrived just in time for the Christmas season: "Boy, I have really been getting packages. I got the two from you that had the lighter, the pen, and the canasta deck, and the one with the candy and nuts. . . . I got the socks, and the loafers, but I haven't put them on yet." Three other packages came to Greene from "Mrs. Barnard, Mrs. Dickson, and Mrs. Fitch." On Christmas the marines were treated to "a meal of ham and turkey." Greene told his mother of the "huge Christmas tree near the mess tent with decorations." A choir of the 5th Marines serenaded Division Headquarters "with carols on Christmas Eve."[5] The entire division observed the holidays with special intensity, for they had much for which to be thankful. Greene told his mother that he was going to start going to church services "as long as there are services available to us."

Along with a spirit of thankfulness, a thread of dissatisfaction concerning the turn the war had taken started to creep into letters home. Barney Barnard declared, around Christmas, that he and his fellow marines "are hoping that the government will make some kind of peace treaty." Gordon Greene concurred with his friend's wish for a quick end to the war. "I sure hope the present situation is settled by some peaceful movement," he told his mother. However, many marines who now lounged around the Bean Patch believed that the war would likely escalate into a global conflict. Wrote one, "We would all like to have a little state-side duty before the Russians jump in."[6] More immediate problems arose, however.

One of the major concerns the recuperating marines now faced was a shortage of equipment. Often the army seemed to be given priority in the matter.[7] In terms of motor transport, the situation was ironic given the fact that the marines had brought out most of the vehicles from the Chosin while the 8th Army had lost so many of theirs. Although the supply situation would slowly improve, the marines never seemed to have as much available to them as the army. Evansville reservist David Graham recalled "how the marines were always short of adequate food, shoes, and clothing. Once, when my boondockers had been completely worn out, I complained to the sergeant, but he wasn't able to help. Then I heard that a nearby army unit was giving their men new boots and piling the old ones up for Korean civilians." Graham hurried over to the shoe pile and found "some better boots than I had. The next day a colonel came to our unit and pulled an inspection. When he saw my army combat boots he shouted, 'What in the hell is this?' and threatened me with a court-martial for being out of uniform." Luckily for Graham, the colonel ordered the sergeant to find the reservist some proper footwear. Graham also recalled a shortage of good food when the marines were not in combat. When Graham's mother saw in several photos how thin her son had grown, she became very upset. "You could count every one of my ribs in one of those pictures," Graham recalled. "When I went in I weighed about 185 pounds. I was down to about 130 in the picture. I'd never been skinny before."

Resting marines also had time to ponder their ambivalence regarding the war and the Korean population for which they were supposed to be fighting. Writing home soon after the brutal Chosin campaign, one bitter reservist from Indiana declared, "We don't want this country. It isn't worth fighting for."[8] Some marines held a low opinion of the Korean people as well, seeing them as "gooks" who could, in the words of one marine, best serve "to wash all my clothes."[9] Coming from a more technically advanced culture, American marines were unprepared for the shock of living in a third world nation. Because the Koreans spread human waste on their fields, for example, there was an odor to the countryside that was difficult for Americans to get used to. "You could smell Korea before you saw it," remembered one Hoosier reservist.[10]

American news media also often conveyed a negative image of Korea to the American public. *Newsweek,* for example, painted a rather sordid picture of Korea and its people: "When the books on the Korean War are written, they aren't going to reflect a backdrop of friendly chateaux, farm houses, and warm barns—convenient back-area cities—as have books on wars in Europe. Korea is not that kind of country. It vaguely resembles the Northwest Frontier of India—rugged, barren hills, tracks instead of highways, wretched huts, and a treacherous peasantry." The article went on to note, "The gray thatched huts are repellent outside, dark, dirty, and malodorous inside." One group of Koreans was described in the article as a "string of natives who seem eternally to be straggling along the roadsides toward some place that couldn't possibly be worth reaching. There are expressionless women, balancing 50-pound bundles on their heads, tough little men, 'A' frames on their backs, scroungers with packing cases under their arms, hurrying home to make a fire, and the inevitable white-clad elders with fly-trap hats, 2-foot pipes, and impenetrable, pathetic dignity."[11]

Closer to Evansville, the local Oakland City, Indiana, paper carried a negative piece about Korea that emphasized the horrible smell that dominated the Korean countryside.[12] Not all newspaper reports, however, were critical. In a syndicated piece, one war correspondent, Hal Boyle, related an especially sympathetic story about the suffering of the Korean people. In a letter addressed to his wife, Boyle wrote of the agony of a Korean mother who gave birth to a baby in a "frozen road side ditch." Such ditches, the reporter noted, "have been the birth bed for many a young Korean in recent weeks." The letter, written around Christmas 1950, added that among some Americans in Korea "there is a sense of guilt about trying to celebrate Christmas in an atmosphere of temporary plenty in a country that lives in perpetual need."[13]

In the minds of some marines, there seemed to be little difference between the North and South Koreans, causing tensions to further rise when marines went out on patrol. Sometimes near-atrocities occurred. In the relatively calm period between the rest at the Bean Patch and the fifth Chinese offensive in April, a marine patrol from Charlie Company, 1st Battalion, came upon a village and encountered a sniper. One marine was shot between the eyes. William Etheridge recalled "how our lieutenant and captain just blew their stacks. 'Flush them out,' we were told. We took our bayonets and ripped doors open and threw in white phosphorous grenades." The marines were "able to gun down about fifteen guerrillas, but once the roofs got on fire the whole village went up in flames." North Korean guerrillas had hidden supplies there, including ammunition in the thatched roofs and "fifty gallon drums buried underneath the floors. It all went up." Syngman Rhee filed a protest over the incident, but the marines, because of the sniper and the hidden enemy supplies, felt the action was justified.

Although cases of outright physical cruelty on the part of the marines toward the Korean civilians were extremely rare, many Americans typically held a low opinion of the people they were supposedly helping. Often this led to humorous but harsh behavior. In his unpublished novel "Boondockers," Gordon Greene related several incidents of marines' abusive treatment of civilians he had witnessed. In one episode a marine riding in a convoy of trucks tossed a lighted match on an old man's straw-loaded A-frame: "The fire spread rapidly until the entire load was ablaze high on his back." As the marine trucks "rounded a bend in the road the [Americans'] last view of the papa-san was one of the old fellow getting out of the A-frame, fanning the flames with his hat, and shaking his fist at the remainder of the passing trucks." The incident, noted Greene in the novel, "was most beneficial to the morale of the Marines on the trucks. For some, it was the first real laugh in weeks."[14] Such behavior is even more disturbing when the Korean emphasis on respect for the elderly is taken into consideration.

Not all the Evansville reservists agreed with the unfavorable assessments of some marines regarding Korea and its people. Carl Barnett remembered the daily life of the Koreans he observed as rural and somewhat exotic: "Farmers used oxen to pull wooden plows. They gathered grain by hand, using scythes and separated the grain by throwing it up into the air." The southern Indiana man recalled that the people seemed to be living "in biblical times." Many marines were amazed at the tremendous amount of weight the Koreans could tote on their A-frames. Barnett, for example, witnessed a little boy "not much over ten carrying a rail road tie strapped to his back" and took a snapshot of the sturdy child because he did not think anyone back home would believe him when he told the story. "They were hardy people," he recalled. "The little kids would skate on wooden skates in the cold winter weather wearing these dresslike outfits, and it would be so cold their skin would just turn blue."

Bob Whitehouse, another Evansville reservist, felt so sorry for the Korean children that he frequently bought apples from them even when his squad had more than enough. Finally his fellow marines grew so frustrated, they began chiding him by saying, "Jesus Christ, Bob, not more apples!" In another instance, Whitehouse and some other marines came across a small band of Korean civilians, "just kids and the very elderly," who were hiding from the Chinese and North Koreans. "We'd been throwing some of our rations that we didn't like over the ridge, and when I saw the condition of those people, I ran back and got our squad to scrounge up the tossed cans. Those people were so hungry it was all they could do to wait while we opened the rations up."

Reservist Bud Fitch's first impression of Korea was also quite different from that of most of the other marines. "We are lying in the harbor," he wrote home. "Korea is a beautiful country to look at, lots of mountains with snow on them." Fitch showed a particular tenderheartedness for the Korean civilians, who had suffered so much. In another letter to his parents, he described one of the few pleasures of his duty: "I like to go down in the valleys and 'liberate' the small towns. The people return to their homes when they see us in the town, and they seem genuinely glad to see us." The young Hoosier, taking a kind interest in the people, added, "I always like to try to talk to them and learn a few words."

Another reservist who came to sympathize with the struggle of the Korean people was William Wright. One of the most disturbing sights

Wright witnessed was how, after a battle, Korean civilians would "tie their dead on their backs and walk with them. They'd squat down once in a while to rest, then get up and keep going. I guess they were bringing a family member home to bury. It's hard to understand how they could bear all the tragedy around them." Wright also witnessed great masses of moving humanity as civilians tried to escape the ravages of war. "They'd carry what few things they had in bundles on their heads. Sometimes you'd see a child leading a person who was blinded, or shot up, by a rope."

The Chinese apparently had little regard for the Koreans. Wright recalled a time when he and some other marines came into a small village that the Chinese had just abandoned: "Everyone in the village was dead and the women had been raped. Even the children were dead." Another time Wright came to a Korean hut and stumbled upon an elderly woman. "This lady was holding a baby and they were both crying," he recalled. "I ran up to see what I could do for her and saw her daughter was lying on the floor, nude, where she had been raped and killed. I was determined that I was going to bring the old woman and child back something to eat." When Wright returned with the food, however, the woman and baby were gone. "I never found out what happened to them." Often Wright observed people "just walking around. They didn't know where they were, you know. They were just dazed." Later Wright and a group of marines adopted a parentless boy of about seven whom they found walking alone and near death. "He was in the street, and we stopped and talked to him, and he couldn't talk, he was so congested. His nose was running, and he couldn't talk. And he was cold, so I put my coat around him and took him back about twenty miles to the jeep, back where our group was, and we took care of him and got him well. He didn't want to leave us."

Perhaps Wright's most vivid memory of the simple humanity of Korean civilians was of the time when his group was pulling out of a village about to be attacked by the Chinese: "As we were leaving this town, an old man and his wife ran out of their house with all their bundles of stuff on their back. They came out their gate and started running down the road to join us. But then the old man stopped and went back and latched that gate before catching up with us. I doubt that house was there when he got back, but he latched that gate anyway. It struck me as something any of us would do who had ever cared for a home. I just prayed his house was there when he got back." Most of those who fought in Korea would always carry a mixed bag of feelings concerning the civilian population. There were those, however, like William Wright, who aggressively tried to make a real difference.

All through the beginning of 1951, the enemy buildup north of the thirty-eighth parallel continued at an alarming rate. By the last day of March, MacArthur estimated that the ground total of enemy forces was just shy of half a million, with about that many more in reserve in Manchuria.[15] Earlier, on 8 January, Gen. Matthew Ridgway, who had replaced General Walker after Walker's death in a jeep accident on 23 December, urgently requested that General Smith send a marine regiment to the central part of the American lines to back up an army unit there. Smith balked at breaking up the division, and, consequently, Ridgway quickly decided not to split the marines into smaller groups. As a result of Ridgway's and Smith's discussions, the entire 1st Marine Division was deployed without delay on a line from Andong to Yondok.[16] Although the marines could have used more precious rest time after the horrors of the Chosin, the need to move the division up to where the action was took precedent. The Chinese had hurled one offensive at the parallel on the western side near Seoul on New Year's Eve, pushing back the American defense line. The move of the 1st Division to shore up the central and eastern side of the main defense line took almost a week.

On 22 January, marine units had their first encounter with the enemy in their new area of operations. William Etheridge's and Albert Dickson's company flushed out a guerrilla force several miles southeast of Andong, but the enemy quickly "disappeared into the winter dusk."[17] Many reservist and regular marines were now growing weary of the fighting. Gordon Greene wrote his mother that "maybe it was meant for me to be in a line company, but I sure wish I could get out of it." In another letter in January, Greene reported hopefully, "We stopped digging our foxholes today. Someone said something about a cease-fire. . . . I sure hope they come to some kind of solid agreement soon." His wish to leave almost came true on 15 January. "Yesterday I thought for a minute I could get out of here," Greene related. While he was riding in a truck convoy, a huge tree limb had struck him. "It shoved off my helmet and hit my arm. The first thing that came to my mind was 'now I can go to Japan.'" When a doctor examined Greene's arm, he found it only bruised "and the muscle swollen. So all I could get out of it was two days and no duty."

Greene wasn't the only marine reservist who had grown tired of the war and wished for home. Greene's Oakland City friend, Barney Barnard, wrote about the same time as Greene's accident, "I am being worked too hard here [and] . . . would like to have a little state-side duty." Barnard also feared he would soon have to go over to China and fight but wished instead "to get back to the States before I'm old and gray." Letters home from marines now often mentioned the possibility of being rotated home, a hope that seemed to replace the former home-by-Christmas wish. Gordon Greene wrote his mother in late January, "We have heard that all the guys who were . . . up north are to be relieved starting March 15, and I hope it is true." Another reservist mentioned the possibility of leaving in a letter home in early February but cautioned his family that such rotations "will be in the future."[18] Meanwhile, the war continued, though in somewhat low-key fashion, for marines. Unknown to them was the preparation being made by the Chinese for one great final push designed to throw the Americans out of Korea.

One thing Gordon Greene thought he would not have to worry about in early January was his best friend Bud Fitch coming to Korea and facing the dangers of combat. "Fitch has a good deal sitting back there in the States," Greene observed to his mother. Indeed, Gordon Greene's friend had made himself a lucky break early in his training. Fitch had gone to communications school out in San Diego in October 1950 and had achieved one of the highest scores among a large group of marines on his final test. That score, coupled with his poor eyesight, offered Greene's friend a chance to stay out of combat. To Greene's surprise, however, he later found out Bud Fitch was coming over anyway. Greene was greatly distressed by his friend's decision, telling his mother that he could not "understand why Fitch is coming over when he doesn't have to. I know he would like to see us, but you have to draw the line somewhere." Years later Greene wrote that "Bud didn't have to go into a combat situation, but had volunteered to do so in order to be able to tell 'sea stories' when we all returned."[19] Before he boarded a ship for Korea, Fitch went home to Oakland City, Indiana, for Christmas furlough. "It is swell that Bud could come home for Christmas," Barney Barnard observed in early January. "At least one of us from Oakland City made it home."

The last night of Bud Fitch's furlough home, a close friend, Bill Barnard, stayed overnight at the Fitch's house on Oak Street. Mrs. Fitch had already experienced a disturbing premonition that she would not see her son again.[20] Barnard recalled how "in the morning Mrs. Fitch asked me to drive Bud down to the train station at Evansville. On the way down, Bud quietly said to me, 'I don't think I am coming back.'" Barnard tried to talk his friend out of his dismal mood, but the teenager seemed to be unable to let go of his own gloomy premonition. Later Fitch seemed to shake off this foreboding state, writing his grandfather upon his return to camp, "Your letter with the money was waiting for me when I got back from Xmas leave, and although I'm a little late, I want to thank you very much for it."

When Bud sailed westward in late January 1951, the marines in central Korea began to see more activity. The weather brought snow, but often a warm sun turned the ground into a muddy mess. "Everything is so muddy that a person can hardly walk around," wrote one marine.[21] Signs were also beginning to appear that new and savage fighting might soon erupt. About this time Evansville reservist Jim Stearsman found himself on a patrol sent out to get the division ready to move north when his group came upon a bridge. The squad quickly moved to check the structure for booby traps: "Suddenly it became evident that there were people under there, and at first we assumed they were either Korean or Chinese. We were pretty nervous at that point, not knowing exactly what we faced. Our interpreter told them that if they came out they would not be harmed." When no one answered, Stearsman, on a hunch, hollered out in English, "'Hey, we're American marines!' Apparently our interpreter's first words had convinced the fellows under there that we were Chinese." Finally two haggard Americans stumbled out from under the bridge. "They had been captured by the Chinese but had somehow managed to escape. One had a severe wound in the leg, and the other one had literally lost his mind from stress." Under the bridge, Stearsman's group found a large cache of ammunition. "You could tell the Chinese were getting ready for a big push." Ironically, among the supplies were boxes of .45 ammo made in Evansville, Indiana, during World War II. The ammunition had been given to the Nationalist Chinese during the late 1940s.

Bud Fitch arrived in Korea on 16 February and was sent as a replacement to the 1st Battalion, 7th Regiment. Gordon Greene grew frantic about seeing his friend and giving him advice regarding combat. "We have been getting a lot of new men in steady now," Greene told his mother. "I go out and ask if there's anyone from Indiana, hoping that Fitch might be one of them." In another letter Greene asked his mother to "send Fitch's address when he gets into an outfit over here so I can look him up." Barney Barnard saw Fitch in late March. "I went over and found Bud Fitch this afternoon. It was really good seeing him again. He had just come off the line three days ago." Barnard noted that his boyhood friend "was in great spirits, but he wants to come home, just as we all do."

In late March, Barnard had an urge to go see Fitch again. "I am going over to see Bud tomorrow," Barnard wrote his mother. "His outfit is moving, and it may be a long time before I get to see him again." Bud Fitch also wrote his parents about the encounter, telling them how "Barney walked up and surprised me the other day. He is about two miles down the road. . . . He gave me an orange, the first one I had since I left the ship." At this same time Gordon Greene was still desperately trying to get in touch with his friend. Greene asked his mother to try again to get his address "in case we're near the 7th sometime." By April, Greene had Fitch's address but was still unable to physically be with his friend to offer advice about combat. At least now, Greene was able to keep tabs on his hometown buddy. "Fitch is on line now," Greene wrote on 8 April. On the twelfth, Greene finally got a letter from Fitch and noted to his mother that his best friend seemed rather subdued but was otherwise "alright." After this time the two young men began to correspond regularly, since it only took "three days to get mail in the Division." Likely the two reservists shared how much they missed the quiet life back in Oakland City.

Bud Fitch's fateful journey in Korea is chronicled in a number of letters he wrote to family members from February to April 1951. He wrote his parents upon his arrival in February, worriedly confiding to them, "I suppose we will be committed before long. Kind of a rude shock. . . . I am assigned to the 7th Marines, although I wanted to be in the 1st, where Gordon [Greene] and Al [Dickson] are." In a letter written about two weeks later, the lonely reservist noted, "Well, the picnic is over. . . . There are nineteen of us in this tent. We sleep on the ground and have gear piled all around. . . . We have some oil lamps and I can't hardly see to write." Somewhat exasperated, Fitch further reported, "After all my training in telephone, then as a rifleman, I got put in mortars."

As time passed, Fitch grew more accustomed to his surroundings. In one letter he wrote, "I got a mat made out of rice straw . . . and it keeps the cold from coming up off the ground. I also got a haircut from a native barber for one package of cigarettes. We get issued packs of cigarettes and they are good for trading." Fitch was especially amazed at the difference between the U.S. Army and the Marine Corps in terms of supplies. "The Army sure has a lot of gear," he noted. "It amazes me all the luxuries they have in their camp. They even have tents with stoves and around their heads. [Even] the Koreans have more candy in their shops than we have in our PXs."

By late February the Oakland City reservist was beginning to experience the difficulties of combat: "It took us three days to move up to the line. . . . We ended up on open trucks all the way. The roads were bad, and we had to wait for hours to ford a stream where a bridge was blown out. It sure got cold, and my rear end is flat. There are some gooks laying around, but they are frozen so they don't smell." On the first month's anniversary of Fitch's arrival in Korea, the teenage reservist sounded more like an old hand, writing his parents, "We are waiting for an air strike on a hill we have to take. The 5th Marines (who have been in reserve) were supposed to take this objective, but they didn't get here in time so the 7th is going ahead. We are now taking the city of Hongchon, which will put us about 8 miles from the 38th. The first battalion is taking the mountains overlooking it. . . . We just came down after fifteen days on the mountain."

Getting supplies turned out to be a difficult task. Fitch related in March how "a lot of times up there they couldn't get chow to us, and there was hardly any water. I thought maybe we would get a chance to wash up when we got down by some water, but we didn't even stop. We found a spring though and had some water to drink. Also we got some candy bars and a half loaf of bread to go with our rations." Fitch also experienced at this time the pain of seeing good friends wounded. "Bob O'Keefe (my buddy from Toledo) got hit in the arm pretty bad," he wrote. "Mortar shrapnel hit him. I think it hit his elbow too. Another buddy from Fort Wayne got evacuated on account of trench foot (the new scourge)." Fitch himself also suffered: "I have a spot on my little toe, but it's not worth turning in for. I got some frostbite that split up the skin on my knuckles but they are about healed now."

At this time the cold became a constant problem for Fitch and his marine comrades. Fitch noted, "I sweat while I am moving and then get cold when I stop. It's hard to write with mittens on." Another difficult element was the terrain upon which they fought. "It is *impossible*," Fitch declared, "to advance more than 3–5 miles during one day through this terrain, even if you don't meet any resistance." The views, however, were often breathtaking. "We will be standing on a ridge and way below is a valley you can hardly see. We go all the way down and all the way up the other side. It takes all day, and you haven't even gone a mile by map." Fitch added, "If someone would have told me a month ago I would be walking the distance I have with the loads I have carried, I would have told them they were crazy."

In late March, Fitch wrote home, telling of a new hope: "If we stop at the 38th, it won't be too long maybe before the war ends." In a letter written about the same time to his father, the eighteen-year-old marine observed, "We have reached the 38th almost all along the line now. If they decide not to cross, the fighting may come to a close." The young man qualified his hope by adding, "It's out of our hands now, for sure." Unfortunately, Fitch's hope would not be actualized. A 30 March letter now related how his outfit was beginning to see renewed action.

Letters from Bud Fitch to his family written in April begin to hint at a worsening situation. The reservist and his comrades were now beginning to stumble upon abandoned but heavily fortified Chinese bunkers. "The Chinese are sure dug in around here. You can sure tell they've been here quite a while." By 7 April, Fitch's group faced increasing resistance. "Just time for a short note," Fitch hurriedly wrote on this date. "The 3rd Battalion passed through us and took up the assault." The teenager's last letter home was written on 11 April, just shortly before he would participate in the biggest battle of the war: "The Chinese opened the gates on a big dam up the way, and the river is so high they can't get supplies across. They are afraid the Chinese will blow the dam and flood the whole valley." This last letter offered a vivid picture of Bud Fitch's life at this time. "It has been raining all day today," he wrote. "I am set up in a trench dug by the gooks and have a shelter over me, so I'm pretty dry." In closing, the young man, who actually was a strong student in high school, reflected, "You know, you are supposed to regret that you played around and didn't study hard in high school, but I don't feel that way at all." The letter was signed "Love, Bud."

While Bud Fitch and the rest of the Oakland City boys grew weary of the war that spring of 1951, the Chinese continued to prepare for the biggest push of the conflict. After two offensives had failed in January and February, the Chinese gathered strength for an even bigger attempt in late April. Toward the middle of that month, the 1st Marine Division had been sent to the area of the Hwachon Reservoir, about twelve miles north of the thirty-eighth parallel and near the middle of the American defense line. On 21 April, the 7th Marines, Bud Fitch's outfit, held the left side of the new marine line. The 5th Marines held the center, and a KMC (Korean Marine Corps) regiment anchored the right. The 1st Marines stood by in reserve. To the left of Bud's regiment, the 6th ROK Division had dug in, but somehow too great a gap between the South Koreans and the 7th opened up.

James Skinner, a Florida native and a member of Fitch's company, remembered how turbulent things were around this time. Skinner had joined Able on April Fool's Day and found the company gaining new replacements like himself at a rapid rate. "The enemy seemed to be dropping back and action was very light, mainly flushing out what seemed to be delaying forces," Skinner recalled. "We moved during daytime and dug in at night. A snow storm occurred one night. I thought I would melt some snow the next day to shave and take a bird bath before we moved out. The experience was so miserable that I never tried that again. It didn't take long for me to get as gamey and bearded as the 'Old' vets." The walking was especially difficult, Skinner remembered. "The terrain was rugged mountainous type. After getting to the top of one ridge there was always another to climb." Sydney Greenwood, a Philadelphia native, had, like Skinner, just come over to Able Company in April. He also remembered how little time existed for personal visits among the small scattered groups. "Many new reservists and regulars were now thrown together in an environment that was about to become hostile," Greenwood recalled. In this regard, the forthcoming battle would be very similar to the Chosin struggle.

On Sunday, 22 April, Louis Main, a member of the Evansville reserve unit, now with the 7th Marines, recalled suddenly seeing movement on the ridge of a nearby hill. A member of a three-man radio team, Main and some other men were setting up their equipment at that time. "Those are Chinese soldiers," Main said nervously, as he pointed to the ridge. "No, no," the other marines replied, "those are South Koreans." Main knew better. "Boys, the shit's going to hit the fan tonight," he predicted. That evening, a few minutes into the darkness, a flurry of bugles, sirens, whistles, gongs, and screams announced a colossal Chinese attack, with wave after wave of Chinese soldiers driving at the UN lines. In sheer numbers, the struggle of the next eight days would be the biggest battle of the war.[22] The 7th Marines took a particularly hard blow, and the marine lines were quickly penetrated. Chinese mortar rounds and hundreds of grenades began to rain down on them. For the next few days marines fought in a struggle "as heavy as anything at Inchon-Seoul or Chosin." The Chinese employed more artillery than usual, as well as using mortars and automatic weapons in support of human wave assaults.[23]

For the marines, the battle began on a perilous note. The 6th ROK Division, to the left of 1/7 and already dangerously separated from the marines, quickly disintegrated in the initial Chinese attack. Now the main enemy effort moved to the left of the 1st Division line where the understrength 7th Marines were dug in. With their flank exposed here, the marine lines were rapidly penetrated by the onslaught of Chinese soldiers. James Skinner would always remember that night of ferocious combat: "On April 22, we were moving up a ridge to get on a crest to dig in. I thought I had about reached my limit of endurance when several rounds of artillery from our rear slammed into our column just above me. I scampered down the ridge a short way and hit the deck." The blasts had actually been short rounds that exploded on top of a observer team, killing several marines. "It was eerie passing those bodies. I had to balance myself in order not to fall off the trail by placing my hands over the dead to move up to the ridge." By this time Skinner had forgotten his fatigue. He and the rest of the marines, after some difficult climbing, finally reached the crest of the hill and quickly prepared for the night. "The terrain was very rocky and I don't recall anyone being able to dig a proper hole," Skinner recalled.

The battle grew more intense as time passed. "It seems like only minutes later, maybe after midnight, small arms and automatic weapons firing started to our front," Skinner recalled. "I saw the muzzle flashes and they seemed to be firing across our front, a couple of hundred yards out, up into Charlie Company's position and apparently unaware of us. The Skipper passed the word to start firing and the enemy started paying attention to us. I scrambled around trying to find some cover to fire from. I got back on the ridge and flopped as low as I could get and pointed in the general direction at a muzzle flash with thoughts to zap that rascal the next time he fired."

Skinner had temporarily forgotten his combat training and initially approached the problem as if he were on the rifle range. However, "the Chinese were moving, so I realized well-aimed fire was not appropriate here. I started firing into the general area with my carbine." Suddenly an explosion rent the air around Skinner. "A sergeant was in the prone next to me, to my left about eight feet away, when a ChiCom concussion grenade went off between us. I just felt the blast real good and he received a small sliver of the casing next to his right eyeball. He said he was alright but was medevaced the next day, and I heard the sliver severed the optic nerve to his right eye." The fighting now began in earnest. "The areas were soon filled with white, blue and green tracers coming at us, thick enough to walk on it seems."

Later, Sydney Greenwood would write in a letter his recollection of that epic struggle: "On Sunday morning, April 22, we jumped off early in the morning. We walked down into a valley where we took a rest and some cold fresh water from a stream. We then walked up and down, through a stream and along a narrow dirt road." Greenwood had a strong feeling that the marines would be hit that night: "At dusk we started up the hill and I was stopped half way up. I spent that night in a building, and we heard the clatter of the weapons all that night. I remember saying to a marine next to me, 'If the chinks break through we will be done.'" The marine responded to Greenwood by reminding him, "Don't forget there are Marines on that hill." Greenwood emphasized, "That remark will last with me forever."

James Skinner remembered the most critical part of the battle that night: "At one point word came that our line had been penetrated on the left. The Skipper directed Lt. Nichols to close the line up again. Lt. Nichols took several marines and a bunch of grenades and did the job. Regretfully, Lt. Curry, and four or five of his marines of the mortar section, had been killed." Killed along with Lieutenant Curry was Bud Fitch. The young man was one day short of his nineteenth birthday. Syd Greenwood believed that the actions of Nichols, Fitch, and the other marines saved "the center of the UN line." Greenwood would later tell the Fitch family in a letter, "I read a New Hampshire paper in which the glaring headlines stated, 'Marines Save U.N. Disaster.' It told all about the heroic fighting your son and the other Marines did on April 22, and what would have happened if they hadn't." Greenwood himself was severely wounded that night. Downplaying the seriousness of his wounds to the Fitches, he told them, "It was not serious to me, as it got me out of that mess. It was a large piece of shrapnel that clipped me in the back of the left shoulder taking away . . . part of my shoulder blade." Greenwood ended his letter to the Fitches by telling them to "feel free anytime to ask any questions. I appreciate doing something for the family of someone who did so much for me on that night."[24]

The 22 April battle continued for several days. Initially the Chinese had been determined to break through the 7th Marine's line, hurtling two thousand men at the understrength battalion.[25] The 7th fought through three hours of furious combat, holding on until reinforcements from the 1st Battalion of the 1st Marines came rushing up to the left of 1/7 where the 6th ROKs had previously been. Now the division's flank was no longer "in the air."[26] In the 1/1 group were Gordon Greene, Albert Dickson, and William Etheridge. "When we left I knew we were going to be in a pretty big fight," recalled Etheridge. "They really loaded us up on the ammo and grenades. We were told we had to go plug up a hole where some ROKs had been." Etheridge's entire battalion "dug in on a hillside, and it seemed like my company, Charlie Company, was right on the end."

The next day Etheridge saw movement on another hill. "I asked the platoon leader if they were Chinese and he said, 'No, those are ROKs,' so we didn't call any artillery down on them." Etheridge had been correct; the men he spied were Chinese. After dark the Chinese attacked in mass against 1/1's positions. A marine officer from Charlie Company told how the Chinese came "in wave after wave, hundreds of them. They were singing, humming, and chanting, 'Awake Marines.' . . . In the first rush they knocked out both our machine guns, . . . putting a big hole in our lines." Charlie Company held "for about fifteen minutes under mortar fire, machine gun fire, and . . . hundreds of grenades." Finally the officer called for Charlie Company to withdraw. "All this was in the pitch-black night with Chinese cymbals crashing, horns blowing, and their god-awful yells."[27]

William Etheridge would never forget the Chinese bugle calls: "They started blowing bugles all up and down the line—one big shrill note." Etheridge's squad was quickly overrun. "A sergeant and I crawled around together up the hill where some more marines were dug in. Pretty soon all three companies, Able, Baker, and Charlie, got all mixed up. They were cut off for a while and did not get organized until daylight." Somehow Etheridge ended up in Baker Company in a foxhole with two other marines. A marine sergeant recalled the attack on Baker Company and how "the Chinese came at our position in waves and were supported by heavy machine gun fire. Much of the action was hand to hand."[28] Just before Etheridge dived into the hole with the Baker marines, a concussion grenade knocked him off his feet. "The other two fellows were glad to see me," he recalled, "glad to have the company with all the Chinese coming at us." Etheridge's new comrades carefully picked grenade fragments from Etheridge's wound and wanted to call for a corpsman. The hardy Evansville man, however, refused to have any help summoned. The next day Etheridge volunteered to go down the hill under gunfire and bring back a wounded marine. "I asked another fellow to watch my sleeping bag—they were invaluable, you know. When I returned, the sleeping bag was gone."

Some time during the 22 April battle, over in the 5th Marine Regiment area, Willard "Bill" Nemer, another Evansville reservist, attempted to rest after the rugged walk to the front lines at the Hwachon Reservoir. Two weeks earlier, Nemer had been approached by a marine reservist from Ohio: "I was scheduled to go off the line in a couple of weeks, and this fellow named Rogers asked me if he could take my place as the head wireman. I suppose he thought it would be a safer job than the one he had, though in reality a wireman's job was quite dangerous." Rogers was "a nice looking fellow who really missed his wife and two children. He was always flashing their pictures around us for everyone to see." When the 22 April battle erupted, the Ohio reservist was down the slope in a narrow valley with a machine-gun section. Nemer "caught a glimpse of the Chinese marching down through the valley, four abreast. They were jabbering away and obviously didn't know we were there. The Chinese ran right into our machine guns." Ross "Pappy" Compton, who worked with the machine-gun section "kept telling Rogers to keep his head down." In spite of the warning, the reservist made the fatal mistake of raising his head to see what was going on and received a mortal wound. Nevertheless, the marine machine guns tore to pieces the Chinese movement in that area. "Bodies were just piled up in front of our guns," Nemer remembered. "Unfortunately, the reservist Rogers and several other marines died in the action."

On the morning of 24 April, orders were received by the marines to pull back to a new defense line. The hurried movement south was again reminiscent of the Chosin campaign. "We walked and walked and walked," remembered William Etheridge. Evansville reservist Robert Egan recalled "being chased. Tex Graham sat at a point where he watched the Chinese massing for another attack. I was on another side of a hill and saw a company of Chinese walk right into our machine guns." Sometime during the late April battle, Tex Graham had led a mortar team up to the line to lend support to the marines fighting off the waves of Chinese. For this quick and valorous action, Graham would receive a Bronze Star. Another Hoosier reservist, Charles Gottman, watched as a great pile of marine ammunition and grenades was booby-trapped. "Shortly after we pulled out we heard this tremendous explosion." Ironically, Gottman would soon come close to death after he was transferred from infantry to the supposedly safer job of motor transport: "I would take a wrecker up into the mountains and bring back breakdowns. Coming back one night I got my windshield blasted out by a sniper."

James Skinner also experienced some difficult moments during the withdrawal. "Early the next morning," he recalled, "the Skipper informed us that when the word was passed we were to run off the hill. This caused me some concern as the bottoms of my feet were one solid blister, and I'm sure most of the others had the same problem. I decided I would hobble the best I could behind the company and if the gooks caught up with me I would expend all my ammo and grenades and try to die bravely." Fortunately for Skinner, "the rain and tanks churning made the mud soft, and I found the going easier on my blistered feet."

When the 22 April battle ended some eight days later, many American fighting men felt the battle had gone to the Chinese. On the contrary, UN forces had slowly been turning the tide of the war since February. Ridgway, in particular, had brought forth a new fighting spirit in the 8th Army, and the marines continued to do their typical excellent work. Although UN forces had ceded about thirty-five miles of real estate and had been forced off the thirty-eighth parallel, Seoul had been defended from the Chinese and the enemy had suffered seventy thousand casualties, compared to seven thousand UN casualties. Clay Blair, the noted Korean War historian, pointed out that the battle was a "magnificent victory" for UN forces. The American effort "had repulsed and savaged" the greatest Chinese offensive. "Beyond that, the battle must have caused great concern in Peking."[29]

As the April battle wound down, marine survivors began to seek out their friends. Gordon Greene and Albert Dickson found one another as they came off a hill to go into reserve. Later that day someone snapped a photo of Greene, Dickson, William Etheridge, and Bob Whitehouse, along with two other marines of the old Evansville reserve group. The photo later appeared in an Evansville paper with the caption "Evansville Marine buddies rejoin after fight." Gordon Greene, who carried the company nickname "Chick" because his youthful face lacked whiskers, looks to have aged ten years in the picture. Greene's greatest concern, however, now centered on what had happened to his best friend from Oakland City, Bud

Fitch. Greene wrote to his mother during the fighting in April, telling her, "You know I told you that we were in reserve in my last letter. Well we were called up during the night to fill in the gaps. Albert is alright, I saw him this morning. I don't know about Bud. We passed through them, but I did-n't have time to inquire about him." In a letter dated on the last day of the battle, Greene wrote, "We're resting today by a little stream. Everybody is stripped and out in the water. Sure is refreshing to get some of the dust and crud off again. We are close to the 7th Marines at present so I'll try to look for Bud whenever I can." Greene added, bitterly, "I've gone through another withdrawal. . . . This is getting mighty old, being pushed back and going up again. Nobody is content anymore."

In early May, Greene wrote his mother that Albert Dickson, who had received a wound in late April was "alright." Alarmingly, however, Greene reported he "hadn't heard from Bud for sometime." By the next letter, Greene was greatly disturbed about not hearing from Bud Fitch: "Every-thing is calm here, we're still sitting up here on the same hill, been here about four days now. Albert went back for glasses. He'll get a rest back there I think. I haven't heard a thing from Fitch. I am getting a little uneasy. Since this counter offensive began, I haven't heard a thing." Shortly afterward, Greene heard the shocking news. "I still can't believe Fitch is gone," he wrote his mother, "but we will just have to face it." Greene seemed to blame himself for Fitch's death. The Oakland City native lamented, "I had gotten two letters from him since he got over here, and I tried but I could never get close enough to his outfit to look him up." Greene ended the letter by asking his mother to "go over and see Bud's parents. They have been very good to me."

In another letter, to some Oakland City neighbors, Greene wrote of the 22 April battle and of the death of his best friend, "I am well, and very thankful to be, for I know of many instances that but for the aid of God I would never have made it. He has truly been good to me. Yesterday was the first official word that I had gotten concerning Bud. As soon as we got back to our present position, I went over to his outfit to check on how he made it, and one of the guys said he didn't. I wasn't going to believe it until I had heard from home, but it has actually happened, I guess. It will sure be hard for his parents. I plan to write them, but it will be a hard letter to write. If I get home soon it would be much easier to talk to them." In a letter written 9 May 1951 to his friend Bill Barnard, Greene, almost beside himself about his friend's death declared, "Boy, I'm so nervous I can hardly write. Your letter was the first to tell me about Bud. I had heard from one of the guys in his company but I sure as hell wouldn't believe it. I guess it happened the night the chinks started their counterdrive on April 22nd. We were several miles from his outfit and fought our way back by the 24th. God is still with me, and I keep praying every day, never missing, that someone will wake up to the fact that one of us has given his life and still nothing has been accomplished."

The news also stunned the other Oakland City boys who had gone so eagerly into the reserve together. Barney Barnard wrote his mother, who was a neighbor and close friend to Mrs. Fitch, "I suppose you have heard the news by now. It has been long enough for the official notice to go through. Bud's section was overrun, and he was the first one to go down. Four others were killed at the same place." William Marshall wrote home from boot camp in San Diego. "It's sure too bad about Fitch. I sent his family a sympathy card yesterday. I didn't say anything, though," the eighteen year old sadly wrote. "There wasn't any use to say anything." Gordon Greene seemed to have the greatest trouble accepting Bud's death. "Is there any more news about Bud? Tell me what news there is about him," he wrote his mother in late May. Greene also tried to assure his mother at this point that he would come home alive: "Now don't worry about me. No Chinaman is going to get me down. It will be about July when I'll be rotated, so I'll get to eat some of the things from your garden."

Albert Dickson, the Eagle Scout and Boy Scout leader, was the next Oakland City lad to suffer. In May, when the 1st Division advanced back north toward the Hwachon Reservoir, Dickson had been sitting down with the three other members of his fire team to eat when a Chinese mortar shell landed in their midst. The blast killed the two South Korean marines and severely injured Dickson and the other American marine. The Oakland City man would lose his spleen and a kidney and receive more than 150 stitches. Dickson was sent to Japan, then quickly back to the United States to convalesce.

Gordon Greene, who had lost two of his closest friends, one to death, grew increasingly homesick. "I sure miss strawberries and watermelon. That's all I'm going to eat when I get back," he told his family in June after Dickson had gone back home. Greene, like so many reservists plucked from home and sent to Korea, now found the monotony, discomfort, and occasional danger of a line company almost beyond bearing. "I'd leap for joy if I could just get out of a line company," he declared to his mother. The young Oakland City man had certainly changed his views since the early days of the war when he wished "to show the communists their place." Barney Barnard wrote in the same vein in late May: "We are all tired from so long on the line, and it seems that we must keep on pushing ahead whenever we can." In late June, Barnard observed, "There is quite a lot of talk about calling a halt to the fighting. That would be great, but not many of the men are getting excited about it. . . . It still looks dark on getting out of Korea. There aren't many replacements coming in, and we are way under strength. I have not let my hopes get too high." In August, toward the end of his Korean tour, Barnard wrote, "I'm not going on any patrols this time—the law of averages you know. I'm going to stay in camp unless ordered out from now on. No more volunteering."

Many years later Gordon Greene wrote of this time in a diary he kept while bicycling across the country to raise money for a monument to Korean veterans: "It must have been May or June of 1951. One of those months of the rainy season. Although fuzzy, I had an image of our platoon winding its way along a finger of a ridgeline during a downpour of rain. Always a finger leading into a larger ridgeline. That was the way it was each day as we plodded onward toward the 38th Parallel."[30] The occasional battles marines now endured were still ferocious. One marine sent home a picture of "some of the Chinks that tried to break through last May. . . . There were nine hundred laying out in front of our lines."[31] Living conditions on the line had not changed either. One reservist told his family back in the United States that he had not bathed in over a month. "In between I wash my face and hands and sometimes my feet," he wrote. "Some days our outfit will pull back, and then we will get a little rest and be able to wash when we want to."[32]

As the war went on, it became more difficult for the marines—reservists and regulars alike—to see why they were fighting in Korea. Especially vocal about the war were some of the veterans who came back after the Chosin. One Evansville reservist, Paul McDaniel, who had been severely wounded up at Yudam-ni, spoke at a meeting of the Evansville, Indiana, Junior Chamber of Commerce in January 1951. Now on crutches, the wounded reservist told his audience that "America should get out of Korea. One American life is worth a million Chinese or Korean, and we ought to save the lives of our boys."[33] Others shared McDaniel's views. Albert Dickson, another severely wounded reservist, wrote back to his college newspaper, the *O.C. Collegian,* in March 1951, telling his fellow students, "I would like to say that Gordon [Greene] and I really miss the students and teachers. . . . Maybe through the teachers and preachers we can do something to educate the people of the evils of war."[34] In an interview with a local Evansville paper, an Evansville reservist, Henry Maley, who had just returned from Korea noted, "A lot of the boys say they are glad to be in Korea, because they might be stopping the Russians from moving. But at the same time they are asking when it's going to end."[35] Reservists' letters written at this time demonstrated the hope many marines had that the war would soon end by some means, even if not by all-out victory.

In January 1951, Gordon Greene complained to a friend, "This damn place would drive Joe Chink himself back into Manchuria. No kiddin', if I don't get out of this place, I'll crack up." Greene's mood darkened throughout the first half of the year. In June the young reservist wrote the same friend, telling him, "Things are getting a little too rough." The Chinese, Greene related, were using "artillery and mortars and we've spotted some tanks." Worse still, Greene told how his company "is shot. We've got a corporal for a platoon sergeant and so many replacements at one time can foul up an outfit when thrown into combat for the first time. The guys they're sending over must be scrubs, for the outfit isn't the fighting unit it was last winter."

In July, Greene wrote that he believed "there might be a chance for a cease fire" but admitted he couldn't "be too optimistic." Then, in August, Greene became despondent again due to the departure of several of his former comrades: "Last night we had a big one for the guys going home[,] . . . some of my best buddies. It's like seeing your brothers leaving." In September Greene's luck finally turned, and he sustained a combat injury to his foot. While recovering in a hospital in Japan, he sat for a local artist to have his portrait drawn. "I'm sending a sketching of myself which was made by a Japanese artist," he wrote his mother in October. Unaware perhaps of the extent of his own grief and pain over Bud Fitch's death and his own suffering, he told his mother that the sketch was "not very good because I think I look as if I were mad at something." Truly the young man had much about which to be angry.

During the last week of August 1951, Barney Barnard received word that he was to be rotated back home. "It is really hard to believe after all these months. I won't feel safe until after I get on the ship. You know anything can happen." Obviously in a good mood, the Oakland City man added, "The sun has just come out and it's really making the tent steam. It feels good though, just for a change. It will be so nice to get out of this country and this weather." Like Barnard, those Evansville reservists who had not been killed or injured while serving in Korea hoped to return home in late summer or early fall of 1951. Many experienced narrow escapes. Jack Burgdorf was spared death in an odd fashion. He was just emerging from a foxhole when an almost spent .30-caliber bullet entered his shoulder. The projectile came to stop in Burgdorf's back. Had the marine received the full force of the bullet, he would have likely been killed. Doctors decided it would be safer to leave the bullet where it was, giving the Evansville man a most unusual souvenir to take home. Bill Nemer was looking through a set of powerful field glasses, calling in artillery fire, when he heard a strange pop. Nemer turned to see a fellow marine, who had been kneeling beside him, laying on the ground and holding his head. "A Chinese bullet had gone through the marine's right eye and came out the forward side of his head at an angle," he recalled. "His other eyeball had been popped out of its socket by the impact and was hanging down on his cheek." Nemer quickly gave the wounded marine blood expander to keep the man from going into shock. Then the quick-thinking Evansville man "gently worked the eyeball back into the socket and wrapped the marine's head in wet bandages." Because of Nemer's quick actions, the wounded marine kept the use of his right eye.

On 31 October 1951, Evansville reservist Jess Thurman trudged down a mountain, breathing a silent prayer of thanks. His squad had just been relieved after a ferocious night's action on the front line. He was one of only seven in his squad uninjured in this battle—his last. It was almost time for the marine to go home to Evansville. First, however, Thurman was assigned to bring some replacements to his squad. After locating a couple of available marines in the valley, Thurman spread his poncho on the ground and knelt to sort rations and ammo for the new men. As he worked, the Indiana native thought of his young bride, Nina, the job waiting for him at International Harvester, and the stock car he and his brother would soon be racing again. Suddenly a powerful force knocked Thurman over backward. "I saw the sky between my feet as I tumbled," he recalled.

Thurman awoke three days later in Tokyo, Japan, strapped to a Striker bed, paralyzed from midchest down. Later he was told what had happened. As Thurman had been sorting the rations and ammo, a South Korean boy of about fifteen (one of several who helped carry the marines' supplies) had picked up a .45-caliber pistol left lying on a blanket after a marine had cleaned it. Curious, the boy had jacked the firing mechanism back, unknowingly loading a shell from the clip, and pulled the trigger. A bullet barreled down the hill, bounced off a water can, entered the front of Thurman's shoulder, and went on to sever his spine. Soon after the shooting, the South Korean police had arrived, wrestled the boy down, and left, purportedly taking him to police headquarters. The boy never got that far. A policeman had stopped on the roadside and shot the boy in the head, leaving him to die in a ditch. To Thurman, this only doubled the tragedy.

During the early portion of 1952, Evansville reservist Henry Orth Jr. would endure ferocious combat in the area around the Punchbowl and Luke's Castle. By this time the war had grown static, and only a few hundred yards separated the marines and their Chinese foe. In one instance Orth recalled how the Americans brought up a tank beyond the front line where the Chinese quickly disabled it. The next day, another tank went forward and got hit. Orth, watching through field glasses, quickly took over a heavy machine gun and fired at the Chinese lines in an attempt to help the disabled tank crew escape. "We went through twenty-two boxes of ammo," Orth recalled. "We saved the crew, but burned out the gun."

Unfortunately, the Chinese were able to zero in their mortars on Orth's position: "We pulled back, but the Chinese apparently still had us zeroed in. One round hit just in front of us, knocking me unconscious. When I woke up, I yelled that I'd been hit." Orth did not want anyone to call for a corpsman just yet, for he knew the Chinese fire would focus on any marine moving around the lines. Nevertheless, a corpsman was called. Orth watched in horror as "a mortar shell came in right on top of him. He disintegrated before our eyes." Orth had a severe head wound and was soon tagged to go back to Regimental Headquarters. On the way, however, the plucky Evansville man turned around and went back to be with the marines, although he did not reach his squad. Because he did not go back to Regimental Headquarters and he was separated from his original group, Orth was reported dead for two weeks. When he finally caught up with his squad, the leader gasped and said, "Orth! You're dead!" The reservist answered back, "Damn it, I ain't dead." Orth remembered that the squad leader then "started running around the other marines yelling, 'Orth's not dead! Orth's not dead!'"

For many reservists, the end time of their tours became a blur of trudging up and down mountainsides coupled with occasional moments of intense combat. William Etheridge recalled, "You were always on the edge." Etheridge remembered seeing a fellow Evanville reservist, Jack Perigo, the young man who had only been married two days before leaving for Camp Pendleton, as stretcher-bearers carefully brought the wounded man down a mountainside. "It was summer and very hot, and I asked Jack if he was okay. We talked for quite a while. The corpsman reassured me Perigo would be okay, and in fact had a 'stateside wound,'" recalled Etheridge. "Later I heard he died of shock." About this time, a thirsty Robert Egan stumbled upon a pool of water and kneeled down to fill his canteen. Egan was suddenly startled by the face of a dead Chinese soldier floating just below the surface of the water. "He seemed to be grinning up at me. Needless to say, I moved elsewhere to get my water." David Graham, another Evansville reservist, recalled this difficult time toward the end of his tour: "You always had hope that over the next hill would be the end of the war."

After leaving Korea, Graham and some of the other reservists had to endure advanced infantry training, even after undergoing months of actual combat. "I went back to Camp Lejeune, where I was supposed to help train the new recruits," Graham remembered. "Instead, they had me and the rest of them playing war games, crawling on our bellies, while they fired machine guns over our heads. I'd been doing this for a couple of weeks when one day I sat under a tree to rest. A drill sergeant came over and started to chew me out. 'We're trying to save your butt, marine, to get you ready for Korea.' I told him, 'To hell with you, I've already been to Korea and I'm not going back!'"

7 *Go Back Home and Tell Everybody
There's a War On*

In the beginning, most Americans believed the Korean struggle
would bring forth the same patriotic fervor on the home front as
World War II had. Certainly for those marine reservists who had
been so abruptly called up, the times were as topsy-turvy as they
had been for the entire nation following the bombing of Pearl
Harbor. For the Evansville men and their families, the few days
between being called up and leaving took on a surreal quality.
Reservists notified schools and employers, and some of the young
wives made arrangements to live with families or friends. A few of
the husbands and wives hatched plans to spend some of their
time in California together. Meanwhile, from the families of the
younger reservists came a flurry of letters to congressmen and
senators as parents desperately tried to buy time for their under-
trained sons to receive more combat instruction.

On 28 August 1950, after the train carrying the men and boys
of C Company pulled out and began its long grinding journey to
Camp Pendleton, the train station at Evansville grew eerily silent.
A few women held their gaze upon the train as long as possible.
An Evansville paper carried an especially haunting photo of a
young woman with a child on either side staring forlornly down
an empty set of tracks. A few men, uncomfortable with the strong

feelings on display, hustled their families toward the parking lot. Many family members left with a nagging fear that they might never see their sons or husbands again.

For some of the women, the train's leaving was only a temporary good-bye, as they rushed to make preparations to leave for California themselves. Some flew, some took later trains, and others traveled by car. While their husbands were at Camp Pendleton, these wives set up temporary housekeeping at apartments and hotels in the nearby town of Oceanside. Several were setting foot west of the Mississippi for the first time in their lives. Despite some nervousness and the quiet dread of a different kind of goodbye in the future, most of these wives were able to spend weekends and some evenings with their husbands for at least the next two weeks. Clinging to the hope that California would be as far as their husbands would have to go, these young women quickly prepared to set out on an adventure.

Young Bonnie Eberle found her long train ride alone a little scary. At one point a strange man who had been drinking sat down right next to her. Fortunately, she had struck up a conversation with the kind Hispanic woman sitting behind her. "I don't think I would have made it without her," Bonnie recalled. "She knew everything about where I was going." When Bonnie got off the train, she rushed, catching the bus to Oceanside just in time, thanks to her newfound friend. Once at the hotel, Bonnie met with Betty Crawford, Becky Compton, Bonnie Hosse, and Betty Ellis, who had flown out earlier. When the husbands arrived, Richard Eberle had just had all of his shots. With his aching arms and a fever, Rich was miserable. Unfortunately, because of Bonnie's long train trip, this was one of only a few nights Bonnie and Rich would have together. He and the other combat-ready-in-two-weeks men were flying out in a few days to Korea. The women weren't allowed to watch the men leave Camp Pendleton, but later, as a plane flew overhead, Bonnie could imagine him in it. Now Bonnie had to turn around and take the long train ride home. She was even more uncomfortable this time because of a nagging pain in her side. She hadn't told her husband about it because he was feeling so badly himself, but as soon as she got home, she went to the doctor, who quickly performed an appendectomy.

The time in Oceanside was more of a break from reality for those lucky reservists and their wives who were able to be together longer than a few days. William and Evelyn Wright recalled a pleasant temporary residence right on the beach, and with help from Wayne Poole, a mess sergeant, they had steak for dinner every night. Nevertheless, the time would pass all too quickly. Although her husband was in the combat-ready-in-four-weeks group, Evelyn could stay out west for only two weeks. She had a job and had already used two weeks' vacation for their earlier trip to Daytona, Florida, in those innocent weeks before they knew their lives would be turned upside down. Although they made the most of their time together in California, Evelyn still felt devastated by the call-up. "I guess I just wanted to deny that this was going to happen," she remembered. "I really didn't think it would come to that. I was twenty-one. . . . You just never had any idea that your marriage would start like this."

Tex and Joan Graham rented a house with the Jim Rausches for two weeks; then after Tex left, Joan stayed four more weeks with relatives who lived nearby. When Tex departed with the rest of the two-weeks group, Joan tearfully saw him off. Two questions kept circling in her mind: What will happen to him, and when will I see him again? After spending four weeks with relatives in California and with only one year's driving experience, Joan made the six-day drive back to Indiana, accompanied by another reservist's wife. After one extremely long day of driving, she got sick somewhere in New Mexico and had an attack of vomiting. Shortly after she returned to Indiana, she discovered that she was pregnant.

Many of the Evansville reservists were leaving behind young wives, as well as, in many cases, babies and young children. While in Korea, after reading some clippings his mother had sent, Gordon Greene wrote back somewhat wistfully, "Boy, all the young ones are marrying. I won't have anyone to run around with when I get back." Greene's boyhood friend, Bud Fitch, also noted all the marriages that were taking place back home. In one letter to his parents he wrote, "I hear Jack and Peg are going to get married in December. If you find out, write me, so I can send them something." This tendency to marry and begin families at a young age was representative of a nationwide trend that had begun immediately following the end of World War II. As to the immediate effect of the Asian conflict on this renewed emphasis on marriage, "New York jewelers reported that the Korean crisis had set off the biggest spurt in the sale of engagement and wedding rings since the end of World War II."[1] By 14 August, "in Knoxville, Tennessee, 200 prospective draftees had gotten married since the outbreak of the Korean hostilities."[2] Evansville reservist Henry Maley and the former Mona Louise Dugan married just two days before he went back into active service. Reservist Jack Perigo and his new bride wed about this same time. Indeed, when the call-up fell, many of the reservists were newlyweds. Jess Thurman summed up their feelings when he noted, "Our honeymoon had hardly started."

The Korean War home front quickly offered the nation unique tensions, especially for the women whose sons, husbands, or brothers had gone overseas. Just five short years earlier, American women had been required to take on new roles for the World War II effort. Now women suddenly found themselves living in a time of growing ambivalence regarding these roles. World War II had, in its duration, liberated women; indeed, it had required them to take on new responsibilities. In the immediate postwar era, however, the pendulum swung sharply back. By 1950, American women faced continuing pressure to conform to society's limited view of a woman's place. Several women's magazines of the day reflected this reactionary tendency.

McCall's celebrated the conservative family ethic when it proclaimed to its white, middle-class readers that women were marrying younger, raising large families, and living in affluent homes. "This powerful commitment to family was accompanied by a widely held belief that men should be the wage earners for their families, and women should tend to the home and children. Women of all racial, ethnic, and class backgrounds faced intense pressure to become wives and mothers after the war, and to make homemaking their primary career." Agnes Meyer expressed these sentiments in 1950 when she wrote in the *Atlantic Monthly*, "What modern woman has to recapture is the wisdom that just being a woman is her central task and greatest honor. . . . Women must boldly announce that no job is more exacting, more necessary, or more rewarding than that of housewife and mother."[3] Other women's magazines of the day certainly did their part to promote this philosophy. The monthly article on "Making Marriage Work" in the November 1950 issue of *Ladies Home Journal* even went so far as to tell women how to get a reluctant man to marry.[4]

Despite the not-so-subtle pressure from society to be a stay-at-home wife and mother, working women were not eager to abandon the labor force: "Four out of five women who worked during the war [World War II] hoped to keep working after the war, including 69 percent of working wives. Although more than 3 million women left their wartime jobs, most were rehired into other occupations."[5] Dorothy Michael, the mother of reservist William Marshall, struggled with the tensions that faced working women who also had families at that time. A music teacher in the public schools, Mrs. Michael was also a single mother who cared for two small children at home. In 1950 she wrote her son, who was serving as a reservist in Seattle, telling him about her difficult life. "Well Thanksgiving is over and I'm back on the job," she stated. "I'm tired already. . . . I had to stay at school yesterday until five o'clock getting grades in because that was my last day there until Thursday." In another portion of the letter, the hurried mother and teacher told of how forgetful she had become because of all the pressures she now faced: "You know the last letter I wrote you I lost for a couple days. I picked it up to mail as I went out to eat on Thanksgiving and that was the last I remembered until I got home and I realized I hadn't mailed it. I raved and I searched and hunted. I could have written ten more letters during the time I spent hunting for it—it just put me out of sorts for the rest of the day, and late Sat[urday] Dixie found it on the coffee table among some magazines. She said 'go mail it now,' so I grabbed up a jacket of hers and dashed out to the mail box then. I do things like that all the time . . . though, I hope when Xmas is over I can get going without being so rushed all the time." Many women of Dorothy Michael's day would be able to identify strongly with this struggling mother and teacher.

Besides the conflicts women faced in regard to their roles in society, the Korean War also witnessed other uncertainties on the home front, many directly connected to the war. The stock market reacted almost immediately to the invasion of South Korea, taking its biggest drop in nearly four years. *Time* reported that "when the New York stock market opened, the day after the Korean fighting started, a huge wave of panicky selling began. By day's end, trading totaled 3,910,000 shares, the heaviest since May 21,

1940, when Hitler's Panzer divisions were sweeping through northern France. The selling sent the Dow-Jones industrial average tumbling 10.41 points, the biggest single day's break since the September crash of 1946."[6] The next morning, as stocks began their recovery, it appeared the worst was over. By noon the market was up by as much as three points until "the news [came] that President Truman had ordered U.S. intervention in Korea, and a huge wave of selling swamped the market. Big and little traders, amateurs and professionals, scrambled to unload."[7] After the "war jitters" of the first days of the Korean conflict had passed, however, "the market recovered its balance, whereupon prices moved steadily upward from July through November 1950."[8]

Along with the stock market's zig-zag reactions, the suddenness of the conflict brought forth unnecessary buying and, eventually, hoarders. In the early days of the Korean War, Americans could not help but remember the shortages of food and manufactured goods brought about by World War II. "Fearing that a new period of shortages might be at hand, Americans went on a veritable buying orgy in the aftermath of President Truman's decision to intervene."[9] The explosion in buying saw the return of that much-maligned character of World War II days—the Hoarder—a 1950s version of a politically incorrect and realistically irresponsible character. A rush began on cars, tires, nylons, washing machines, refrigerators, bedding, soap, sugar, toilet paper, and cigarettes. Cartoons, newspapers, and magazines quickly made their opinions known on this issue. *Life* ran a short article under the title "Nobody Loves a Hoarder," with pictures of a reporter from the *Atlanta Journal and Constitution* posing as a hoarder in an Atlanta supermarket. One picture showed another customer frowning indignantly at the reporter's full cart: "At the sugar counter the reporter greedily picked up 10 large-sized bags and thereupon was several times insulted, three times reported to the manager of the store and once accosted by two husky young men who hoped to provoke him into a fight." When he asked the salesgirl for twenty-five cartons of cigarettes, she first stood and glared at him with her hands on her hips. Then she began counting them out in a voice loud enough for everyone in the store to hear.[10]

Some patriotic grocers made well-intentioned efforts to discourage hoarding: "Max Rosenthal of Washington, D.C., . . . decided to teach people a lesson by boosting his sugar prices from the normal 49 cents for a five-pound bag to 98 cents. To his surprise and horror, people came in and bought it at the double rate." Grocer Ernest Murphy of Wayne, Michigan, was inspired after reading an article in the paper about hoarders to design a jumbo shopping bag marked with the word "Hoarder" in giant letters. After receiving the bags with his design from the printer, however, he found he didn't have the heart to hand them out to his good neighborhood customers. After other grocers had likewise declined their use, Murphy said wistfully, "It was a good idea. If everyone had used these bags, hoarding would have been stopped overnight."[11] Many Americans felt nothing but disdain for the hoarders but sometimes were unable to see past the end of their own noses. In Chillicothe, Missouri, a man left this note for his grocer: "Give me 100 pounds of sugar before those hoarders get it."[12]

The Federal Reserve Board provided the first rough measure of how much scare buying had been set off by the war, reporting that in July 1950, "installment purchases of automobiles, refrigerators and other durable goods had sent consumer credit soaring to $660 million, well above the $457 million rise in May and $550 million in June to a total of $20.3 billion. It was the first time in history that consumer debt had crossed the $20 billion mark."[13] The outcome of scare buying—"not only by anxious housewives and motorists but also by manufacturers and processors who envisioned shortages of the materials required to sustain their operations"—was inflation.[14] Truman had tried relying on monetary and credit controls to deal with the problem. These efforts, however, failed. When "government officials reported at the end of September that prices of twenty-eight basic commodities had gone up 25 percent since the outbreak of hostilities in Korea . . . it was evident that the cost-of-living index soon would surpass the record set in 1948."[15] Local Hoosiers were soon feeling the squeeze caused by rising prices. One mother wrote her reservist son, telling him, "You were talking about hamburgers being high—everything is high. Coffee is 95 cents a pound and I use quite a bit. I guess I'll have to drink plain water."[16]

While prices rose, big business boomed, but they were far from the sole beneficiaries. "The demand for skilled workingmen, particularly die makers, machinists, and aircraft workers, quickly exceeded the supply; unemployment dwindled; and it was estimated by spring of 1951 less than 2 percent of the national labor force would be out of work."[17] *Time* declared, "The war in Asia made its first impact on the U.S. economy last week. Personnel managers, worried about manpower, began totting up the Reservists and draft eligibles on company payrolls."[18] In the Evansville area, a headline in the *Evansville Press* noted, "One in ten men teachers could be called to service."[19] In addition to the teachers who departed Evansville with C Company, there were many who left other jobs as well. Dave Schellhase had to turn in his mailman's uniform, Bill Wright left a job with the telephone company, and Jess Thurman left his job at International Harvester. Some of the reservists, such as the school teachers, knew their jobs would be waiting for them when they came back from the war. Others had no such certainty. Because he was supply sergeant and had to arrive at Pendleton before the other reservists, William Nemer was only able to give his boss a few hours notice. "You've got to be kidding me," was his boss's reaction.

For those who did not go off to war, these were great times to be in the labor force: "In August 1950, to discourage its workers from jumping to more remunerative jobs, Chrysler Corporation granted substantial pay increases, a move that touched off a wave of similar wage hikes throughout the industry. Millions of other working people received cost-of-living raises in accordance with union contracts." In fact, the only groups who didn't really benefit from the boom were farmers and those in the construction industry.[20]

By early 1951 the effects of mobilization seemed to sweep the nation. Under the headline "Our Blueprint for Western Survival," *Newsweek* stated that "America's immediate future began to take a recognizable form this week. . . . Many of its plants are to be devoted to production of the machinery of war. Civilian goods turned out by remaining plants will be enough to satisfy normal demand, so there will be price and wage controls to guard against runaway inflation. Taxes will be high enough to pinch every citizen."[21] This aura of total mobilization, however, would soon prove to be illusionary.

Another significant concern on the home front accelerated by the war was the fear many Americans had regarding the spread of communism and the possibility of nuclear war. Both worries had increased since the end of World War II, but with the fall of the Chinese government to the Communists in 1949, a new sense of panic emerged. Once the Korean War broke, fear of Communist domination deepened. *Newsweek* asked, "Where would the Communists stop? Memories of Munich, of the Axis's piecemeal conquest which preceded the second World War, were still alive. On street cars, buses, and suburban trains, the parallel was being drawn: 'If we don't stop them now, the Russians will be all over the Pacific by the time they get set for an all-out war against us.'"[22] A Gallup poll taken six months before the war broke showed that 70 percent of U.S. citizens believed the Soviets were scheming to become "the ruling power of the world."[23] Local leaders in Evansville also fretted over the Communist threat, as the area had always possessed a conservative streak. One of the city's newspapers carried a story that declared that the FBI knew where local Communists were "and how to find them." The article added that "local FBI men periodically visit an Evansville business office checking up on a former woman employee either known or suspected of being a communist."[24]

Potential Soviet use of the atomic bomb also gave Americans nightmares. Hearing of the horrors of Hiroshima and Nagasaki drove Americans to seek information about what to do in case such attacks did occur here at home. Responding to these concerns, the government released a series of documents for civilians about nuclear war. One of the earliest, very simplistic and somewhat insulting to the average American's intelligence, was called *You Can Survive*. Published in 1950, this pamphlet can still be found in some public libraries. "Survival," it stated, "is virtually ensured if you 'KNOW THE BOMBS TRUE DANGERS. KNOW THE STEPS YOU CAN TAKE TO ESCAPE THEM!' Avert contamination," it urged, by "simply taking refuge inside a house or even by getting inside a car and rolling up the window." The pamphlet went on to note that "should you happen to be one of the unlucky people right under the bomb, there is practically no hope of living through it."[25]

Pamphlets such as this seemed to be dealing with the public need for information while addressing the reader as if he were a child and playing down the true horrors of a nuclear blast. In August 1950, the Department of Defense and the new Atomic Energy Commission (AEC) released a semitechnical, more straightforward, 456-page report that instantly became a best-seller. It described in detail the nature of an atomic blast and what it would do to buildings, utilities, and people. Quoting the report, *Life* magazine noted, "To the man in the street the first warning of an air blast will be the blinding flash of a terrible light brighter than a hundred suns. Everyone within half a mile almost certainly will be killed instantly or die soon after. Those who are still alive," the article stated, "should do three things—if possible within the first second: cover face, neck and hands; take the nearest cover if it is not more than a step or two away or, if in the open, drop to the ground and curl up."

The AEC did not hesitate to relate how awesome a nuclear explosion would be. The blast, the agency noted, "takes place in less than a millionth of a second. In that time it develops a temperature of a million degrees, unleashes deadly radiation, builds up an air pressure hundreds of thousands of times greater than that of ordinary atmosphere, then forms into a rapidly expanding ball of fire. The gamma rays, powerful enough to penetrate thick concrete walls, attack the body's blood cells and cause fatal radiation sickness. The scorching heat of the explosion radiates for three seconds, then is over. The shock wave, strengthened by its own reflection from the earth's surface, thrusts outward at 1000 miles an hour, crushing buildings in its path. In ten seconds its damage is done."[26] This more graphic picture of the results of the nuclear blast was tempered with illustrated instructions on minimizing the damages.

Time quickly called the AEC's work "the ABCs of atomic disaster." If a Russian bomb was dropped on an American town, the article warned, "the great majority of those within a half-mile radius of the blast will die. . . . Preparation and precaution," the magazine added, "may mean the difference between life and death for tens of thousands."[27] Evansville papers took up a similar theme. In early August one paper asserted, "Russia May Move *Now* to Take World." The article went on to relate that the United States could be "fighting for survival soon."[28] The next week the same paper warned, "U.S. Tells Nation How to Prepare for Atomic Bomb Blast."[29] Around the time of these disturbing headlines another issue of the paper sought to reassure nervous citizens that an explosion on the edge of Evansville "was not an atomic detonation."[30] America's Civil Defense plan had not yet begun locating public fallout shelters, but in the spirit of capitalism, entrepreneurs began building private fallout shelters for those who could afford them. In California, a whole variety of shelters were available by 1950. They ranged from the economical $13.50 foxhole model to the luxurious $3,500 version with phone and Geiger counter.[31]

With the specter of nuclear holocaust hanging over their heads, it's no wonder the American people wanted to take some kind of preventive action. *Time* declared, "When a man knows he has a good chance to be a-bombed, nothing can stop him from wondering if there isn't something he can do to prevent it."[32] Stopping the Communists in Korea seemed like a step in this direction. This action—called variously a war, a conflict, and a police action—was considered the opening round of World War III, according to 57 percent of the American population in a Gallup poll released in September 1950.[33] Americans seemed relieved to be finally confronting the perceived Russian menace. Thus the high level of support for Truman's actions in the early days of the war.

In August 1950, *Newsweek* asserted that the ripples of the Korean War would be affecting most Americans in their daily lives. "The House of Representatives gave President Truman sweeping power to put the home front on a wartime basis," the article declared. "The administration got virtually all the powers it had requested plus stand-by rationing, price, and wage controls the President agreed to accept only in the face of a bipartisan drive sparked by strong public demand. An almost identical bill was nearing a vote in the Senate."[34] Conversely, *Time* noted the puzzling dichotomy that quickly seemed to be forming regarding the war: "The quickening of U.S. mobilization . . . could hardly be seen last week in the August sun. The peaceful look of U.S. cities, the countryside and the beaches contrasted oddly with the ferocity of battle in Korea."[35] News reporters, perhaps more than any other group, wanted to discern the true effects of the war on the American home front. For their 1 September 1950 issue, *U.S. News and World Report*, for example, sent a member of their Board of Editors to Hamilton, Ohio, a city of fifty-eight thousand, which they considered representative of the country as a whole and therefore a good indicator of how the Korean War was affecting the country. "Hamilton, proud of its record in the last war, is doing all that is expected of it in this one. But there is no enthusiasm for war among the draftees and reservists who are being called upon to fight it. Korea seems far away, war a little unreal. There is reluctance among some people to make the sacrifices the war requires, but on the whole they are taking the sacrifices in stride."

At this point in the war, the article reported, the majority of people in Hamilton were carrying on as usual. Some voiced concern about inflation and shortages, although the scare-buying from the early days of the conflict had tapered off. For young draftees and reservists, the "shattering of plans for marriages, homes, careers, education and many other things are the upsetting part of mobilization in Hamilton and elsewhere." Barring full-scale war, the reporter noted, "the burden of the Korean conflict was being carried largely by young draftees, Reservists and their families."[36] The weight of that burden became painfully clear in the first weeks of the Korean conflict. Almost immediately after the opening days of America's commitment in Korea, a national magazine reported, "In Texas, in Washington and in a remote country hollow in West Virginia, the families of three U.S. men got the inevitable news—brought by radio, or by friends, or the regretful telegram from Washington. An American bomber had gone down after a scrape over Korea, and its two crewmen were dead. An enemy tank had opened up on a 19-year-old American boy who had helped fire a bazooka at it in a South Korean village, and the boy was dead."[37] *Time* noted that "of the first 249 U.S. casualties in Korea, 192 were listed as 'missing'—presumably captured."[38] Americans shuddered at such news, but oddly enough, would eventually fail as a nation to become greatly stirred about the war. Few, however, could have imagined at that time how quickly concern over the war would fade in the eyes of Americans not directly affected by it.

On the day that the reservists from Evansville left for Camp Pendleton, California, an issue of *Time* emphasized what most of the reservists' families were finding out: "The Korean War was being fought by a small segment of the U.S. people. The U.S. forces on the battle line were not as big as the baseball crowd that jams Yankee Stadium, and only a minority of Americans—servicemen outside the battle zone, families of men in action and civilians subject to military duty—were directly concerned even in a secondary way. For all its savagery and import, the Korean conflict was working little more hardship on most citizens than the Battle of Wounded Knee." Regarding the booming economy, *Time* added, "The nation so far seemed to accept this plethora of prosperity and plenty with none of the qualms of conscience which had afflicted it during World War II. . . . There had been no revival of such phrases as 'the home front' and 'don't you know there's a war on?'"39 The magazine had certainly hit upon something entirely strange about this war. Indiana, in America's heartland, also seemed to follow the national trend of quickly disregarding the conflict in Korea. William Hasselbrinck, for example, then a student at Indiana State University at Terre Haute, remembered how at the onset of the war "stores in town placed signs in their front window referring, as in World War II, to 'the duration of the war.'" Within a few weeks, however, Hasselbrinck observed that the signs had disappeared, and things went on as usual.

While the rest of the country quickly began to lose interest in the war, the Evansville marine reservists in California were, according to one hometown newspaper account, "getting a real taste of what life is like in wartime. . . . Food, quarters, the familiar 'hurry up and wait' routine and training—or lack of it—and all are coming in for their share of cussing." Within two weeks of arriving at Camp Pendleton, many of the men had already left for Korea by way of Japan. Most of the wives who had visited their men in California brought back news when they returned. "Some of the men are being shipped out so suddenly they don't even know what specialty they are supposed to have," complained Mrs. Edward Hosse, the wife of a private first-class. "They know they have been given ratings as machine gunners or mortar men, or squad leaders, for example, but they are told to 'wait until you get where you're going' to find out." Regarding the men's experiences at Camp Pendleton, the wives reported, "It isn't at all like they thought it would be." Perhaps already sensing the lessening of the impact of the war on the American conscience, the men themselves sent this message home with their wives, "Go back home and tell everybody there's a war on."40

As soon as the C Company reservists left for Camp Pendleton, finances were an immediate and major concern for almost all of their families. Most of the working men—many with wives and children—would be taking a big cut in pay. Some of the younger men, like Gordon Greene, helped aging parents with money and with labor. On the date that C Company departed from Evansville, the *Press* ran an article entitled "Tough Times Are Ahead for Reservists' Families." In this piece, marine reservist wife Mrs. Edwin J. Savage explained that under the bill Congress was currently considering to provide family allowances for servicemen's families, she would be left with only $110 per year to feed and clothe herself and her son, plus meet any emergency expenses. She sent letters (along with a list of her itemized expenses) to Rep. Winfield K. Denton and Sen. Homer Capehart "explaining how they and other Reservists' families are being pinched by the recall order."[41]

The allowance, or "allotment" as it was called by most of the servicemen, would be a sore topic for many of the families over the next year, not only due to the low dollar amount they received, but also because of the difficulty in getting payments started and coming regularly to their families. The problem quickly became a primary theme in the correspondence between many of the reservists and their families. Only four days after leaving Evansville, Gordon Greene wrote to his elderly mother, "Is your money holding out? . . . I'm going up today to see about the allotment." On 12 September, he wrote to say, "I checked on the allotment last night, and you will get $75.00 per month. Just when it will start I don't know." Obviously concerned about his mother's financial situation and maintenance of their home, Greene wrote on 26 September, "How does the roof look now? I really don't know when the allotment will begin, so I'll send some when I can." The young Greene's anxiety would not be quickly soothed. His letter of 16 October sounded somewhat frantic: "Are you receiving any money? If not, how are you making out? Did Mrs. Dickson [the mother of Greene's friend Al] come to see you?" The tone of a letter written in late October resounded with resignation: "I hope you are doing the best you can because your allotment won't come through until the first of November. . . . We are due to be paid tomorrow, so I'll be sending some money. I don't see how you can make it, but I'll do my best."

Whereas Gordon Greene's worries revolved around his elderly mother being able to make it on her own, Evansville reservist Paul McDaniel, because of his hasty departure, had to leave a wife and young child living

with his parents. An early letter from his mother fretted, "I guess the allotment don't amount to a thing. It's awful to take you away and not even
take care of your baby." And on 17 November: "We sure are sore because
they are not paying [your wife] for all that time you've been in that Hell
over there." A week later McDaniel's mother wrote and complained, "I
know you are going to really think of dirty deals when you hear the back
pay isn't to be paid. I sure was mad. Still am. . . . I thought that would
almost clear up the loan." Because of governmental red tape, allotments
were painfully slow in arriving. Still very frustrated by the matter, Mrs.
McDaniel wrote to her son in late November, "What do you think of the
allotment checks not starting like we expected them? Guess Truman gave
it to some other country."

Young Gordon Greene, whose high school classmates had described
him as fun-loving and a jokester, now carried an extra burden of concern,
for he knew his mother's house was not in the best of shape. He had
intended to repair it late that summer, but the call-up foiled his plans. In
his letter of 26 October he worriedly asked, "How much did the roof cost
you? I don't think you should have the house painted this fall because the
allotment might not come through." Even after the Chinese had entered
the war and battles were raging near the Chosin Reservoir, Greene was trying to straighten out the allotment snafu. On 3 December, immediately
after his group was surrounded, Greene wrote, "I hope you are feeling
better and aren't worrying too much. About your allotment, I will try to get
down to battalion today to get it straightened out. It will probably be slow
in coming through, but I have two months back pay due, and I will send it
as soon as I get paid." It would be 19 April 1951, seven months after the
young man had been called up, before he could write, "Glad to hear that
you finally got your full allotment. I know that you are in bad need of it.
Only wish you could've gotten it sooner." Greene's Oakland City neighbor,
William Marshall, also saw his family struggle with paying bills. When an
aunt wrote and complained to the Oakland City teenager that his mother
desperately needed money, Marshall wrote back, saying, "If my mother
needs any of my money at all, give it to her. I'll have plenty to come home
on when I get out of here."

It must have been difficult to deal with financial crises while the rest of the country felt hardly any effects of the war; however, money problems were not the reservists' families' only hardship. Worry and uncertainty about their loved ones' well-being most often overrode everything. The loved ones of the Evansville group must have felt they were on a monstrous roller coaster. The highs looked to be an end of the war and seeing their sons and husbands again soon, while the lows brought the dreaded fear that they might never see them alive again. People have a variety of ways to cope with anxiety, and the families of the reservists were no different. Bonnie Eberle hung a large map of Korea in her home and used push pins to mark where she thought her husband, Richard, was at any given time. She also cut out every article she could find relating to the war in the two local papers.

Letters between Bonnie and Richard Eberle were frequent, although Richard, like most other reservists, didn't describe just how bad things were. When Bonnie received a letter, she would call Ross Compton's wife Becky and Ross's parents to let them know what was happening, and they would do the same for her when they received a letter from Ross. She also stayed in touch with Betty Crawford, another reservist's wife. Bonnie stayed in the same apartment she and Rich had fixed up—a former doctor's offices. It also helped that this apartment was attached to her parents' home. Evelyn Wright continued in her job but moved in with friends while Bill was gone. This helped to ease the loneliness for her and was an occasional distraction from her constant worry. She and her husband exchanged letters almost daily. Evelyn often went home on weekends to visit family and friends. During this time she had to become more familiar with driving since she had driven very little up until then. Recalling that difficult time, she said, "You just tried to get through it the best you could." Joan Graham lived with her parents in Terre Haute while Tex was gone. Being close to her family and friends was comforting as she went through her pregnancy.

The separation was especially hard on the youngest and most recently married couples. One reservist wrote a letter asking a family member to "try and pep" his wife "up a little. She must feel lonely living by herself after we were together all the time." Raleigh McGary especially longed to be back with his wife. Writing her on Thanksgiving Day from near the Chosin, he told her, "According to the latest word we are supposed to leave Korea by the 15th day of the new offensive which was to have started this morning. . . . MacArthur is supposed to be over here now and he seems anxious to get the M.C. [Marine Corps] home. I hope so! If we leave here in 15 days it won't be too long. Of course we shouldn't plan on it but it makes the separation more bearable if you keep thinking—well, it's only for another month."

While at Camp Pendleton, Gordon Greene tried to ease his mother's worries about his absence. "I know it's very difficult being alone, but you can make it until I get back," he wrote. In spite of his own difficulties, Greene always seemed to be aware of the hardships on his mother. In October 1950, he wrote, "It's beginning to get cold here now, and it is at home too, I suppose. Have you any coal? It's going to be bad this winter for you to have to go up and down the steps, so take care of yourself the best you can. I know it's tough on you, and I wish you didn't have to because you aren't able." On top of the worries about his mother's difficult situation, Greene soon found himself fretting over other relatives' misfortunes. In one instance, Greene's brother found himself out of work. Greene asked his mother in one letter home about the situation, "Is Harvester still on strike? Golly, what's Tony doing to take care of his family?" Other reservists also heard from parents who struggled in their sons' absences. "I do wish you were home," wrote one reservist's mother. "I just can't seem to hold out on things. I have so much pain in my chest, and I'm afraid it's my heart."[42]

The families of the men who went to Korea were not the only ones whose lives were drastically disrupted. The Evansville men who were not sent overseas drew stateside duty, most of them at Camp Pendleton. Reservist David Schellhase, who served in the 87th Infantry, 3rd Army during World War II, had suffered a hearing loss from the concussion of an artillery explosion shortly after the Battle of the Bulge. When called up as a marine reservist in 1950, he was assigned to be a mail clerk at Camp Del Mar, part of the Pendleton system. After finding renters for their Evansville home, his wife Marjorie, and sons David, six, and Michael, four, moved to California and joined him in September to live on the base. With the confidence that they would return to their house after his tour of duty and that his postal job in Evansville would be waiting for him, David and Marjorie felt the move was probably hardest on their kids. While at Camp Del Mar, David Jr. enjoyed following around the marines who cut the grass at the camp, alarming his mother, who knew that those men were on work release from the brig. David was also one of six students in the first grade at the marine school that year. Because of the school's small enrollment, sons and daughters of the marines found the atmosphere to be laid back and pleasant. David Jr. did well in that environment, but the following year, when his family moved back to Evansville and he attended a parochial school, adjustment was not easy. Going right to the pencil sharpener, David was struck by a nun for rising from his seat without asking permission. He further inflamed the wrath of his teachers when he rebelled against singing "America the Beautiful," wanting instead to sing the Marine Corps Hymn.

Several other marine reservists of the Evansville group also served stateside during the war. Many, such as William Marshall, were only seventeen when the call-up came. For these younger reservists, the experiences that came from being so far away from home for a prolonged period of time were difficult. Marshall, for example, was soon sent from Pendleton to Seattle, where he spent much of his time "dealing with prisoners in the brig or guarding ocean piers." Two of the piers were the longest wooden piers in the world. As with other reservists, Marshall had to endure the complaints from the regular marines regarding the soundness of the reservists. On top of that, the Oakland City teenager found himself completely separated from his other friends from Indiana and, consequently, experienced long bouts of homesickness. On 1 May 1951, just nine days after his eighteenth birthday, Marshall arrived in San Diego for boot camp. "We have to do a lot of silly things here," he wrote in a letter home the next day, "but it isn't too bad." The young man was especially proud of some of his achievements at boot camp. He told his family, "I took a test to be a radio man earlier in the week and passed it. . . . Only about 10 out of 75 passed the test." Often Marshall's letters home concerned music, a passion his entire family shared. In one letter he asked how his younger brother Jim liked "some of the song books I sent home. The one, '30 Years, 30 Hits,' is the one I meant to bring home to Mother. It was the first one I bought." Marshall's mother found her son's absence especially trying. In one letter written shortly after Thanksgiving, she told her son, "I don't think this is much of a letter, but at least you've heard from me and know I'm thinking of you. I took your picture to school with me. It sure is nice Billy, and I can at least smile when I look at it because you are there smiling right at me."

Barney Barnard of Oakland City missed being able to help one of his younger brothers, Bill, who was a senior back at Oakland City High School and who suffered the problems typical of that age. "School may seem rough to you," Barney wrote, "but it is nothing like life over here. As soon as you get out of high school, start into college. If I were you I would take a summer course at Oakland City. Perhaps you can beat the draft." In another letter, Barnard advised his brother to keep up his grades: "You don't have anything to worry about now but your school work. Don't fall down in the home stretch." In yet another letter, the elder Barnard informed his brother that he would take care of one particular bully. "Sorry you got into it up at Jasper. Just remember what he looks like, and it will be taken care of when 'the boys come back from over here.'"

Bud Fitch missed his big brother role as well. A decade older than his brother Gordon and his sister Jane, Bud often asked about or made mention of "the kids," as he called them. "I was glad to hear the kids did so well on their cards," he wrote in a March letter to his parents. Two weeks later he wrote how happy he was that his younger siblings had joined 4-H. "It will be a good way to learn a lot," he said. Fitch was also concerned about his parents' well-being. His mother had recently returned to college, and Bud wrote from training camp, lovingly encouraging his mother in her endeavor. In one instance he wrote, "Your reactions to school were about the same as mine to high school. It doesn't pay to worry about your grades if you do your best." So much did the young reservist miss his family that he wrote, "Don't worry writing about trivial things because that is what I want to hear. I don't wade through them. I save them and read them over many times. Just news about the family, etc. is what I want to hear about."

For the reservists who were already in Korea, the families' worry was constant. After receiving one of Paul McDaniel's letters early in November, his mother wrote, "We were so glad to hear from you we all had tears in our eyes. The last we had was written 15 October—when you were in Inchon harbor. We thought you were around the neighborhood of Wonsan, but we were so very worried. . . . We listen to the news a lot and read the papers." Mrs. McDaniel also stayed in contact with some other parents of other reservists. She told her son, "Mrs. Ellis says Jack is in Osaka, Japan, and Bill is in Korea." In a letter dated 27 November, just before things turned really grim for McDaniel and thousands of others near the Chosin Reservoir, the Evansville mother told her son, "We have the little radio on and the Korean news don't sound good. We hope it's not where you are."

Letters and packages from home meant the world to the young men in Korea. In Gordon Greene's many letters to his mother, he mentions his or others' getting or not getting letters, packages, and/or news from home in almost every single one. In another letter to a teenage friend, Greene reported how important packages from home were: "Man, I received your package yesterday, and I can't explain just how much I did appreciate it. It's really a good feeling to know that you have buddies back home, true buddies I mean." Bud Fitch also wrote to his mother regarding packages and letters, "I have been getting a lot of mail and sure appreciate your steady writing. Dad and Beth are sure coming through too. . . . I got your box . . . and I sure enjoyed it. It was just exactly what I liked. I never thought of cocoa, but it sure is good." Some reservists got downright cranky when they didn't receive mail. Raleigh McGary complained, for example, "Here it is Sunday and still no mail, but I might get some today. I heard a rumor there were four bags for this company. I sure need something to snap me out of this mood I'm in. I've started this letter, but I don't know anything to say."

For those servicemen with children back home, letters gave them a chance to witness their children growing from a distance. Paul McDaniel's mother said of Paul's baby daughter, "I don't know what I would do without her to help me forget about the war for a few minutes." She told Paul a little about Paula Gail in almost every letter: "She is so sweet and meddlesome. Ha! . . . She still calls you, and we can tell she wonders where dada is." In the next letter McDaniel heard how his daughter "walked several steps at a time last night." Later in October his mother reported, "I went upstairs the other night and she tried to cry after me, and in a few moments I thought she sounded closer and looked down the stairs and here she was coming up the stairs. Joe Nell saw it and stayed just behind her to catch her if she fell. . . . Well she came up as fast as you could, all the way up. Then she sat and laughed at us. . . . We had 36 Halloween kids here Halloween night and the baby sat in the front door and looked them all over; she wasn't afraid of any of them." In November came the news that "the baby is having her first birthday in a few days. . . . She is so cute toddling around." The little girl could be contrary too, as she continued to grow up in the absence of her father: "Well your little meddlesome Mattie is a busy gal. You can trail her through the house by everything in her reach being on the floor. She walks everywhere and does look so cute. When the music is a bit catchy she shakes a mean hip. She waves her hand if we even speak of going someplace."

Newspapers from home were also read voraciously. In a letter to his mother from Camp Pendleton, Gordon Greene noted, "I received the *Journal* [Oakland City newspaper] today, so I really hit the jackpot." He was also excited because his address was listed in this edition of the local paper. "That's the first time I ever made the front page of the *Journal*," he said, "really surprising." He and Al Dickson shared every *Oakland City Journal* they received, and Greene related that the other Oakland City resident in his company, William Cunningham, "received the *Winslow Dispatch*." It must have given Greene and other reservists a small measure of normalcy to be able to keep up on the events back home. Hoosier reservists especially followed their local basketball teams. In late winter, Greene reported to his mother that he had "heard all the sectional results. [I] guess Winslow went wild over winning the sectional." And later, "Give me all the clippings on the state high school championship. There's a boy in my platoon from Jeff of Lafayette with whom I have a five dollar bet that Jeff won't win the state."

The holidays were especially difficult for families back home. It was shortly before Thanksgiving that the home-by-Christmas rumor grew strongest, and many of the families of reservists had very high hopes. One local paper carried headlines reading "Allies Drive to Win War by Yuletide" and reported "a massive offensive to end the war in Korea quickly and have the American soldiers 'home by Christmas.'" A little later, however, news media dropped the disappointing news. "Gen. Douglas MacArthur said . . . his home-by-Christmas forecast merely expressed the 'universal hope' for an early end to the Korean War," one national magazine reported.[43] Not everyone at home was actually convinced that the home-by-Christmas promise would come true anyway. Paul McDaniel's mother wrote to him, "There's been a lot of remarks about MacArthur mentioning you being home for Christmas. They seemed to think he needed his head examined." Nevertheless, his mother added wistfully, "Well we hope you do get home by Christmas." A Thanksgiving article in the *Evansville Courier* conveyed the longings of many reservists' families over the holidays: "In many a home across the great reaches of America, Thanksgiving 1950 must seem merely a day of more penetrating ache. The warmth of thousands of firesides is chilled by drafts from North Korea. The chairs of sons, brothers and husbands are empty. Some will be filled again in a more joyous time, but others, never. Some are still filled, but around the heads of their occupants play the fears of families who don't know where they will be next Thanksgiving."

Christmas was even more difficult for reservists' kin. Once more the war looked to be a long one for those in Korea. Still, everyone tried to make the occasion as happy as possible. One reservist wrote, "I suppose everyone is very busy doing their late Christmas shopping. Sure wish I were there for the celebration."[44] A local paper reported that "the men who carry the soldier mail in Korea are working 24 hours a day to insure that fighting men receive their Christmas packages in time."[45] This was obviously important for morale. By Christmas Eve, for example, Gordon Greene's mood was a little more upbeat: "Boy, I have really been getting packages. . . . I have been getting mail everyday so far. So all in all I have hit a lucky streak on the mail and package deal." Greene's friend, Bud Fitch, still in training in California, thought often about his Oakland City friends and what their holidays must be like in Korea. "I sure am glad you sent those boys those Xmas packages," he wrote to his mother. "I know how much they will appreciate it, and I think it was a fine thing to do. It will be bad enough being here for Xmas, so you can imagine how it would be over there."

Sometimes reservists' families just were not able to overcome the pain of the separation. Paul McDaniel's mother wrote in a letter dated 14 December, "I guess we won't have much of a Christmas without you. The baby is too young to know much about it, and we don't have money to do with either. . . . I know we will be having our Christmas when we can have that sweet face of yours to look at." Her sentiments were also echoed in thousands of letters written during the season by much younger writers and addressed to "Santa Claus." Since so many letters to Santa were directed to the Santa Claus, Indiana, Post Office, members of the Evansville local American Legion Honor Society assisted by answering all letters that gave a return address. Five-year-old Larry Slamons asked Santa, "Please bring my two brothers home. One is in the navy, the other in the air corps." Jimmy Fishel, three, of Attica, Indiana, wrote, "If . . . you could, I wish you would bring my daddy home for Christmas." One little girl wrote to St. Nick in care of her local paper: "I am a little girl 9 years old, and I'm in the fourth grade. I guess all the little boys and girls have written you what they want for Christmas. So please let me tell you what I want too. I don't want any toys or clothes. My two little brothers don't neither. We want our daddy Joseph Earl Hall who is in the navy, to come home for Christmas. You can find him somewhere near Korea, for he is on a ship that carried ammunition and supplies to Korea."[46]

Home-front reaction regarding Korea, carried in local newspapers, seemed to wax strongest at the beginning of the war and when the Chinese came into the conflict. The 26 July 1950 issue of the *Evansville Press* ran the headline "President Calls for Sacrifices," and the *Oakland City Journal* carried an editorial on 27 July entitled "The Pinch Is Coming." The latter article asserted "people right here in Oakland City are daily realizing the seriousness of the situation." Foreshadowing the call-up of some of her own sons, the article ended by stating, "those who will feel it most are those with sons or close relatives in the conflict." The Oakland City College paper, the *O.C. Collegian,* also responded to the war's seriousness. The little Baptist school's monthly bulletin declared, "Once more America is embroiled in a great armed conflict and as always the struggle is perpetuated in the difference of two ideals. The clashing of good and bad and of right and wrong, but this time it's the opposition of the two extremes; the confirmed belief and faith in God, and atheism."[47]

Local reaction to the war often turned bitter after the beginning of 1951. "Why is it," began one letter to the editor of an Evansville paper, "more than ever before this country needs leaders, and the leaders have time for everything else but leading the people. . . . Why not tell the people what is happening to our men in Korea?" The writer suggested using an atomic bomb but believed President Truman "would rather let the war go on for a while so the prices will stay up." The letter ended by asserting, "Korea has never done this country one whit of good."[48] Another letter in the same issue lamented "we will find ourselves short of men because we lost them in Korea, China, and other police actions. We will be short of arms because we shipped them to other countries. . . . Last but not least we will be short of friends because of the bungling of Washington."[49] The *O.C. Collegian* carried another article on the war in January 1951 after one of its students, Albert Dickson, wrote about his difficult times at the Chosin. The article carried some of Dickson's letters under the title "Big Al Is Okay." After excerpts from the letters were offered, the editor chided the readers, saying, "Now, fellow students, when you think the going is pretty rough and the professors are showing you no mercy, let's all stop and think of our boys in Korea who would gladly exchange their troubles for yours. And as Al suggested, let us each and everyone pray for all our boys who are fighting for the cause of freedom and democracy."[50]

While their loved ones served in Korea, almost all the families of reservists read the newspapers and news magazines, listened to the radio, and watched the news on television. Television news was in its infancy at this time. *Newsweek* said of this novice media in its 21 August 1950 issue, "Television newscasts have not lived up to radios. But television coverage of public affairs is a different story." One of the first international events covered by television was the UN Security Council's struggles with the Korean mess. "Here," *Newsweek* stated, "television offers a sense of participation that radio cannot give. This has been clearly and excitingly evident in the meetings of the UN Security Council under the president-ship of Jacob A. Malik. Video viewers can now actually see what they've been reading

about—Russia versus the US."⁵¹ This live UN broadcast was the first time a
large number of Americans viewed a news event in unison: "Everywhere
that direct broadcast or co-axial cable could reach, Americans sat glued to
their sets watching the exciting big show at Lake Success, from which the
Security Council's proceedings were telecast without even a pause for a
sponsor."⁵²

Television news from the front lines in Korea, *Newsweek* reported, was
rather primitive: "Mutual, which had a stringer in Seoul when the war
broke out, managed a three-fifths network live show on July 23, but the
first scheduled program was not until August 18, when ABC stringer John
Rich spoke straight to the states over the phone in a Taegu schoolhouse."
With the relative absence of live newscasts, the networks had to depend
"chiefly on tape recordings. . . . Depending on the urgency of the news, the
tape can then be flown to Pusan and played back over the phone to Tokyo,
from where it is relayed to the states; or it can be flown directly to Tokyo,
San Francisco, or New York for editing and playing back."⁵³ Radio offered
the freshest news about happenings in Korea. One reservist received a
note from his family telling how his father was "always glued to the radio
when home, wondering where you are and how you are. . . . Dad sits up
every night until the late news is over."⁵⁴ Regardless of whether families
with loved ones in Korea got their news from television, radio, or the old
reliable local newspaper, they latched onto every source that might supply
news concerning a family member.

Perhaps the most disturbing news media accounts for families of
reservists came after the Chinese plunged into the war. As American
marines and Chinese fought desperate battles all up and down the MSR in
northeast Korea, the rest of the world reeled from the dramatic change of
events. The abrupt and shocking information delivered by magazine and
newspaper accounts could not have painted a grimmer picture. *Newsweek*
called the quick and stunning turnaround "the worst military licking since
the battle of the Bulge or . . . Pearl Harbor." The magazine went on to say
glumly that the situation loomed as the worst military disaster in American history. "Barring a military or diplomatic miracle, . . . the U.S. Army
. . . might have to be evacuated in a new Dunkirk to save them from being

lost in a new Bataan."[55] By mid-December the same magazine suggested that the Chinese thrust could be the opening battle in "a third world war."[56] *Time* reported that the United States stood "at the abyss of disaster." The Chinese, noted *Time,* had brought about "the worst defeat the U.S. had ever suffered." A real possibility of the "Atomic Horrors of World War III" hovered just on the horizon. Of more immediate concern was the fate of U.S. fighting men now potentially trapped in Korea. "As it becomes apparent that 140,000 U.S. troops . . . face possible annihilation, the disaster and implications became the subject of endless shared conversations. . . . Men on the street," *Time* went on to report, "sometimes simply stare at each other, and then voice the week's most often repeated phrase—'it looks bad.'"[57] The *New York Times* spoke of "hordes of Chinese Reds" sweeping down upon vastly outnumbered U.S. troops.[58] The primary paper for the region in which the families of Evansville reservists lived, the *Evansville Courier,* also offered a gloomy assessment of the situation in Northeast Korea. One headline noted that X Corps, which included the 1st Marine Division, was now "trapped" by as many as three hundred thousand Chinese.[59] The next day the same paper announced that X Corps was surrounded and their only supply route had been cut.[60]

Now the traumatized families could only watch television, listen to the radio, and pour over the newspaper and magazine articles describing the horrifying situation in which the marines now found themselves. Many wives and parents who had been receiving letters from the troops on a regular basis found that mail from the front lines suddenly stopped cold. Nevertheless, relatives desperately checked the mail each day, hoping for word from their loved ones but finding nothing to ease their growing panic. Joan Graham remembered contacting anyone that she thought might be able to find out something about her husband, Tex. Becky Compton sadly informed her husband's family at their Thanksgiving dinner that Ross was most likely among the men trapped by the Red Chinese. Evelyn Wright, whose husband William struggled to stay alive at Hagaru, remembered repeating in her head, "They'll surely get out—they'll surely get out." For her, Christmas was terrible "because we still didn't know if they had escaped." Ruby Etheridge, not knowing if her son Bill was still alive or not, sent him a Christmas card saying, "Bill darling, I will be the happiest woman in the U.S.A. if I hear from you this week, for then I will know you are safe. Love, Mom."

Bud Fitch wrote his father from communications school in San Diego at the time of the Chinese entrance to the war: "It's Sunday night, so I have some time to catch up on my letters. I'm listening to Jack Benny now, and I'm getting a big kick out of it." However, Fitch added, "after hearing Walter Winchell tonight, it's kind of hard to enjoy it. . . . I guess the Oakland City boys are right in the middle of it." Like so many other Americans, Fitch now wondered if atomic weapons should be employed in Korea. "I wasn't much for dropping the atomic bomb, and I don't think it is too effective against troops, but now I think we ought to drop it." Still upset over what was happening to his boyhood friends, Fitch added, in a bit of dark humor, "I wouldn't care if one dropped right on the White House, by mistake of course." Interestingly, the young reservist also noted to his parents how some marines were now attempting to escape a tour of duty in Korea: "We have twelve men 'over the hill' out of our company . . . and they won't let you out of the gate anymore." Sadly, Fitch observed, "It's not like it was in the last war. We don't have a united spirit to defeat the enemy."

The community of Evansville was particularly upset by the grim news of the Chinese entrance into the war. Responding to mounting inquiries by family members of reservists, Capt. George Schmidt, marine inspector-instructor in Evansville, told a local reporter, "The families of Evansville Marine Reservists, members of C Company called to active duty last August, can fairly well tell where the men are by the news dispatches coming out of Korea. . . . The first Marine division is the only Marine ground unit operating in Korea, and any man who is with that unit will have Korea in his address." Captain Schmidt further related that most of the marines with the local unit went overseas "within a few weeks after leaving here. . . . Another group went out some time later. . . . It would be almost impossible to tell what percentage of the local men are in the fight without contacting each individual family," he noted. "Casualty lists reaching here since the unit was recalled had named one local Marine killed in action and four others wounded."[61]

At this time, panic also mounted among reservists' families in other parts of the country. In Birmingham, Alabama, wives and mothers of the local Marine Corps Reserve unit sent telegrams to President Truman, asking him to use "every weapon necessary" to save their loved ones. They pleaded with the president and Alabama's congressional delegation to "'evacuate our troops immediately.' The message was drafted at a tearful mass meeting . . . sponsored by the local Marine Corps League Auxiliary and attended by some 300 relatives of members of almost all branches of the armed forces. Many of the parents who had family in Korea expressed their anxiety in spontaneous speeches at the Jefferson County Court House. They blamed 'bad leadership' for the plight of 'our boys' and urged that the troops not be 'left to the slaughter of Chinese Reds.' Some were so choked with emotion they could hardly talk."[62] Pleas for action now went up throughout the country for all the troops. "In St. Louis, mothers advertised in the Post Dispatch for 'parents, wives, sweetheart and friends' to 'flood Truman and Congress with telegrams' to save our troops. . . . In Wolfe Pointe, Montana, a selective service board refused to draft any more Roosevelt County boys until an atom bomb was dropped in Korea. When the board was asked to resign, it was deluged with appreciative letters." In towns and cities across the country, citizens organized in support of the use of atomic weapons: "The Denver Post front-paged a letter from a retired Army captain, Eugene R. Guild, whose boy had been killed in Korea. 'I let my boy down because I did not help him here at home by fighting against the cowardly appeasement policies of those in Washington,' he wrote."[63]

As the agonizing days passed, Evansville reservists' families finally began to hear bits and pieces of information regarding their loved ones. Newspaper articles carried many heartrending stories. The wife of Mason Wiers finally received two letters, the first reporting that Lieutenant Wiers was "hit in the hand with a concussion grenade, and slightly wounded." Wiers also reported that "he had one frozen foot and was near pneumonia." His second letter came from the hospital, and in it he explained that he had originally been evacuated from Hagaru, near the Chosin Reservoir, to Japan.[64]

Mrs. Gene Koonce received word that her husband had been wounded a second time, this time by shell fragments in the right arm, and he had barely escaped the trap. He did not give details, but his mother, Amy E. Koonce, told a newspaper reporter, "He's right-handed, so if he could write, it can't be a very bad wound." Indeed, she could not have guessed how bullet-ridden her son really was. Pfc. William H. Etheridge wrote to his mother that both he and Pvt. Richard Bost, a former neighbor, were safe and were in the process of boarding ships at Hungnam.[65] Another Evansville marine, Pfc. Curtis A. Richardsville, twenty-two, wrote his parents that he had safely escaped the Chinese trap in Northeast Korea and was boarding a ship at the UN beachhead. He had not been heard from since Thanksgiving, when the division moved up to the Chosin Reservoir. He wrote that after being on the front fourteen days, "I'll never forget the things I saw. . . . I was plenty scared—we couldn't hear anything but machine guns and explosions, airplanes roaring and big guns going off."[66] Pfc. Glendal [Jeep] Ellis, twenty-one, wrote his parents that his feet were swollen to twice their normal size after being frozen. He was on a hospital ship in Hungnam harbor.[67]

Another frantic family who got a letter in time to celebrate Christmas were Mr. and Mrs. Ralph Inkenbrandt and their daughter-in-law, Mrs. Donald Inkenbrandt. Private Inkenbrandt, twenty, was now on a hospital ship after walking for eleven miles with frozen toes. Pfc. Ronald Burton wrote his family that he was safe and sleeping in a bed for the first time in weeks after having to carry dead buddies down a mountainside during the retreat.[68]

Other good news followed. Nina Thurman received word that her husband, Pvt. Jess Thurman, was safe and in good health after escaping the Chinese trap. He wrote of the difficulties of the ice and snow in keeping the road clear for supplies to get through. He added, "We were surrounded by at least four divisions of the enemies. . . . We took our toll on them. We walked and walked for 20 straight hours[,] . . . no chow and no sleep." He was happy to report that as he wrote this letter he was in a big tent with an oil heater and had as much food as he could eat.[69] Pfc. Chester Krueger wrote to his parents, Mr. and Mrs. Arthur H. Krueger, telling them he was all right and asking them to please tell Mr. and Mrs. Lee Roy Graham that their son Pfc. David Graham was all right but too busy to write. Pvt.

Charles Deffendall wrote to his parents, Mr. and Mrs. James Deffendall, that he was on a ship headed for Pusan.[70]

Sometimes news of a loved one's survival came to family members in odd ways. Mr. and Mrs. Ray Mitchell Sr. were very grateful to America's amateur radio operators. They received word through the ham radio channels that their son, Pfc. Raymond Mitchell Jr., eighteen, was safe in a naval hospital in Yokohama, Japan. Their last letter from him had been dated 21 November; in it he told them he was in combat with the 1st Marine Division. An Evansville ham radio operator, Earl Greer, heard a CQ called on his radio receiver saying there was a message for someone in Evansville, Indiana. Greer took the message, which was being sent by an Indianapolis ham radio operator who received it after it had been relayed from station to station from a trunk line from Yokohama. Private Mitchell's message assured his family that his wounds were "nothing serious."

In one instance, an Evansville reservist who fought at the Chosin Reservoir was used by the national news media to convince American civilians to go to the Red Cross and help fill blood banks for use on the wounded in the war. Pvt. Emmanuel Hester had volunteered his thanks to the Red Cross according to a United Press article. The piece reported that Hester had been "given 27 pints of whole blood after receiving severe wounds in the back and shoulder . . . in Korea." According to the article, Hester told his doctor, "Just tell the folks, whoever they are, that a little country boy from Indiana is grateful [for the blood]. I wouldn't be here to tell you if it weren't for them."[71]

Paul McDaniel's family received a letter from him on 13 December telling of his narrow escape. His mother immediately wrote back: "We were so very thankful to get your letter yesterday. No one will ever know how glad—for it could've been worse—we have wondered and worried because we could hear and read so much and knew if it was possible you would write. . . . Hope you aren't hurt too bad and can get over it all. We have one consolation: you are in out of the cold and being cared for. If you can only be sent back here. . . . We never received any war office news of you. I guess it's better we didn't. It's better we got a letter in your writing. Dad always says if he can see your handwriting, he feels better."

To their delight, McDaniel's family received the best possible Christmas present—he got to come home for the holidays. A local Evansville paper carried the story of his return: "Cpl. McDaniel was allowed to come here from the Philadelphia Naval hospital for a few days. He suffered frozen hands and feet and got a bullet through his ankle during the fighting retreat from the Chosin Reservoir to Hungnam. Cpl. McDaniel's leg is in a cast, but he can hobble about, he said today at his home. . . . 'I don't know how long I'll have this cast on. . . . Right now I'm getting reacquainted with my wife and year old daughter. I hardly recognized the girl when I walked in the door—she didn't know me at all. It's wonderful to be back, and being away makes me appreciate our country all the more,' he says."[72]

Not all word coming back to family members regarding an injured son or husband was good, but in one instance, heartbreaking news was premature. In the early months of 1951, Henry Orth Jr., the Evansville reservist who had been knocked out by a mortar round, bandaged, and then tagged to be sent back to Regimental Headquarters, returned to the front after deciding his comrades still needed his help. Because neither Orth nor his body showed up at headquarters, it was assumed that the marine had been killed in action. A lieutenant wrote a letter to Orth's mother telling of her son's death. On top of the letter, the woman received official notification that her son had been killed. She painfully grieved for two weeks before she was informed that there had been a tremendous mistake and her son was still alive. "My mother never really got over the shock of thinking I was dead," Orth recalled.

Sadly, for most families who received tragic news, the information was true. Around the same time as other families were hearing from their loved ones of miraculous escapes from the Chosin, Mr. and Mrs. Clyde W. Grove received a telegram notifying them that their son, Pfc. William Clyde ("Billy") Grove, had been wounded in action on 2 December. The telegram was worded in the same way as those others had received, saying, "The nature of the wound and further details have not yet been reported." The marine's mother recalled that it was the first word they had received from him since 20 November, when he had asked for a pair of gloves. Before that time he had written at least once a week. "It is a relief to know he's still alive," Mrs. Grove told a newspaper reporter at the time. However, as the days passed, and the Grove family failed to hear further word, some of Grove's Evansville buddies finally contacted the family. In a newspaper interview, Mrs. Grove related how the marines had told her that her son had been "left for dead on the battlefield when they had to make a sudden retreat. They thought someone might have found him later and taken him to a hospital if he had not been killed." Mrs. Grove then wrote to Sen. Homer Capehart and Rep. Winfield K. Denton, requesting assistance in locating her son. Both men were unable to trace him. Then a second report arrived saying Grove was missing in action. "He wanted a pair of warm gloves," Mrs. Grove recalled, "and we sent him some fur-lined ones." They would never see their son alive again.[73]

In late April 1951, the community of Oakland City received shocking news about their own Bud Fitch. Almost everyone in the small town was familiar with the well-kept, cottage-style house in which Henry and Garnet Fitch had made a loving home for their family. Their oldest child, Beth, was a student nurse at Ball Hospital in Muncie. The Fitches also had two younger children—Gordon and Jane—almost ten years younger than Mary Beth and Bud. This family was one of the most well liked and respected families in the small college community. Garnet Fitch, however, had been gravely concerned ever since Bud's unit had been called up for the Korean War. Though thrilled to see him on leave over the Christmas holidays, the family had an even harder time saying goodbye than before he left for Pendleton. Garnet was afraid she would never see him again.

On 22 April, the headline in the *Princeton Clarion* (a nearby town) reported, "Joint Chiefs to Tell of Differences with General MacArthur."[74] The next day's headline hit the families whose sons and husbands were still fighting in Korea like a punch to the stomach: "700,000 Reds Opened Counter Drive—U.N. Troops Withdraw."[75] By the time that headline appeared, the unthinkable had already happened. Robert "Bud" Fitch had been killed in the mammoth 22 April battle, just a day prior to his nineteenth birthday. On 26 April his parents received the telegram telling them of the death of their beloved son. Younger son Gordon Fitch, about ten years old at the time, remembered playing at a friend's house in the neighborhood when the telegram came. The play was interrupted by his little sister who told him to come home at once, that "something terrible had happened." The message in the telegram drove brutally to the point: "Deeply regret to inform you that your son Pfc. Robert Stuart Fitch USMC died 23 April 1951 of wounds received in action in Korea in the performance of his duty and service of his country." After hearing his grief-stricken mother read the telegram and not knowing what to do, Gordon went to his room.[76]

The entire town reeled from the devastating news. Helen Robertson, a neighbor, remembered what a blow it was to the people of Oakland City. The death of the likeable Eagle Scout "was like losing somebody out of your own family," she recalled. Gene Holderbaugh, another neighbor, remembered hearing the terrible news from her young nephew, who arrived at her door breathless and upset. A memorial service was held for Bud in May, but the funeral would not take place until October when his body was finally returned. At the latter ceremony, young Gordon Fitch stepped forward to receive the American flag that had been taken off the casket holding the remains of his brother.

Bud's father, Henry Fitch, dealt with his loss by seeking information from anyone who was near Bud at the time of his death. Sydney Greenwood, one of the marines from Able who was present at the 22 April battle, spent over a year in the hospital recovering from his wounds. While convalescing, he came across a desperate plea in the *Marine Corps Gazette* asking for information regarding Able Company's struggle on the night of Bud Fitch's death. The request came from Henry Fitch. Greenwood soon wrote to Bud's father, sharing his recollections of the battle with the heartbroken man.

In December, shortly before Christmas, Henry Fitch sent a reply: "Dear Marine, I received your letter and I want to thank you for taking the time and trouble to write as we are very sad about our son." Mr. Fitch added that "any news we hear . . . seems to help." Mr. Fitch described his son as a "large boy, [who] weighed 200 and [was] six feet tall and wore glasses." This information, Henry Fitch hoped, would help Greenwood "place him, although I know that when in combat you have little time to visit and get acquainted." Greenwood, however, was sorry to report to the Fitches that he had not really had the opportunity to get to know their son. Yet Greenwood would always feel a special bond to Bud Fitch, believing as he did, that Fitch and the other marines who lost their lives on 22 April helped turn the tide of battle on that fateful night.

Not giving up on finding out more about his son's last day, the elder Fitch told Greenwood, "If you can give me the name and address of the Marine that was with you for awhile in the hospital and also from 'A' Co., I could write him and see if he was near my son on April 23rd." The fatherly Fitch ended the letter to the wounded marine by saying, "You stated in your letter that you were wounded but not seriously on April 22nd. I was wondering if you were wounded more seriously later and as a result you are now in the hospital. I hope you are on the road to complete recovery and will be able to spend Xmas in your home. I have great respect for veterans who saw action in Korea, as our son told of some of his experiences in his letters." In fact, Greenwood would spend a year recovering and lose much of the use of his left arm.

Some of Bud's friends from Oakland City, such as Gordon Greene, noticed how Mrs. Fitch had difficulty accepting Bud's death: "She maintained the hope that there had been some mistake and he would appear at the front door."[77] However, through this difficult period she remained the wonderful mother she had always been. One neighbor recalled frequently seeing Garnet in the warm glow of light from the Fitches' front room, reading to her two younger children.

While the Fitches and others who lost family members in Korea struggled to deal with the death of a loved one, the war continued. In May 1951, UN troops had once more pushed just north of the thirty-eighth parallel. Little movement would occur on the battlefield for the next two years. Americans now had "little stomach for pressing on with the 'police action[,]'. . . for in the aftermath of China's intervention it was manifest that Americans have lost their enthusiasm of the previous summer for the bloody affair in East Asia. A Gallup poll taken in early February 1951 reported that only 39 percent of those interviewed believed America's intervention in the Korean conflict had not been a mistake."[78]

Eventually Americans became "disenchanted with the armed conflict which no longer seemed likely to end in a magnificent victory."[79] For much of the nation, there seemed to be a "switch from urgency to complacency."[80] Ironically, through the act of arming itself to prevent a third world war, the United States had already succeeded in lessening world tensions. Faced with the reality of forty divisions in Western Europe by 1953, the Communists had become less aggressive. The possibility of a Soviet attack now appeared remote even in the Far East. The fear that Communist China would seize Indochina and all of Southeast Asia had disappeared. With those fears allayed, many Americans were no longer in the grip of war. The North Koreans and Chinese had grown tired of fighting as well. In July 1953, three years after the war had begun, U.S. general Mark Clark signed the truce document for the UN forces. News media carried little about the truce signing. Reflecting the bitterness many Americans felt after so little gain following so much sacrifice, General Clark declared, "I cannot find it in me to exalt at this hour."[81] Within a decade the war would fade from most Americans' memories.

Two teenage reservists having fun at a two-week summer camp in the late 1940s. *Top bunk:* Richard Whitfield of Evansville, Indiana. *Courtesy of Richard Whitfield*

Four Evansville reservists who participated in Operation Santa Claus Land in December 1948. *Standing, left to right:* Henry Maley, Robert Egan, and Paul McDaniel; *seated,* William Mangrum. *Courtesy of Paul McDaniel*

Seven of the ten Oakland City boys at a farewell party given on 22 August 1950. *Back row, left to right:* Albert Dickson, Robert "Bud" Fitch, Garold Sheetz, Forrest Miller, and William Cunningham. *Front row:* William Marshall and Gordon Greene. *Courtesy of William Marshall*

Several of the reservists who were called up had recently been married. Pictured above on their wedding day are Jess and Nina Thurman of Evansville. *Courtesy of Jess and Nina Thurman*

The Barnard family of Oakland City, Indiana, say goodbye to their oldest son, Charles "Barney" Barnard, 28 August 1950. *Left to right, back row:* Barney Barnard, Kenneth Barnard, William Barnard; *front row:* Betty Ann Barnard (wife of Barney), Neva Barnard, and Charles Barnard. *Courtesy of William Marshall*

Teenage reservists often left behind much younger siblings. Here Oakland City native William Marshall holds his sister Dixie Michael and his brother Patrick Michael on the day he left for active duty. *Courtesy of William Marshall*

Best friends since grade school (*left to right*), Glendal "Jeep" Ellis, Arthur Hart Jr., and William Ginger stand before the Evansville Reserve Headquarters on the day they left for active service. *Courtesy of Arthur Hart Jr.*

Eight boys from Oakland City line up for a last snapshot before their train leaves for Camp Pendleton. *Left to right:* Forrest Miller, Robert "Bud" Fitch, Gordon Greene, William Marshall, Charles "Barney" Barnard, Albert Dickson, Donald Corn, and Garold Sheetz.

Family and friends of C Company reservists linger on the platform on an overcast day as their loved ones board the train for Camp Pendleton, 28 August 1950. This scene would be repeated in more than 120 cities across America when Marine Corps Reserve companies were hastily activated. *Courtesy of Denning Campbell*

Anita Campbell, a proud but concerned mother, stands by her son Denning as he waits to board the train. *Courtesy of Denning Campbell*

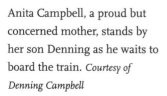

Evansville reservists arrive at Camp Pendleton. *Courtesy of Bonnie Eberle*

A few of the Oakland City reservists getting together at Tent Camp Two shortly before some of them were sent to Korea. *Left to right, back row:* Albert Dickson, Donald Corn, Kenneth Dougan, and William Cunningham; *front row:* Gordon Greene and William Marshall. *Courtesy of William Marshall*

Alice Whitfield, wife of an Evansville reservist stationed at Camp Pendleton, stands on a California beach. *Courtesy of Richard and Alice Whitfield*

Reservist Richard Eberle and his wife Bonnie in front of the hotel where they stayed during his brief preparation at Pendleton to go to Korea. *Courtesy of Bonnie Eberle*

Some Evansville reservists did their entire service at Camp Pendleton. Those with families often stayed in Quonset huts on base. Here the Schellhase family—Marjorie and David Schellhase Sr. with their sons David Jr., six, and Michael, four—stand in front of their living quarters. *Courtesy of David and Marjorie Schellhase*

A group of reservists taking a break from training at Camp Pendleton. They and others like them would soon be shipping off to Korea. *Courtesy of Richard Whitfield*

An excited Gordon Greene prepares to board the USS *General Walker*, bound for war. *Courtesy of William Cunningham*

Snapshot of the USS *General Walker* leaving California for Japan. A number of C Company reservists traveled on this ship on the first leg of their journey to Korea. *Courtesy of William Cunningham*

Reservist Richard Eberle shortly after his arrival at Wonsan, Korea, October 1950. At this point in the war, many reservists thought they would be home by Christmas. *Courtesy of Bonnie Eberle*

Three marines stand in front of a tent at Hagaru, North Korea, a day before the break south began. On the right is Evansville reservist William Wright. *Courtesy of William Wright*

Richard Eberle standing in the kind of deep snow that so hindered fighting efforts at the Chosin Reservoir. *Courtesy of Bonnie Eberle*

Somber reservist Raleigh McGary shortly after escaping the Chinese trap at the Chosin Reservoir. *Courtesy of Raleigh McGary*

Christmas card photo of Oakland City reservist Robert "Bud" Fitch. On the back of the card Fitch wrote, "I may have a chance to see some of the boys before long." Fitch was killed in the 1951 Chinese spring offensive. *Courtesy of William Cunningham*

Reservists were often amazed by the amount of weight Korean peasants could carry on their A-frames. *Courtesy of Raleigh McGary*

Six former C Company reservists who survived the April Chinese offensive in 1951 come together shortly after the battle. *Left to right, back row:* William Etheridge, Richard Lockridge, Gordon Greene, and Albert Dickson; *front row:* Robert White-house and Ronald Burton. *Courtesy of Robert Whitehouse*

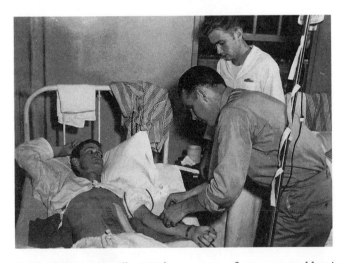

Oakland City native Albert Dickson recovers from a mortar blast in a Japanese hospital in May 1951. The young man had more than 150 stitches, losing his spleen and a kidney to the blast. *Courtesy of William Cunningham*

Four convalescing marines in Japan. Standing on the left is William Etheridge of Evansville, and sitting on the left is Gordon Greene of Oakland City. To the right are marines Gobel and Strode. *Courtesy of William Etheridge*

A marine camp in the area of Luke's Castle. *Courtesy of Henry Orth Jr.*

A group of marines getting ready to shoulder their heavy packs and go up a hill into combat in the Iron Triangle area, June 1951. *Courtesy of Henry Orth Jr.*

Reservist David Graham, somewhere in Korea. The photograph captures the mix of marine bravo and youthful innocence teenage reservists often possessed.
Courtesy of David Graham

A group of marines dig in at a Korean rice paddy sometime during the summer of 1951. In the foreground is Robert Whitehouse's squad.
Courtesy of Robert Whitehouse

Many marines were disturbed by the suffering of the Korean people, especially the children. Evansville reservist William Wright (in white shirt) is shown here with a Korean orphan boy his squad adopted. *Courtesy of William Wright*

Marine snapshot of young Korean child. *Courtesy of Raleigh McGary*

Evansville reservist Henry Orth Jr., who was reported as killed in action for two weeks before his mother was informed otherwise. *Courtesy of Henry Orth Jr.*

Philadelphia reservist Sydney Greenwood shortly before the 22 April 1951 battle in which Bud Fitch was killed. Greenwood would later correspond with Fitch's grieving parents. *Courtesy of Sydney Greenwood*

The Evansville Korean War monument, built through the efforts of C Company veterans. *Courtesy of Henry Orth Jr.*

Members of C Company who attended the 1992 reunion. *Courtesy of Jess Thurman*

8   *Every Time I See a Marine . . .*

Coming home. For men who have been away to war, no other words sound as sweet. Relief and joy, however, are always tempered by the memory of those who did not make it. The surviving men of C Company would find themselves returning home changed, both physically and emotionally; they were no longer the boys and young men who left Evansville on 28 August 1950. For those who fought in Korea, the return to the United States usually meant boarding a plane for Japan then taking a long journey by boat to California. After a two-week processing period, the men were generally allowed a thirty-day leave before reporting for duty at their stateside assignment.

When David Graham first arrived home on leave and set foot on Hoosier soil, he received a warm family welcome: his dad, mom, aunts, grandma—everybody was hugging him. Though he was extremely happy to be alive and grateful to at last be home, Graham was "surprised that the country wasn't more war-spirited. Except for the families with men in the war, I saw nothing much that would tell people that a war was going on." Members of David Graham's family were not the only ones glad to see him at home. Graham had run around with a large group of friends before he left for the war, and some of the girls in this crowd had corresponded with him frequently during his tour of duty. One of the girls, Betty Lawson, was a student nurse at St. Mary's Hospital. At lunchtime she and some other student nurses would often walk several blocks to downtown Evansville. One day, as they strolled, she spotted Graham getting out of his car in his uniform, home on leave. She was struck by how handsome and trim the young marine looked. Soon the youthful couple were engaged.

William Marshall, who had been called up while still a high school student, had always dreamed of playing professional baseball like his Oakland City neighbor and Baseball Hall of Fame member, Edd Roush. Upon his release from the service in the spring of 1952, the young man had an opportunity to try out for a Cincinnati Reds minor league team. Marshall hitchhiked to Columbia, South Carolina, for the camp, where he realized his dream of playing in a professional baseball game. However, he soon found himself "growing homesick. I wasn't really in shape for the tryout either," Marshall recalled, "so I went home after a couple of weeks." When an opportunity to try out for the Washington Senators arose, Marshall had to choose between going to spring training in 1953 with a minor league team or completing his senior year at Oakland City High School, which he had started in the fall of 1952. Remembering his promise to his mother to complete his education, and perhaps matured by his military experiences, Marshall elected not to go to the tryout camp. He graduated from high school and then went on to earn a degree from Oakland City College. A few years later the young man entered law school at Indiana University, where he graduated with honors.

Bill Etheridge enjoyed a pleasant homecoming when he came back to Evansville on leave from Great Lakes Naval Base. While on the train south from Chicago, he met a young man whose father owned a business in Evansville. After discovering that the rider across from him was a Korean War veteran, the young man asked how the marine was getting home from the train station. Etheridge said he would call a cab, but the young man declared, "No, you're not going to call a cab. . . . My dad's going to pick me up. We're going to take you home." Etheridge responded in his easygoing manner, "Oh, that isn't necessary." But the young man was emphatic: "No, you guys are heroes. . . . We're going to take you home." When the young man's father arrived and found his son with a Korean War veteran, he wanted to buy the young marine lunch. "When they finally dropped me off at home," Etheridge remembered, "the father said to me, 'Now, when you get ready to go back, you give me a call, and I'll come and pick you up in a Cadillac.'"

Once finished with his service, Etheridge returned to work at the telephone company in Evansville and later married. Another bit of good fortune for the young man, on his return from fighting, was the opportunity he had to work alongside two other Evansville reservists who had served in Korea, William Wright and Bill Nemer. Although none of the three felt at ease talking in great detail about the war, it was comforting to know that others who shared similar difficult memories were near. In one instance, shortly after the three men had returned to their jobs, their boss asked them to write down their war experiences for the company newspaper. Anxious to put the war behind them, the three men's unanimous response was a resounding "Hell, no!"

Tex Graham, one of only two officers of the original Evansville group who served in Korea, experienced an unusual homecoming. Once back in California, he and five other men sought the quickest transportation to Great Lakes Naval Base in Chicago, where they were to be stationed. "A sign on the barracks bulletin board saying, 'Drive Straight Through,' drew our attention," Graham remembered. "We called about the service and decided that was the fastest way to get home." The deal promised that a limousine would pick them up at their barracks the very next day. Joan Graham was already anxiously waiting in Chicago for her husband and was happy to hear of any travel plans that would speed his appearance. "The next morning we grabbed our gear and hurried to meet the limo and driver." The six marines gratefully climbed in and settled back for a long, but relatively comfortable, drive. The deal, however, turned out to be different than what they had been led to believe: "When we got to the edge of the city, we got a real surprise. The driver stopped at a gas station and told us we had to switch vehicles." The men's mouths fell open when they saw the pint-sized Nash waiting for them. Despite their irritation, this still seemed the fastest option, so they squeezed in for the hard ride.

Unfortunately, cramped conditions were not their only problem. Later in the journey, the marines found their driver falling asleep and drifting all over the road somewhere in Oklahoma. He would not allow anyone else to drive, so as Graham recalled, "we took turns punching him to keep him alert." Reckless, even when awake, at one point in a driving rain, the driver began passing a large truck near a curve. As the Nash approached the front end of the truck, the occupants spied a car coming straight for them. The oncoming car swerved wildly to avoid hitting them. When their driver kept going, Graham protested, "You've got to stop and see what happened to that other car!" Inexplicably, the driver continued. Fed up, Graham and another officer from the group ditched the car and driver at the next city. Graham purchased a train ticket and called his wife to tell her of the change in plans. Rushing through the call, he barely caught her saying something about the possibility of their appearing on a radio show.

Graham had never set eyes on his baby daughter, Susan, except for photographs, and he could hardly wait to see her. However, they had planned that Joan's mother would keep the baby while Joan and Tex spent their first night together alone in Chicago. Consequently, when the marine arrived at the train station, he was surprised to be met at the platform by strangers, who said they would take him to see Joan. Graham was somewhat apprehensive, but eager to see his wife as soon as possible, so he reluctantly accepted the ride. Astonished to find that the car had a motorcycle escort, the curious marine could not persuade anyone to tell him exactly what was happening. The motorcade pulled up to the back entrance of an enormous building and, after being rushed through a back kitchen and long hallway, Graham found himself "shoved through a door and onto a radio sound stage." The marine looked around and realized that he was center stage on the nationally popular show *Welcome Traveler*. "As I tried to get my bearings," he said, "a stranger carrying a crying baby girl thrust the wailing child into my arms. At that moment, I was totally confused."

Not until he saw his wife Joan did Graham realize what was happening—the radio station was broadcasting his reunion with his family live. Though still a little disoriented, Tex was thrilled to see Joan and the baby. As part of their appearance, the radio station showered the Grahams with gifts, such as a Tappan range and a layette for the baby. Although it was an unusual and startling homecoming, Graham, like others from the Evansville group, was overjoyed to be home. Like other reservists, Graham also put the war aside and quickly got on with his life, returning to teaching and coaching at Evansville Central High School after finishing his stateside duty.

When Gordon Greene's ship docked at San Francisco in December 1951, he got down on his hands and knees and kissed the earth. Greene's 1994 novel, *A Star for Buster,* contains a version of his return home. Greene told of taking a slow train from California and stepping off at the Oakland City depot at ten o'clock on Christmas Eve. A clean, white layer of snow accentuated the silence of the small station. The thankful reservist strolled down Main Street toward an all-night diner to grab a bite to eat before he surprised his family. Suddenly, however, Greene realized that there was now no "Roll of Honor" board to salute the dead and wounded, such as his friend Bud Fitch, as there had been during World War II. Greene sadly began to understand that the Korean conflict would somehow be a different kind of war in the minds of the American people.[1] Gordon Greene, too, went on with his life, believing he could somehow forget the war. He finished his bachelor degree at Oakland City College and went on to complete a doctoral degree, eventually becoming a professor of education at the University of Nebraska.

Such were some of the homecomings of the Evansville reservists. Many of the reservists also had to spend time in hospitals recuperating from war wounds. For some, such as Albert Dickson, it was nothing short of amazing that they survived. Several others of the Evansville group would always carry pieces of shrapnel in their bodies. Jack Burgdorf lived with a .30-caliber slug embedded in his back. One injury very common in the Chosin campaign—frostbite—would plague many of the veterans for the rest of their lives. For reservists and regulars alike, the scale and degree of physical problems caused by this injury was not recognized until the first meeting of the national Chosin Few organization in 1985: "The former Marines and soldiers had met to reminisce. But as they looked around, they were dumbfounded." The vets were having trouble getting up and walking. They soon realized that many of them had the same symptoms: "excess sweating, malformed toenails, infected stumps, skin cancer and cold sensitivity. Many had moved South to escape cold winters." Numerous Chosin veterans, who quietly overcame their injuries after returning from Korea, were "left with damaged blood vessels and nerves. Later the natural forces of aging, such as impaired circulation . . . [made] once-manageable ailments intolerable."[2]

One member of the Evansville group whose recovery exemplified heroic strength of spirit was Jess Thurman. After being struck by a bullet accidentally fired by a South Korean boy in October 1951, Thurman spent several days in a MASH unit, knocked out by morphine. When he finally woke, he found himself in Yokasuka Hospital in Japan, "strapped to a Stryker bed, covered in ice packs to bring down a raging fever." Three doctors and a Marine Corpsman appeared to tell him that he had been shot in the shoulder and that the bullet had severed his spine. The taller doctor of the trio said softly, "You are paralyzed from midchest down." Thurman soon realized that he was also unable to move his left arm. The immediate crisis, however, was a collapsed lung and the blood filling his chest cavity. As he again drifted in and out of consciousness, he thought of his young wife Nina and wondered if she knew.

Each day for the following nineteen days, doctors inserted a long needle in Thurman's side to drain the blood, an excruciatingly painful process. For every pint drained, they gave him a pint through transfusion. In surgery, a doctor removed the bullet from his back and later gave it to the young reservist. Ironically, the bullet would be nearly the only item he brought back from Korea, the rest of his gear having been stolen somewhere en route home. To add further injury, even a Purple Heart would elude him. Thurman was told he did not qualify for this award because he had not been in a combat area when the bullet tore through his spine. As Thurman began to recover, a corpsman told him, "We are going to get the use of that left arm back." Strengthening this arm became Thurman's initial focal point. He and the corpsman began undertaking a grueling workout with his left arm two to three hours each night.

During this period he was finally able to talk to his wife, Nina, by phone. She had been notified by the Defense Department that he had been shot and was paralyzed from the neck down. Thurman explained to her that the paralysis was from midchest down, and although he was also unable to use his left arm at this point, he planned to change that. He told her he wanted to say two very important things: "First, don't feel sorry for me, and second, we're going to live our lives just as we planned." Nina's strength of spirit was quickly apparent too. She said simply, "Alright. What do we do next?"

During Thurman's recovery in Tokyo, a fellow reservist, Gordon Greene, visited and explained to the wounded marine how it came about that the young Korean boy shot him. While at the Tokyo hospital, Thurman also received visits from boxer Joe Louis and actor Errol Flynn. The reservist spent nearly a year of recuperation and rehabilitation at the hospital in Japan; however, this was only the beginning. Next he was flown to a hospital in California, where he "felt I was laid aside to die. Even the hospital personnel did not know what to do with my kind of injury." Once there, though, Thurman was at least reunited with his wife, Nina, who had flown in from Indiana to be with him. Later Thurman was moved to the Veterans Administration hospital in Hines, Illinois, where he was initially considered not ready for a wheelchair. After he had regained movement of his left arm, "A corpsmen gave me two canes and put me on my stomach on a gurney." Soon Thurman was navigating the hallways, "propelling myself with a cane in each hand." The recovering marine also participated in a woodworking class, making an elegant tray with inlaid veneer, all the while lying on his stomach. "When the hospital decided I was ready for a wheelchair, I started harassing them to let me go home," Thurman remembered. A couple of months later the Evansville man was on his way.

The world Jess Thurman returned to was much different than the world we know today, where making the environment wheelchair-accessible is the law. In the 1950s there were no curb cuts in sidewalks, and six inches—the normal height of a curb—was enough to stop a wheelchair in its tracks. Thurman found even more obstacles indoors, where, he recalled, "most doorways were not wide enough to accommodate a wheelchair. A multiple-story building without an elevator was impossible." The Veterans Administration had sent him home with hand controls to convert a car for his use; however, climbing from the wheelchair to behind the wheel of the car was extremely difficult. Despite his tremendous upper-body strength, his left arm was still somewhat weak. Besides the physical hurdles, the Thurmans also had to overcome the attitudes of the times. "I felt like people thought that I should go home and hide," Thurman recalled, "so that others wouldn't have to deal with my disability."

The rest of the Thurman family tackled the situation with the same head-on determination as Jess and Nina. As soon as Jess was able to return home, his father went to work building ramps at all the family homes. Skilled as a mechanic, the elder Thurman also modified the car kit to make it more workable. International Harvester, where Jess worked before the war, gave him a job inspecting M1 rifle parts. The large factory was ahead of its time in also providing a wheelchair-accessible rest room.

Thurman soon found that navigating Evansville's city streets meant using alleys, often taking him far out of his way, but giving him access to the sidewalks. Everything else became a matter of reach: "Anything I could reach, I would do, from painting [devising his own extension tools] to laying concrete blocks, to trimming shrubs. Only the highest reaches required help." People in their neighborhood became accustomed to seeing Thurman carrying out all kinds of jobs, using whatever means it took. The Evansville man still faced many challenges, some he recalls as humorous. For example, once Thurman was home by himself "hanging Christmas lights on the shrubbery, when I leaned too far in my wheelchair and flipped it over." The accident left Thurman sprawled partially out in his driveway. Seeing a neighbor coming down the street in a truck, the fallen man frantically waved his hat. Thinking that this was just one more way Jess had found to get a job done, the neighbor just smiled and waved back as he drove past. "You quickly learn to look on the humorous side of situations like that," Thurman mused.

Shortly after International Harvester sold out, Thurman went to work for twenty-seven and a half years in inventory control at Brandeis Industries. Throughout this time, he helped Nina raise their two children, performed much of the maintenance on their house, and used his woodworking skills to create furniture and large decorative cutouts for every holiday. He also continued as mechanic for the stock car he and his brother, and later his son, owned and raced. It bothered Thurman's reservist comrades to no end that the marine was not awarded the Purple Heart for his injury in Korea. However, as a constant reminder of that defining moment, the jagged slug that struck Jess Thurman those many years ago hangs framed in Jess and Nina's home; his own private sort of Purple Heart.

Though not as obvious as the physical injuries, most of the men would have lingering emotional scars from their ordeal in East Asia. Few if any of them would recognize this pain for many years. Korean War veterans came home to no hero's welcome and quietly went back to school or work. As Gordon Greene observed, "Like so many Korean War veterans, I returned home, placed my war experiences on the back burner, went to college on the GI Bill, got a job, married, and raised a family."[3] Pushing back the trauma and anguish they had endured in their recent past, these men quietly slipped back into their former lives. Almost to a man, all they wanted to do was forget, and as it became apparent that Korea would become the "forgotten" war, it seemed no one else wanted to remember either.

But the horrors of war would not simply go away. Among the reservists who came from the Evansville unit, even though they did not speak of their experiences in Korea, there were still signs of unresolved trauma. Robert Whitehouse, while working at Servel "in a white shirt and tie," recalled walking along a production line "when a loud noise caused me to hit the floor and roll under a bench. At first, several workers laughed, until a World War II vet came over and scolded them. 'If you'd experienced what this man had, you wouldn't be laughing,' he said." Other signs of deeply buried pain haunted many of the former reservists as well, such as recurring nightmares, depression, and bouts of moodiness. One reservist found that for almost thirty years after the war, he could not go outside on a snowy night without being overcome by memories of another winter those many years ago in Korea. Such flashbacks left him unable to sleep.

The loss of friends or family to the war also created memories almost too painful to bear. Bill Etheridge, who "lost three good buddies in Korea," could not recall the war without thinking about his friends and what it would be like if they had lived. Gordon Greene, too, found most of his pain bound up in the loss of his best friend, Bud Fitch. Greene carried the loss of his friend like a great weight on his soul, much like the Korean peasants with their overloaded A-frames. In addition to his own pain from Bud's death, Gordon also bore guilt for the grief of the Fitch family. He often wondered what might have happened if he had been able to give Bud some advice for fighting on the line. More painful still, Greene carried the burden of knowing he helped influence Bud to join the reserves. As time passed, Greene tried to make sense of it all, and because of his verbal abilities, he was able to leave behind a body of work documenting his quest for peace and understanding.

One of Gordon Greene's earliest attempts to make sense of his time in Korea was his novel "Boondockers," in which, after experiencing all the brutalities of combat, the main character dies when a mortar round lands in his foxhole. It was dedicated, not surprisingly, "To Bud, who didn't make it." Acknowledging that most of the situations, but not the characters, were based in truth, Greene described his purpose as "revealing the various attitudes for making emotional and psychological adjustments to combat."[4] An interested editor suggested that Greene change the ending of his book and let the main character live. Greene later explained, "I would not do this [make this change]. That was the point of the whole book. I wanted readers to know these men, and know the tragedy. The book was never published. I again buried the feelings . . . [and] pulled myself up by my bootstraps."[5]

Through the next fifteen years Greene continued to use writing as a way of battling the old demons. He wrote many poems about his time in Korea, such as "Waiting," a poem that touches upon the paralyzing fear that descends just before combat:

> They're coming!
> Down by the creek
> Nee saw two of them
> Silhouetted by the flares.
>
> Straining—it's difficult to see
> Too many boulders
> The heavy 30's are silent
> Discipline is the word . . .
>
> Wonder what time it is?
> No one ever knows—

What difference does it make?

It's one eternal night.[6]

In "The Five Paragraph War," written in 1987, Greene vented his frustration regarding the forgotten status of the Korean War:

Oh the Five Paragraph War
A run-o-the-mill fling;
Two frozen feet
An arm in a sling.

Ice up my nose
Two ruddy cheeks;
Ice in my beans
No B.M. for weeks.

Chesty asked for beer
"No!" said the W.C.T.U.;
Wade through a rice paddy
Step in honey pot stew.

Oh the press was in Tokyo
Standin' at the bar;
Findin' the front
Was a ridge too far.

The Five Paragraph War
Was a minor bash;
Remembered by most
As a farce named M.A.S.H.[7]

On 28 August 1984, the thirty-fourth anniversary of the day the Evansville
reserve unit left for Camp Pendleton, Greene penned a letter to his lost
friend, Bud, reminiscing about their younger days together: "The summer
of 1950. Remember how we talked about combat as we rode double on
your motorcycle through the countryside while waiting for the departure
date?" The letter went on to describe to Bud a recent trip Greene had taken
back to Oakland City: "My youngest son [Ben] and I went back home this

summer. Very few there would know you or me. People and buildings have come and gone. . . . Your home is still neat and trim. . . . Those yews at the north end of the front yard are gone. They made a miserable end zone for football! Your mom looks great! Even though beyond 80 years, there is that twinkle in her eyes." Mournfully though, he also noted that Mrs. Fitch still seemed unreconciled to Bud's death. Addressing his friend, Greene closed the letter by saying, "She remembers, Bud. Probably every day since the telegram, she remembers."[8]

At the age of fifty, Greene "suffered an aneurysm and a subsequent depression." As he recovered from the aneurysm, but not from the depression, his wife Marynelle, already a dedicated bicyclist, convinced him that the sport of bicycling could be just what he needed to "get back on track." Marynelle had been wise about her husband's needs, and the bicycling led to another sort of therapy for Greene. On one of his cross-state bicycle trips, he made a side trip to Marshalltown, Iowa, to visit the brother of his platoon sergeant, Ernie Umbaugh, who was killed in the Chosin campaign. After visiting the Umbaugh family, a thought returned again and again to Greene's mind: "What a shame it is that Ernie Umbaugh and others like him had been forgotten. Ernie, at the old age of twenty-seven, was the father figure for his platoon of eighteen, nineteen, and twenty year olds. Yet now, no one remembered Ernie Umbaugh but the immediate family, and a few of his 'boys,' who were now approaching sixty."

Greene continued to ruminate on this subject until he hit upon the idea of a bike ride across the country on the thirty-eighth parallel to call attention to the men and women who had served in Korea. Greene decided that the fortieth anniversary of the beginning of the war would be an appropriate time to draw notice to it. He began to work in conjunction with a group raising funds for an international Korean War monument in San Pedro, California. Greene planned to set up a miniature version of the monument on his stops across the country to solicit donations, and the organization agreed to provide vans and drivers to escort him. He found one veteran, Rik Yoshizawa (Charlie Company, 19th Infantry) to accompany him the whole way, and many others joined them for various stretches across the country.

The thirty-eighth parallel begins roughly at Washington, D.C., and runs across the country to San Francisco, California. Interestingly, it cuts right through Evansville, Indiana, one of many stops where Greene would be provided with food and sleeping quarters, along with some familiar friendly faces. Gordon made his trip a metaphor for the Korean War, from training to uniform to depending on his fellow vets. He kept a journal of his experiences, and in his introduction noted one tremendous difference in his mental training for this trip as opposed to the mental training required for war: "Combat training demanded a fixed and precise mental focus—a mind attuned to handling the tasks at hand; one that did not consider softening for sentimental moods or retrospective thinking. One's ability to function as a soldier required that his mind stay within the necessary parameters." In contrast, Greene said that for sixty year olds "on this bicycle mission, retrospective and sentimental thinking not only went unsuppressed but, when it was present, became the focus of our attention. So, although on this trip I encountered many situations that, in one way or another, reminded me of Korea, the differences would be obvious from the start of our training; the purpose of our training this time was not to get in shape to fight in a war, but to get in shape to remember those who did."9

The most poignant part of the journey had to be the day that Gordon Fitch, younger brother of Bud and now a professor of business administration at the University of Kansas, joined Greene as he rode through Kansas. Greene later recalled, "That particular day was a proud one for me in that I knew Bud would have been with me had he made it. . . . The many discussions that Gordon and I shared along the 80 mile segment will always remain with me. It was a day of sharing information about his brother and my friend. It was a day of sharing stories that helped Gordon to get to know the older brother that he did not have for 40 years of his life." Perhaps of even greater consequence came a request from Mrs. Fitch, who in a phone conversation asked Greene to serve as her remaining son's big brother. Greene later wrote that there was "no higher compliment" he could receive. Unstated in his description of the overwhelming emotions he felt, was his gratitude for the beginnings of a long-hoped-for absolution.10

At about the time Greene began to envision a way to remind the country about America's sacrifices in Korea by a cross-country bicycle ride, Richard Eberle, the World War II vet who had been sworn into the

Evansville marine reserve unit while he slept at the YMCA, began to experience a deep longing. Like most of the others from the Evansville group, Eberle had scarcely spoken of the difficult times in Korea. However, as the feeling persisted, he eventually came to realize that this yearning, almost forty years after the war, centered around the desire to reunite with other members of the reserve unit and share experiences. For the first time, Eberle started going through all the clippings his wife Bonnie had painstakingly collected back during the trying days of 1950 and 1951. This work led to three large scrapbooks. For a couple of years the former reservist silently nurtured the idea of a reunion, sometimes finding himself misty-eyed without knowing exactly why. When he finally shared his heart's desire with Bonnie, she helped him act on it.

Finding all the members of C Company turned out to be a daunting task. First the Eberles contacted Paul Torian, the former company commander, to see if he had a master list. Interestingly, Torian had recently set about doing the same thing himself, though without much success. Still determined, Bonnie continued to pour through all the clippings in the scrapbooks to make a list of the names she could find there. After making contacts in St. Louis and Washington, D.C., and waiting for a year, she was notified that she could get a list by serial number on microfilm.

In the meantime, Richard Eberle had contacted several of the reservists: Roy Jolly, Tex Graham, Don Lindenberg, Paul McDaniel, and Ross Compton. The Eberles, along with these men and their spouses, began a series of monthly meetings at which they would be assigned unlocated reservists to find. After exhausting all avenues, they produced a considerable list. As the group began contacting C Company members, they received a variety of reactions. Some of the men wanted nothing to do with the endeavor. After repressing the memories for so long, they were afraid of being overwhelmed by the events from their past. One of the wives recalled her husband's first reaction. He told her, "I don't think I can get involved . . . because I don't want all that brought back, you know. I just want to forget it ever happened." But this reservist, like many others, relented and was among the eighty who attended the first reunion in 1990.

If you ask any of the men and women who attended that first reunion of C Company, 16th Infantry Battalion, United States Marine Corps Reserve what they remember most about that meeting, almost every single one would say "the crying." Men who had never discussed the trauma of their war experiences suddenly found themselves with buddies they had not seen in forty years, including some who had traveled all the way across the country for the event. Stories and tears flowed. Several spoke of "a cathartic effect" and "a release." After forty years they were ready to tell the stories of that time of their youth, spent in a cruel place, fighting a savage enemy. It was an eye-opening experience for many of the wives, most of whom had never heard their husbands tell these tales of war. The experience brought many of the couples closer. Shortly after, for example, Richard Eberle dusted off his old maps and began to share his Korean ordeals with his wife Bonnie.

Most of all, the first reunion was a time of healing. Some of the veterans described it as "a weight being lifted" or "a feeling of freedom." Perhaps Gordon Greene best summed up the need the Korean veterans had to meet and heal when he noted, "During [my cross country] trip, I realized the affinity of honoring the dead and celebrating the living. The good men who sacrificed their lives in Korea would certainly want the values they died for to live on; yet they would not have wanted to be remembered only in somber or even only in patriotic sentiments. They knew how to band together with fire in their hearts for a common cause. They also knew how to have a good time in the company of good men."[11] C Company reunions have become just such an event.

At the first reunion of C Company, Richard Eberle presented the idea of raising funds for a Korean War monument in Evansville. The group quickly embraced the idea and planning began. Several of the men who had been reluctant to participate decided to join in the task. Some of the money was collected from the veterans themselves, but the overwhelming majority of the cost had to be raised. Paul McDaniel suggested Steve Shields of Hopkinsville, Kentucky, as sculptor after seeing his statue of a soldier at Pennyrile State Park in Kentucky. After being contacted about putting together a design, Shields grew enthusiastic and set about making a model. Donating the plastic for the job, M&M Plastics of Evansville made small replicas of the model to be used for fund raising. Attractive postcards of the design were sent to everyone who mailed a donation. The veterans also worked hard going door to door and collecting money in buckets placed at various locations around the area. Hoping to have the monument ready to dedicate at the 1992 reunion, the men marched in parades, worked at festivals, and held gun shoots and raffles. Finally, after eight months, more than ninety thousand dollars had been raised. The result of all the hard work was an impressive and stirring copper monument depicting two soldiers helping a badly wounded third soldier. A beautiful site was located on the Evansville riverfront, the monument was erected, and the dedication took place on 21 August 1992. The C Company veterans have maintained funds and rotated responsibility for its upkeep ever since.

In addition to the biannual reunions in August, many of the men of C Company and their wives meet for dinner on a monthly basis to visit and conduct business relevant to the reunions and the memorial. Within this distinguished, active group there is a powerful bond. Hugs and handshakes are a part of every gathering. Ross "Pappy" Compton, at eighty the oldest, is the unofficial dad and chaplain for the group. Ralph Hargrave, whom they were all relieved to see back after a grave illness, is the current president. Glendal "Jeep" Ellis keeps comprehensive minutes of each meeting and reports them in a deep ringing voice. Occasionally differences of opinion emerge, but the men always remember they are on the same side, with a shared history duplicated by very few. Asked to describe the meetings, one of the reservists said, "I told my wife . . . I feel like I've been to church when I leave."

The members of C Company, 16th Infantry Division, United States Marine Corps Reserve answered the call for an unexpected journey in the summer of 1950. They were ordinary men given an extraordinary task. Despite the suddenness of the call and the limited training, despite the cruel environment and the sheer numbers of the enemy, they acquitted themselves with bravery and honor. Gen. O. P. Smith, commander of the 1st Marine Division at the time of the Evansville reservists' tour, commended this and other reserve units when he noted, "When I was detached from the Division in April of 1951, 51 percent of the Division was composed of Reserves, and in my opinion it was a better Division than the one I brought to Korea."[12] No higher praise could be offered.

The Korean War Monument on the Ohio River in Evansville, Indiana, is dedicated to all branches of the military that served in the Korean War, and the men of C Company are proud to be numbered among them. However, the enduring camaraderie and pride of the Marine Corps will always beat strongest within their hearts. Their profound sentiments about the Corps are deeply held and difficult to describe, but former reservist William Wright may have put it best when he said, "Every time I see a marine, I just have to go shake his hand."

Appendix

Final Disbandment Roster, C Company,
16th Infantry Battalion, USMCR

19 September 1950, Camp Pendleton, California

OFFICERS

1st Lt. James W. Graham, 1st Lt. Marion U. ("Tex") Graham, Capt. John P. Long, 1st Lt. Jimmy L. Rausch, Maj. Paul T. Torian, 1st Lt. Mason Wiers, 1st Lt. Herman H. Will, 1st Lt. Harold W. Willis

ENLISTED MEN

Pvt. Donald Anderson, Pvt. Robert Anson, Pfc. Edward R. Ansted, Pfc. Albert Ashley, Pvt. Bobby Baker, Pfc. Charles R. ("Barney") Barnard, Pvt. Carl Barnett, Pfc. Henry L. Bates, Sgt. Elmer C. Beal, Pfc. Charles F. Belwood, Cpl. George Bendzen, Pfc. Richard Bennett, Pfc. Taylor D. Bennett, Pfc. Henry V. Berlin, Pvt. Richard A. Bost, Pvt. Robert A. Bowman, Cpl. Gene Brandt, Pfc. Prentice Brenton, Pfc. David O. Bright, Sgt. Charles E. Brown, Pfc. Hassell E. Brown, Pfc. William J. Brown, Pfc. Louis S. Bruchsel, Pvt. George M. Brunson, Pfc. Lowell E. Buchanan, Pfc. Robert C. Buehler, Pfc. Jack G. Burgdorf, Pvt. Ronald J. Burton, Pvt. Denning B. Campbell, Pvt. Ellsworth Campbell, Pfc. Trimble M. Cavins, Pvt. Reginald Champlain, Cpl. Guy E. Clark, Sgt. William E. Combs Jr., Cpl. Ross L. Compton, Pfc. Michael L. Cook, Pvt. Donald L. Corn, Cpl. Horace E. Cox, Pfc. Norman R. Crabtree, Cpl. James D. Crawford, Pfc. Donald R. Crouse, Pfc.

James E. Crouse, Pfc. William T. Cunningham, Cpl. Preston A. Dassell, Sgt. James F. Davis, Pfc. Charles V. Deffendall, Pfc. Albert S. Dickson, Pvt. Kenneth E. Dougan, Pfc. James D. Dunn, Cpl. Richard Eberle, Cpl. Robert Egan, Pfc. Paul A. Ehrmann, Cpl. John M. Elliott, Pfc. Robert A. Elliott, Pvt. Glendal R. ("Jeep") Ellis, Pvt. Jack S. Ellis, Sgt. William J. Ellis, Pvt. Raymond A. Elmore, Pvt. Richard E. Englert, Pvt. William H. Etheridge, Pvt. Frank S. Fischer, Pfc. Robert S. ("Bud") Fitch, Pvt. Morton A. Flowers, Pvt. James D. Floyd, Cpl. Joseph O. Floyd, Pfc. Ralph C. Floyd, Pvt. George O. Franz, Pfc. Elmer L. Fulkerson, Pfc. Charles E. Gibbs, Pvt. William R. Ginger, Pvt. William O. Goings, Pvt. Charles J. Gottman, Pfc. David G. Graham, Cpl. Ralph W. Grass, Cpl. Robert E. Grass, Pfc. Robert O. Green, Pfc. George G. ("Gordon") Greene, Pfc. Norman L. Griess, Cpl. William A. Griffin, Pvt. William C. Grove, Pfc. William T. Hall, Pvt. William H. Hardesty, Cpl. Ralph Hargrave, Pvt. Arthur Hart Jr., Cpl. Harry R. Henley, Pfc. Emmanuel R. Hester, Pvt. William H. Hester, Ssgt. Walter C. Hoepner, Pfc. Charles W. Horr, Pfc. Edward J. Hosse, Pvt. Jimmy W. Hudson, Ssgt. Melvin C. Huebschman, Pfc. Donald Inkenbrandt, Cpl. Raymond L. Jarvis, Pvt. James T. Johnson, Pfc. James C. Joines, Cpl. Roy E. Jolly Jr., Pvt. Glen F. Jones, Pfc. Alfred R. Keerl, Sgt. Charles H. Kelley, Cpl. Roy A. Kincheloe, Pvt. Edward F. Koehnen, Pfc. Charles Koestring, Sgt. Elbert E. ("Gene") Koonce, Pfc. Ebert Krohn, Pfc. Chester J. Krueger, Ssgt. Eli M. Krueger, Pfc. Walter W. Lampkins, Pfc. George A. Land, Pvt. Harry L. Land, Pfc. John Leslie, Pfc. Donald L. Lindenberg, Cpl. John D. Lively, Pfc. Richard Lockridge, Pfc. Louis W. Main, Sgt. Henry W. Maley, Cpl. Charles D. Malpass, Pvt. William J. Marshall, Pfc. John T. Mayes, Pfc. Arthur B. McCaffrey, Cpl. Paul L. McDaniel, Pfc. Raleigh E. McGary, Pvt. Francis J. Memmer, Pvt. George Middleton, Cpl. Gilbert Miles, Pvt. Robert L. Millay, Pvt. Forrest L. Miller, Pfc. Oscar M. Mills, Cpl. Richard J. Minnette, Pvt. Raymond J. Mitchell, Pvt. Charles E. Moad, Pvt. Edward J. Moehlenkamp, Cpl. Marion R. Mooney, Pvt. Ernest W. Morris, Pfc. George E. Muensterman, Pfc. Wilburn E. Muensterman, Cpl. Willard E. Nemer, Cpl. William R. Norvell, Pvt. Henry A. Orth Jr., Pvt. Frank P. Parker Jr., Cpl. Isaac Patmore, Pfc. Paul I. Paulson, Sgt. Jack R. Perigo, Cpl. John W. Perry, Pvt. Paul K. Perry, Ssgt. Harvey A. Peterson, Cpl. Gilford Pinkston, Cpl. Larry C. Pipken, Ssgt. Wayne G. Poole, Cpl. Louis J. Rausch, Pfc. Dennis G. Rhoades, Pfc. Curtis Richardville, Pvt. Carroll Richard, Pfc. Floyd V. Riggs, Pvt. Lorie W. Risley, Pvt. Billy L. Robertson, Cpl. Herbert Robertson, Pvt. Charles Ryan, Pfc. Dale W. Sauer, Cpl.

Edwin J. Savage, Tsgt. Raymond P. Savage, Sgt. David G. Schellhase, Pfc. Robert L. Schnautz, Pvt. Virgil L. Scott, Pfc. Garold G. Sheetz, Ssgt. Ignatius B. Shoemaker, Pfc. Leon G. Simpson, Pfc. Walter G. Sitzman, Pvt. Richard H. Smith, Pvt. Myron F. Snyder, Pvt. Sherman Southwell, Pfc. James W. Stearsman, Pvt. Donald K. Steinmetz, Ssgt. James R. Stephens, Pfc. Joe T. Stephens, Cpl. John K. Stephens, Pfc. Ray E. Sunn, Ssgt. Charles Thalmueller, Cpl. William C. Thompson, Pfc. Jess R. Thurman, Pfc. Billy G. Townsend, Tsgt. Alfred Travers Jr., Pvt. Donald R. Vandeveer, Sgt. Frederic J. Walter, Cpl Robert J. Walter, Pvt. Byron E. Watson, Pvt. Charles T. Webb, Pfc. Ralph H. Weber, Pfc. Robert E. Weber, Pvt. Leo J. Weiss, Pfc. John Weyer, Pfc. Robert Whitehouse, Cpl. Eugene Whittaker, Pfc. Albert L. Williams, Pfc. Samuel J. Williams, Ssgt. Jerry Wilson, Pvt. Robert H. Wilson, Pfc. Russell Wilson, Cpl. Raymond Wirthwein, Cpl. William E. Wright.

Notes

Introduction

1. Leuchtenburg, *Great Age of Change*, 11.
2. *U.S. News and World Report*, 6 January 1950.
3. *Evansville Courier*, 5 December 1950; *Time*, 21 August 1950.
4. In Goulden, *Korea*, 3.
5. Geer, *New Breed*, 103.
6. Manchester, *Glory and the Dream*, 672.
7. *U.S. News and World Report*, 20 October 1950.
8. *Leatherneck*, June 1947.
9. *Marine Corps Reserve*, 167.
10. Ibid.
11. Ibid.
12. *Evansville Press*, 28 August 1950.
13. Owen, *Colder than Hell*, xv.
14. *Marine Corps Reserve*, 179.
15. Hopkins, *One Bugle No Drums*, xi.
16. Appleman, *East of Chosin*.
17. *Marine Corps Reserve*, 179.
18. Mrs. Homer H. McAtee to Sen. Margaret Chase Smith, 9 September 1950.

CHAPTER 1. An Eddy on the Stream of Events

1. In Peduzzi, *America in the Twentieth Century, 1940–1949*, 670.
2. Ibid., 669.
3. *Evansville Courier*, 1 October 1947.
4. Ibid., 13 September 1947.
5. Martin, *Indiana*, 258.
6. Faux, *Memorable Days in America*, 292.
7. Martin, *Indiana*, 258.
8. McCutchan, *At the Bend of the River*, 91.
9. Martin, *Indiana*, 258–59.
10. Ibid.
11. McCutchan, *At the Bend of the River*, 91.
12. Martin, *Indiana*, 258.
13. Donaldson, *Truman Defeats Dewey*, 14.
14. *Time*, 24 July 1950.
15. Hopkins, *One Bugle No Drums*, 15.
16. *Marine Corps Reserve*, 102.
17. Moskin, *U.S. Marine Corps Story*, 665.
18. Ibid.
19. Millett, *Semper Fidelis*, 467.
20. *Marine Corps Reserve*, 113–25.
21. Ibid., 102.
22. Ibid., 107.
23. Ibid., 113.
24. *Leatherneck*, February 1950.
25. Wills, *John Wayne's America*, 149.
26. *Marine Corps Reserve*, 107.
27. Ibid.
28. *Leatherneck*, April 1949.
29. Paul McDaniel, interview with authors, 20 January 1998.
30. *Evansville Courier*, 19 September 1947.
31. Col. Joseph Alexander, correspondence with authors.
32. Manchester, *Goodbye Darkness*, 211.
33. *Evansville Courier*, 18 September 1947.
34. *Marine Corps Gazette*, September 1947.

35. Mrs. Homer H. McAtee to Sen. Margaret Chase Smith, 9 September 1950.
36. In *History of "C" Company.*
37. Ibid.
38. *Devil Dog,* 29 June 1950.
39. *Marine Corps Reserve,* 143.
40. Greene, "Reflections on People, Places, Things," 74.
41. *Oakland City High School Acorn* (yearbook), 1950. In the possession of William Marshall, Oakland City, Indiana.
42. Greene, "Reflections on People, Places, Things," 16.
43. Greene, *Star for Buster,* 53.
44. Greene, "Reflections on People, Places, Things," 17.
45. *Marine Corps Reserve,* 119.
46. Ibid., 133.
47. Moskin, *U.S. Marine Corps Story,* 468.
48. *Leatherneck,* March 1950.
49. *Marine Corps Reserve,* 143.
50. *Devil Dog,* 24 June 1950.
51. Commandant of the Marine Corps to Maj. Paul Torian, 30 June 1948.
52. *Evansville Courier,* 21 August 1998.
53. Ibid.
54. *History of "C" Company.*
55. Gordon Greene to Rada Mason, 27 June 1949.
56. Alexander correspondence.
57. *Leatherneck,* December 1947.
58. Ibid.
59. Ibid., July 1948.
60. Ibid., January 1950.
61. Ibid., May 1950.
62. *Marine Corps Gazette,* February 1948.
63. Ibid., May 1948.
64. Ibid., March 1949.
65. Ibid., October 1948.
66. Ibid., January 1949.
67. *Marine Corps Reserve,* 127.

68. Heller, *Korean War,* 112.

69. *Time,* 26 June 1950.

70. Ibid.

71. Ibid.

72. *Evansville Press,* 18 June 1950.

73. Ibid.

CHAPTER 2. Like Lightning Out of a Clear Sky

1. Knox, *Korean War, An Oral History,* 8.

2. *U.S. News and World Report,* 20 January 1950.

3. Goulden, *Korea,* 25.

4. *U.S. News and World Report,* 6 January 1950.

5. Ibid., 5.

6. *Newsweek,* 23 April 1950.

7. *Newsweek,* 3 July 1950.

8. *Life,* 24 January 1950.

9. Goulden, *Korea,* 46.

10. Phillips, *Truman Presidency,* 289.

11. Ibid., 297.

12. *Esquire,* August 1971, 56.

13. In retrospect, the invasion more likely involved the intense desires of North Korean leader Sung Il Kim to unify the nation. South Korean strongman Syngman Rhee would likely have invaded the north for the same purpose had he possessed the means.

14. *U.S. News and World Report,* 7 July 1950.

15. Heller, *Korean War,* 114.

16. *New York Times Magazine,* 30 July 1950.

17. Ibid., 16 July 1950.

18. *Newsweek,* 3 July 1950.

19. Truman, *Memoirs by Harry S. Truman* 2:332–33.

20. Knox, *Korean War, An Oral History,* 6.

21. Ibid.

22. In Coudrey, *United States Army in the Korean War,* 3 (emphasis added).

23. Knox, *Korean War, An Oral History,* 6.

24. Ibid., 8–9.

25. Ibid., 9.

26. *Time,* 10 July 1950.

27. Ibid.

28. Ibid.

29. *Newsweek,* 10 July 1950.

30. Goulden, *Korea,* 85.

31. *Time,* 17 July 1950.

32. Ibid. Shadrick was mistakenly reported to have been the first to die in combat. See Goulden, *Korea,* 121.

33. *Evansville Press,* 20 July 1950.

34. *Time,* 24 July 1950.

35. *Newsweek,* 24 July 1950.

36. *Life,* 24 July 1950.

37. Ibid., 14 August 1950.

38. *Time,* 31 July 1950.

39. United Press International, 23 November 1950.

40. MacDonald, *Korea,* 39.

41. *Time,* 14 August 1950.

42. *U.S. News and World Report,* 7 July 1950.

43. *Newsweek,* 24 July 1950.

44. Ibid.

45. Ibid.

46. *Evansville Press,* 4 October 1950.

47. United Press International, 6 November 1950.

48. Ibid.

49. Goulden, *Korea,* 139.

50. Ibid., 140.

51. Hopkins, *One Bugle No Drums,* 19.

52. Oddly, Truman would have a poor relationship with the Marine Corps during much of the Korean War due to an offhand remark he made in a letter to a U.S. representative. Truman wrote the letter in reply to the congressman's proposal that the Corps be given a larger role in America's defense plan. Truman answered that the marines were simply the navy's police force and complained further that the Corps possessed "a propaganda machine almost equal to Stalin's."

53. *Marine Corps Reserve*, 165.

54. *U.S. News and World Report*, 18 August 1950.

55. Daily Intelligence Summary, Far East Command, 4 February 1951.

56. *Evansville Press*, 28 July 1950.

57. Charles Gottman, interview with authors.

58. Marine Corps Bulletin no. 4-51, *Marine Corps Gazette*, June 1951.

59. *Leatherneck*, July 1951.

60. Ibid., November 1951.

61. Ibid., February 1951.

62. Ibid., November 1951.

63. Ibid.

64. Ibid., January 1952.

65. *U.S. News and World Report*, 20 October 1950.

66. Greene, "Reflections on People, Places, Things," 104.

67. *Orr Iron Company Newsletter*, Evansville, Indiana.

68. *Time*, 21 July 1950.

69. *Evansville Press*, 21 July 1950.

70. Ibid., 29 August 1950.

71. Ibid.

72. Ibid.

73. *Evansville Courier*, 28 August 1950.

74. Ibid.

75. *Evansville Press*, 29 August 1950.

76. *Evansville Courier*, 29 August 1950.

77. *Evansville Press*, 29 August 1950.

78. Ibid.

79. Ibid.

80. *Evansville Courier*, 29 August 1950.

CHAPTER 3. All the Boot Camp You Want

1. *Evansville Courier*, 29 August 1950. All twenty names are carried in the article.

2. William Etheridge, interview with authors.

3. Bonnie Eberle scrapbook, 1950–52.

4. *Time*, 28 August 1950.

5. *U.S. News and World Report,* 1 September 1950.

6. McDaniel interview.

7. Card from Gordon Greene to Rada Mason, 29 August 1950.

8. Ralph Hargrave, interview with authors.

9. William Marshall to Madge McAtee, n.d.

10. Etheridge interview.

11. Owen, *Colder than Hell,* 16.

12. Ibid., 15.

13. Etheridge interview.

14. William Marshall, interview with authors.

15. Hopkins, *One Bugle No Drums,* 21.

16. Owen, *Colder than Hell,* 15.

17. Wilson, *Retreat Hell!* 26–27.

18. Geer, *New Breed,* 104.

19. *Marine Corps Gazette,* 19 September 1951.

20. Ibid.

21. Hopkins, *One Bugle No Drums,* 21.

22. Geer, *New Breed,* 105–6.

23. Hargrave interview.

24. Eberle scrapbook.

25. Hopkins, *One Bugle No Drums,* 27–28.

26. Brainard, *Then They Called for the Marines,* 9.

27. Eberle scrapbook.

28. Owen, *Colder than Hell,* 16.

29. Ibid., 24.

30. West, *William Styron: A Life,* 195–97.

31. Owen, *Colder than Hell.*

32. Greene, "Reflections on People, Places, Things," 106.

33. Ibid.

34. Garold Sheetz to Peg Sheetz, 5 October 1950.

35. William Marshall to James Marshall, 14 September 1950.

36. Owen, *Colder than Hell,* 45.

CHAPTER 4. Just the Night Before, We Were Laughing

1. Hastings, *Korean War,* 68.

2. Ibid., 99.

3. Toland, *In Mortal Combat*, 175.

4. Hastings, *Korean War*, 99.

5. Charles "Barney" Barnard to "Mom," 22 September 1950.

6. Charles "Barney" Barnard to "Dad," 27 September 1950.

7. Ibid.

8. Ibid.

9. Charles "Barney" Barnard to "Mom," 25 October 1950.

10. *Time,* 9 October 1950.

11. Toland, *In Mortal Combat*, 230.

12. Acheson, *Present at the Creation*, 445.

13. Blair, *Forgotten War*, 327–28.

14. Spurr, *Enter the Dragon.*

15. Ibid., 64.

16. Ibid., 68.

17. Blair, *Forgotten War*, 336.

18. *Time,* 9 October 1950.

19. *U.S. News and World Report,* 6 October 1950.

20. *Newsweek,* 9 October 1950.

21. Ibid.

22. Cohen and Gooch, *Military Misfortunes*, 165.

23. *Newsweek,* 30 October 1950.

24. Ibid., 13 November 1950.

25. Ibid., 2 October 1950.

26. Ibid.

27. Hastings, *Korean War*, 118.

28. Ibid., 121–22.

29. Toland, *In Mortal Combat*, 223.

30. Ibid., 239.

31. Goulden, *Korea*, 253–54.

32. Owen, *Colder than Hell*, 104–5.

33. Charles "Barney" Barnard to "Mom," 25 October 1950.

34. Etheridge interview.

35. Montross and Canzona, *Chosin Campaign*, 36.

36. Goulden, *Korea*, 252.

37. Charles "Barney" Barnard, untitled letter, 31 October 1950.

38. Montross and Canzona, *Chosin Campaign*, 39.

39. Charles "Barney" Barnard to "Dad," 5 November 1950.

40. Charles "Barney" Barnard, untitled, 31 October 1950.

41. Greene, "Boondockers," 11.

42. Montross and Canzona, *Chosin Campaign,* 96.

43. Blair, *Forgotten War,* 387.

44. Ibid., 388.

45. Ibid., 459.

46. Murphy, *Korean War Heroes,* 89.

47. Appleman, *East of Chosin,* 12.

48. James Dill diary, 24 November 1950.

49. Wilson, *Retreat Hell!* 67.

50. Appleman, *East of Chosin,* 5.

51. Wilson, *Retreat Hell!* 69.

52. Greene, "Boondockers," 36.

53. Goncharov, Lewis, and Litai, *Uncertain Partners,* 182.

54. Toland, *In Mortal Combat,* 237.

55. Spurr, *Enter the Dragon,* 161.

56. Ibid.

57. Hoyt, *Day the Chinese Attacked,* 85.

58. Spurr, *Enter the Dragon,* 167–68.

59. Ibid., 169.

60. Montross and Canzona, *Chosin Campaign,* 88–89.

61. Cohen and Gooch, *Military Misfortunes,* 177.

62. Hopkins, *One Bugle No Drums,* 113.

63. *Newsweek,* 13 November 1950.

64. *Time,* 6 November 1950.

65. *Newsweek,* 13 November 1950.

66. *U.S. News and World Report,* 10 November 1950.

67. Spurr, *Enter the Dragon,* 163.

68. Ibid., 260.

69. Hoyt, *Bloody Road to Panmunjom,* 65.

CHAPTER 5. Home by Christmas

1. Gordon Greene to Rada Mason, 26 November 1950.

2. Wilson, *Retreat Hell!* 72.

3. Owen, *Colder than Hell,* 193–94.

4. Appleman, *East of Chosin,* 52.
5. Montross and Canzona, *Chosin Campaign,* 147.
6. Accounts vary regarding the number of survivors. This work relied heavily upon Appleman's definitive work, *East of Chosin.*
7. Montross and Canzona, *Chosin Campaign,* 197.
8. Wilson, *Retreat Hell!* 70.
9. Montross and Canzona, *Chosin Campaign,* 151.
10. Wilson, *Retreat Hell!* 77.
11. Ibid., 79.
12. *Time,* 4 December 1950.
13. Blair, *Forgotten War,* 433.
14. *Time,* 4 December 1950.
15. Blair, *Forgotten War,* 433.
16. *Newsweek,* 4 December 1950.
17. Montross and Canzona, *Chosin Campaign,* 154.
18. Ibid., 157.
19. Ibid., 158.
20. *Volunteer Soldier's Day,* 29.
21. Montross and Canzona, *Chosin Campaign,* 159.
22. Ibid., 160.
23. Ibid., 161.
24. Ibid.
25. Hopkins, *One Bugle No Drums,* 128.
26. Ibid., 169.
27. *Evansville Press,* 28 December 1950.
28. Montross and Canzona, *Chosin Campaign,* 168.
29. Ibid., 171.
30. Wilson, *Retreat Hell!* 106–7.
31. Montross and Canzona, *Chosin Campaign,* 192.
32. In *Volunteer Soldier's Day,* 29–30.
33. Montross and Canzona, *Chosin Campaign,* 180.
34. Ibid., 182.
35. Ibid., 191.
36. Ibid., 197.
37. Ibid., 198.
38. Ibid., 207.

39. Ibid., 201.

40. Ibid., 208.

41. Ibid., 210.

42. Hammel, *Chosin,* 158.

43. Montross and Canzona, *Chosin Campaign,* 211.

44. Ibid., 221–47.

45. Appleman, *East of Chosin,* 187.

46. Murphy, *Korean War Heroes,* 112–13.

47. Appleman, *East of Chosin,* 194.

48. General Headquarters, Far East Command. General Orders no. 201. Distinguished Service Cross Award, 7 August 1951. See also Randy Mills and Roxanne Mills, "His Valorous Conduct: The Story of a Hoosier Hero in the Korean War," *Indiana Magazine of History* (forthcoming).

49. See Appleman, *East of Chosin.*

50. Wilson, *Retreat Hell!* 186.

51. Montross and Canzona, *Chosin Campaign,* 255.

52. Ibid.

53. Montross and Canzona, *Chosin Campaign,* 255.

54. Hammel, *Chosin,* 256.

55. Montross and Canzona, *Chosin Campaign,* 258.

56. McDaniel interview.

57. Hammel, *Chosin,* 257.

58. Toland, *In Mortal Combat,* 325.

59. Ibid., 326.

60. Hammel, *Chosin,* 272.

61. Montross and Canzona, *Chosin Campaign,* 263.

62. Toland, *In Mortal Combat,* 343.

63. Montross and Canzona, *Chosin Campaign,* 260.

64. Hammel, *Chosin,* 271.

65. Ibid., 268.

66. Montross and Canzona, *Chosin Campaign,* 277.

67. Spurr, *Enter the Dragon,* 261.

68. Montross and Canzona, *Chosin Campaign,* 285.

69. Appleman, *Escaping the Trap,* 291.

70. Montross and Canzona, *Chosin Campaign,* 314.

71. Appleman, *Escaping the Trap*, 291.
72. Hopkins, *One Bugle No Drums*, 175, 218.
73. Brainard, *Then They Called for the Marines*, 132–33.
74. Ibid., 133.
75. Greene, "Boondockers," 86–87.
76. Montross and Canzona, *Chosin Campaign*, 320.
77. Gordon Greene to William Marshall, 15 December 1986.
78. Greene, "Reflections on People, Places, Things," 28.
79. Greene, "Few Old Men," 82–83.
80. Montross and Canzona, *Chosin Campaign*, 351.
81. Cohen and Gooch, *Military Misfortunes*, 186.
82. Hopkins, *One Bugle No Drums*, xi.
83. Robert Taplett to the authors, 18 April 1999.
84. Spurr, *Enter the Dragon*, 267–69.

CHAPTER 6. It Looks as if I Were Mad at Something

1. Toland, *In Mortal Combat*, 369.
2. Montross, Kuokka, and Hicks, *East-Central Front*, 5.
3. Gordon Greene to Rada Mason, 24 December 1950.
4. Charles "Barney" Barnard to "Dad," 10 January 1951.
5. Montross, Kuokka, and Hicks, *East-Central Front*, 5.
6. Charles "Barney" Barnard to "Dad," 26 January 1951.
7. Montross, Kuokka, and Hicks, *East-Central Front*, 11–14.
8. Charles "Barney" Barnard to "Dad," 26 January 1951.
9. Gordon Greene to Rada Mason, 26 December 1950.
10. Carl Barnett, interview with authors.
11. *Newsweek*, 20 December 1950.
12. *Oakland City Journal*, 1950.
13. *Evansville Courier*, 26 December 1950.
14. Greene, "Boondockers," 197–98, 167.
15. Blair, *Forgotten War*.
16. Ibid., 619.
17. Montross, Kuokka, and Hicks, *East-Central Front*, 51.
18. Charles "Barney" Barnard to "Dad," 7 February 1951.
19. Greene, "Few Old Men," 104.
20. Mary Beth Fitch Fanning, interview with authors.

21. Charles "Barney" Barnard to "Dad," 9 March 1951.

22. Blair, *Forgotten War*, 854.

23. Rees, *Korea*, 247.

24. Sydney Greenwood, interview with authors. We came across several versions of Bud Fitch's death. Greenwood's seems likely to be the most exact.

25. Montross, Kuokka, and Hicks, *East-Central Front*, 106.

26. Ibid., 107.

27. Ibid., 113.

28. Knox and Coppel, *Korean War*, 164.

29. Blair, *Forgotten War*, 855.

30. Greene, "Few Old Men," 12.

31. Charles "Barney" Barnard to "Dad," 27 July 1951.

32. Ibid., 21 May 1951.

33. *Evansville Press*, 5 January 1951.

34. *O.C. Collegian*, 2 March 1951.

35. *Evansville Courier*, n.d., Eberle scrapbook.

CHAPTER 7. Go Back Home and Tell Everybody There's a War On

1. *Time*, 24 July 1950.

2. *Newsweek*, 14 August 1950.

3. May, *Pushing the Limits*, 53.

4. *Ladies Home Journal*, August 1950.

5. May, *Pushing the Limits*, 54.

6. *Time*, 3 July 1950.

7. Ibid., 10 July 1950.

8. Heller, *Korean War*, 121.

9. Ibid., 115.

10. *Life*, 21 July 1950.

11. Ibid.

12. *Time*, 24 July 1950.

13. Ibid., 10 July 1950.

14. Heller, *Korean War*, 119.

15. Ibid., 120–21.

16. Dorothy Michael to William Marshall, 28 November 1951.

17. Heller, *Korean War*, 120–21.

18. *Time*, 17 July 1950.

19. *Evansville Press*, 2 August 1950.

20. Heller, *Korean War*, 121.

21. *Newsweek*, 15 January 1951.

22. Ibid., 10 July 1950.

23. Heller, *Korean War*, 114.

24. *Evansville Press*, 15 September 1950.

25. Miller, *50s*, 49.

26. *Life*, 28 August 1950.

27. *Time*, 21 August 1950.

28. *Evansville Press*, 5 August 1950.

29. Ibid., 13 August 1950.

30. Ibid., 8 August 1950.

31. Miller, *50s*, 51.

32. *Time*, 18 September 1950.

33. Heller, *Korean War*, 115.

34. *Newsweek*, 21 August 1950.

35. *Time*, 21 August 1950.

36. *U.S. News and World Report*, 1 September 1950.

37. *Life*, 17 July 1950.

38. *Time*, 17 July 1950.

39. Ibid., 28 August 1950.

40. *Evansville Press*, 24 September 1950.

41. Ibid., 28 August 1950.

42. Paul McDaniel from his mother, 17 November 1950.

43. *Time*, 4 December 1950.

44. Gordon Greene to Rada Mason, 24 December 1950.

45. *Evansville Press*, 14 December 1950.

46. *Evansville Courier*, 13 December 1950; 18 December 1950.

47. *O.C. Collegian*, 1 December 1950.

48. *Evansville Press*, 6 January 1951.

49. Ibid.

50. *O.C. Collegian*, 19 January 1951.

51. *Newsweek*, 21 August 1950.

52. *Life*, 21 July 1950.

53. *Newsweek*, 4 September 1950.

54. Paul McDaniel from his mother, 17 November 1950.

55. *Newsweek,* 11 December 1950.

56. Ibid., 18 December 1950.

57. *Time,* 11 December 1950.

58. *New York Times,* 28 November 1950.

59. *Evansville Courier,* 30 November 1950.

60. Ibid., 1 December 1950.

61. *Evansville Press,* 1 December 1950.

62. Ibid., 6 December 1950.

63. *Newsweek,* 18 December 1950.

64. *Evansville Courier,* 15 December 1950.

65. *Evansville Press,* 20 December 1950.

66. *Evansville Sunday Courier and Press,* 24 December 1950.

67. *Evansville Courier,* 22 December 1950.

68. Ibid.

69. *Evansville Press,* 29 December 1950.

70. Ibid., 27 December 1950.

71. *Evansville Courier,* 13 December 1950.

72. *Evansville Press,* 27 December 1950.

73. Ibid., 3 January 1951.

74. *Princeton Daily Clarion,* 22 April 1951.

75. Ibid., 23 April 1951.

76. Greene, "Few Old Men," 136.

77. Ibid.

78. Heller, *Korean War,* 142.

79. Ibid., 144.

80. *Newsweek,* 19 March 1951.

81. *Time,* 3 August 1953.

CHAPTER 8. Every Time I See a Marine . . .

1. Greene, "Star for Buster," 102–4.

2. *Detroit News,* 28 April 1996.

3. Greene, "Few Old Men," vii.

4. Greene, "Boondockers."

5. Greene, "Few Old Men," 103.

6. Greene, "Reflections on People, Places, Things," 27.

7. Ibid., 30.
8. Ibid., 104.
9. Greene, "Few Old Men," vii–viii.
10. Greene, *38th Parallel Revisited,* 15.
11. Greene, "Few Old Men," 158.
12. *Marine Corps Reserve,* 180.

Bibliography

Personal interviews provided the bulk of the data used to write this book. The following people shared their insights and experiences through these interviews: Col. Joseph Alexander, USMC (ret.), Maj. William Barnard, USMC (ret.), Carl Barnett, Jack G. Burgdorf, Denning B. Campbell, Don Cochren, Ross Compton, Becky Compton, James Crouse, William Cunningham, Charles V. Deffendall, Albert S. Dickson, Kenneth Dougan, Bonnie Eberle, Robert Egan, Glendal K. Ellis, William H. Etheridge, Mary Beth (Fitch) Fanning, Gordon Fitch, Charles Gottman, Betty Graham, David G. Graham, Joan Graham, Marion "Tex" Graham, Sydney Greenwood, Ralph Hargrave, Arthur Hart Jr., William Hasselbrinck, Gene Holderbaugh, Roy Jolly Jr., Elbert Gene Koonce, Louis Main, William J. Marshall, Paul L. McDaniel, Raleigh E. McGary, Dr. James W. Murray, lieutenant colonel, USMC (ret.), Bill E. Nemer, Robert O'Keefe, Henry A. Orth Jr., Helen Robertson, Dave Schellhase, Garold Sheetz, James Skinner, James Stearsman, Col. Robert Taplett, USMC (ret.), Jess R. Thurman, Nina Thurman, Paul Torian, Peg Warnsman, Robert Whitehouse, Richard H. Whitfield, Evelyn Wright, and William E. Wright.

A great portion of this work was also shaped by letters written to and from Korea by Marine Corps reservists and their families. Robert "Bud" Fitch sent over a score of letters home to Oakland City to his family while training in California and later while serving in Korea.

Copies of several of Bud's letters were kindly provided by his brother, Gordon Fitch, and his mother, Garnet. Gordon Greene wrote more than 125 letters to his mother, Rada Mason, of Oakland City, Indiana, between 29 August 1950 and 18 March 1952. Greene's letters were provided to the authors by his widow, Marynelle Greene of Lincoln, Nebraska. William Marshall of Oakland City, Indiana, lent the authors more than a score of letters he wrote as a teenage marine reservist to his family, as well as several letters written by his aunt, Mrs. Homer McAtee; his mother, Dorothy Michael; U.S. senators Margaret Chase Smith and Homer Capehart; U.S. representative James Noland; Marine Corps commandant Gen. C. B. Cates; and columnist Drew Pearson. Betty Ann Risley generously shared a number of letters written from Korea by her late husband Charles "Barney" Barnard to his mother and father Neva and Charles Barnard of Oakland City. Another important contribution came from Maj. William Barnard, USMC (ret.), who shared a number of letters written to him by teenage reservists. These letters to teenage friends back home lent a more earthy slant to marine reservists' experiences. Raleigh McGary shared several letters he wrote his wife while enduring the rugged Chosin campaign. This correspondence gives insight into some of the longings spouses experienced during the war. Home-front concerns were made more vivid through letters made available by Paul McDaniel written by his mother, Mary McDaniel, of Evansville, Indiana. Other correspondence of significance came from Peg Warnsman and Sydney Greenwood.

Information from interviews and letters were made more reliable for this work by consulting three important sources: *Marine Corps Reserve: A History,* published by the U.S. Marine Corps Division of Reserves Headquarters, and two volumes of *United States Marine Operations in Korea, 1950–1953* published by the U.S. Government Printing Office. A more complete bibliography for these materials appears below.

Several newspapers, including the *Evansville Press,* the *Evansville Courier,* the *Oakland City Journal,* and the *Princeton Clarion,* were used extensively for this work. They are available on microfilm at the Indiana State Library in Indianapolis, Indiana. The *O.C. Collegians* used in this work were provided by the Oakland City University Library, Oakland City, Indiana. Copies of *Leatherneck* and the *Marine Corps Gazette,* two other important sources of information, are readily available at Indiana University Library, Bloomington, Indiana. Copies of *Life* magazine used in this work are also available at Indiana University

Library, as are copies of the *Ladies Home Journal.* Bound volumes of *Newsweek, Time,* and *U.S. News and World Report* were obtained at Oakland City University Library, Oakland City, Indiana.

A final source of data for this work came from a series of newspaper clippings compiled from 1950 to 1952 by Bonnie Eberle. Bonnie faithfully cut out every article she read in the *Evansville Courier* and the *Evansville Press* that concerned the Evansville reservists. In 1994 she placed the clippings in three large volumes of scrapbooks.

PUBLISHED AND UNPUBLISHED WORKS

Acheson, Dean. *Present at the Creation.* New York: Norton, 1969.

Alexander, Bevin. *Korea: The First War We Lost.* New York: Hippocrene, 1986.

Appleman, Roy. *East of Chosin.* College Station: Texas A&M University Press, 1987.

———.*Escaping the Trap.* College Station: Texas A&M University Press, 1990.

Bachrach, Deborah. *The Korean War.* San Diego, Calif.: Lucent Books, 1991.

Blair, Clay. *The Forgotten War: America in Korea.* New York: Times Books, 1988.

Brainard, Morgan. *Then They Called for the Marines.* Rutland, Vt.: Academy Books, 1989.

Cohen, Eliot A., and John Gooch. *Military Misfortunes: The Anatomy of Failure in War.* New York: Vintage Books, 1991.

Coudrey, Albert E. *United States Army in the Korean War.* Washington, D.C.: Center for Military History, 1987.

Devil Dog. C Company, 16th Infantry Battalion. Evansville, Indiana. July 1950.

Donaldson, Gary A. *Truman Defeats Dewey.* Lexington: University Press of Kentucky, 1999.

Faux, William. *Memorable Days in America, 1819–1820.* In *Early Western Travels,* edited by Reuben Gold Thwaites. Cleveland: Arthur H. Clark, 1905.

Fehrenbach, T. R. *This Kind of War.* New York: Macmillan, 1963.

Geer, Andrew. *The New Breed.* New York: Harper, 1952.

Goncharov, Sergei N., John W. Lewis, and Xeu Litai. *Uncertain Partners: Stalin, Mao, and the Korean War.* Stanford, Calif.: Stanford University Press, 1993.

Goulden, Joseph C. *Korea: The Untold Story of the War.* New York: Time Books, 1982.

Greene, Gordon. *The 38th Parallel Revisited.* Lincoln: Department of Nebraska Marine Corps League, 1990.

———. "Boondockers." Unpublished novel, 1972.

_____. "A Few Old Men: Bicycling the 38th Parallel." Unpublished diary, 1995.

_____. "Reflections on People, Places, Things." Unpublished manuscript.

_____. *A Star for Buster.* Huntington, W.V.: University Editions, 1994.

Halberstam, David. *The Fifties.* New York: Fawcett Columbine, 1993.

Hammel, Eric M. *Chosin: Heroic Ordeal of the Korean War.* San Francisco: Presidio, 1990.

Hastings, Max. *The Korean War.* New York: Simon & Schuster, 1988.

Haynes, Richard F. *The Awesome Power.* Baton Rouge: Louisiana State University Press, 1973.

Heller, Francis H., ed. *The Korean War: A Twenty-Five Year Perspective.* Lawrence: Regents Press of Kansas, 1977.

History of "C" Company. Booklet assembled for the C Company reunion. N.p., n.d.

Hopkins, William B. *One Bugle No Drums: The Marines at Chosin Reservoir.* Chapel Hill, N.C.: Algonquin Books of Chapel Hill, 1986.

Hoyt, Edwin P. *The Bloody Road to Panmunjom.* New York: Stein & Day, 1985.

_____. *The Day the Chinese Attacked.* New York: McGraw-Hill, 1990.

Knox, Donald. *The Korean War, An Oral History: Pusan to Chosin.* New York: Harcourt Brace Jovanovich, 1985.

Knox, Donald, and Alfred Coppel. *The Korean War: Uncertain Victory.* New York: Harcourt Brace Jovanovich, 1988.

Leuchtenburg, William E. *The Great Age of Change.* New York: Stonehenge Books, 1964.

MacDonald, Callum A. *Korea: The War Before Vietnam.* New York: Free Press, 1986.

Manchester, William. *The Glory and the Dream: A Narrative History of America 1932–1972.* Boston: Little, Brown, 1973.

_____. *Goodbye Darkness, A Memoir of the Pacific War.* Boston: Little, Brown, 1979.

Martin, John Bartlow. *Indiana: An Interpretation.* New York: Alfred A. Knopf, 1947.

May, Elaine Tyler. *Pushing the Limits: American Women, 1940–1961.* New York: Oxford University Press, 1994.

McCutchan, Kenneth P. *At the Bend of the River.* Woodland Hills, Calif.: Windsor Publications, 1982.

Miller, Douglas T. *The 50s.* Garden City, N.Y.: Doubleday, 1977.

Millett, Allan R. *Semper Fidelis.* New York: Macmillan, 1980.

Montross, Lynn, and Nicholas A. Canzona. *The Chosin Campaign.* Vol. 3 of *United States Marine Operations in Korea, 1950–1953.* Washington, D.C.: GPO, 1957.

Montross, Lynn, Maj. Hubard D. Kuokka, and Maj. Norman W. Hicks. *The East-Central Front.* Vol. 4 of *United States Marine Operations in Korea, 1950–1953.* Washington, D.C.: GPO, 1957.

Moskin, J. Robert. *The U.S. Marine Corps Story.* New York: McGraw-Hill, 1977.

Murphy, Edward F. *Korean War Heroes.* San Francisco: Presidio, 1992.

Owen, Joseph R. *Colder than Hell: A Marine Rifle Company at Chosin Reservoir.* New York: Ivy Books, 1996.

Paige, Glenn D. *The Korean Decision.* New York: Free Press, 1968.

Peduzzi, Kelli. *America in the Twentieth Century, 1940–1949.* New York: Marshall Cavendish, 1995.

Phillips, Cabell. *The Truman Presidency: The History of Triumphant Succession.* New York: Collier-Macmillan, 1966.

Rees, David. *Korea: The Limited War.* New York: St. Martin's Press, 1964.

Reserve Officers of the Public Affairs Unit. *Marine Corps Reserve: A History.* Washington, D.C.: Division of Reserve Headquarters, U.S. Marine Corps, 1966.

Russ, Martin. *The Last Parallel.* Signet, 1957.

Spurr, Russell. *Enter the Dragon: China's Undeclared War Against the U.S. in Korea, 1950–51.* New York: Newmarket Press, 1998.

Toland, John. *In Mortal Combat.* New York: William Morrow, 1991.

Truman, Harry S. *Memoirs by Harry S. Truman.* Vol 2. New York: Doubleday, 1956.

A Volunteer Soldier's Day: Recollections by Men of the Chinese People's Volunteers in the War to Resist U.S. Aggression and Aid Korea. Peking: Foreign Language Press, 1961.

West, James L. W. *William Styron: A Life.* New York: Random House, 1998.

Wills, Garry. *John Wayne's America: The Politics of Celebrity.* New York: Simon and Schuster, 1997.

Wilson, Dick. *The People's Emperor.* New York: Doubleday, 1980.

Wilson, Jim. *Retreat Hell!* New York: William Morrow, 1988.

Wright, David, and Elly Petra Press. *America in the Twentieth Century, 1950–1959.* New York: Marshall Cavendish, 1995.

Index

About the Authors

Dr. Randy K. Mills is an associate professor of history at Oakland City University in Oakland City, Indiana. He has had numerous pieces on both history and the teaching of history published in professional journals and is also the author of a book on American frontier religious history, *The Story of America's Frontier General Baptists*.

Roxanne Mills is an instructor of English at Oakland City University. Her articles on writing have been published in various professional journals and she is also the author of several short stories.